Change at Work

D0208359

Change at Work

Peter Cappelli

Laurie Bassi   Harry Katz   David Knoke

Paul Osterman   Michael Useem

New York   Oxford
Oxford University Press
1997

658.406
C456
1997

Oxford University Press

Oxford New York
Athens Auckland Bangkok Bogota Bombay Buenos Aires
Calcutta Cape Town Dar es Salaam Delhi Florence Hong Kong
Istanbul Karachi Kuala Lumpur Madras Madrid Melbourne
Mexico City Nairobi Paris Singapore Taipei Tokyo Toronto

and associated companies in
Berlin Ibadan

Copyright © 1997 by Oxford University Press, Inc.

Published by Oxford University Press, Inc.
198 Madison Avenue, New York, New York 10016

Oxford is a registered trademark of Oxford University Press

All rights reserved. No part of this publication may be reproduced,
stored in a retrieval system, or transmitted, in any form or by any means,
electronic, mechanical, photocopying, recording, or otherwise,
without the prior permission of Oxford University Press.

Library of Congress Cataloging-in-Publication Data
Change at work / Peter Cappelli . . . [et al.].
p. cm.
Includes bibliographical references and index.
ISBN 0-19-510327-0
1. Organizational change—United States. 2. Corporate
reorganizations—United States. 3. Downsizing of organizations—
United States. I. Cappelli, Peter.
HD58.8.C452 1996
658.4'06—dc20   96-23911

1 3 5 7 9 8 6 4 2

Printed in the United States of America
on acid-free paper

Foreword

This study was sponsored by the Committee on New American Realities (NAR), a private sector group established in 1981 by the National Planning Association to promote a more competitive U.S. economy and to focus on both macroeconomic strategies and ways to use human resources more effectively. NAR Committee members are senior leaders drawn from business, labor, and academia.

The book is part of the NAR Committee's examination, extending over a period of many years, of the forces that are changing the workplace and work organization, including the relationship between employers and employees. In 1991 Oxford University Press published *Turbulence in the American Workplace*, another NAR Committee–sponsored study, which provided a comprehensive and compelling account of how economic turbulence is changing the U.S. labor market and workplaces. *Change at Work* offers a broader look at workplace changes and their impact on employees, employers, and work organization.

Change at Work is a major attempt to gather and use systematic data on the changing nature of employment and to develop a better understanding of emerging employment relationships. It describes a far-reaching workplace transformation that is taking place in the United States and that has important implications for businesses, employees, and the nation's economic performance.

Through open, nonpartisan analyses and examination of U.S. economic performance, the NAR Committee defines shared inter-

METHODIST COLLEGE LIBRARY
Fayetteville, N.C.

ests and concerns and fosters a broad-based consensus from which effective national policies and private-sector initiatives can evolve. Although Committee members understand that consensus is not always possible, they believe that frank, informed discussion of key issues is always beneficial. The Committee's sponsored studies, such as *Change at Work*, are meant to help private- and public-sector leaders better understand the complex economic and social issues facing the nation.

All NAR Committee members do not agree with every point raised in this important study. They do, however, believe the authors have done a very valuable job in examining the metamorphosis that is taking place in the relationship between employers on the one hand and employees and work organizations as a whole on the other. We recommend this study to anyone seeking a serious analysis of these issues.

Alan MacDonald
Chair, New American Realities Committee

Acknowledgments

We gratefully acknowledge the Committee on New American Realities (NAR) of the National Planning Association (NPA), which provided financial support, guidance, and constructive criticism throughout our work on this project. Our deepest thanks go to James A. Auerbach, vice president and director of the NAR Committee. Jim helped us develop our proposal for the project, brought it to the Committee, and shepherded it through each step of the way. Special thanks also go to Charles R. Lee, chairman and chief executive officer of the GTE Corporation, who chaired the Committee when the project began, and to Alan S. MacDonald, executive vice president of Citibank, who assumed that position while the project was being completed. Chuck and Alan read the manuscript at several stages in its development and provided helpful comments. We also appreciate the administrative support and encouragement given to us by Malcolm R. Lovell Jr., president and chief executive officer of NPA, and his staff. Mac has a long history of work with academics, and we are grateful for his assistance on this project as well.

We met with the NAR Committee many times to discuss the project and benefited from those conversations. In particular, we thank the members of the Project Advisory Committee that was created to help us with the study: John Caron of Caron International, Stephen Goldmann of Exxon Corporation, Jack Golodner from the AFL-CIO's Department of Professional Employees, Charles

Johnson from Pioneer Hi-Bred International, Inc., William Ket-
chum of AT&T, Barry Leskin, now a private consultant, Nick
Nichols from the Communications Workers of America, Rudy Os-
wald of the AFL-CIO, Beth Shulman from the United Food & Commercial Workers International Union, Hal Tragash of Genesis Associates, and Raymond Thumm, Director of Human Resource
Relations, GTE Corporation. It would be fair to say that the committee members did not always see eye to eye on everything, but even
the disagreements were instructive. We appreciate their help and
patience.

The work for this project began with a series of seminars that
the National Center on the Educational Quality of the Workforce
(EQW) held in Washington, D.C., for the Office of Educational Resources and Improvement of the U.S. Department of Education. We
benefited both from the administrative support provided by the
EQW Center—thanks to Margy Hoover and Joanne Saporito in
particular—and from its research on related issues. Finally, we are
grateful to Herb Addison and his associates at Oxford University
Press for their encouragement and especially to Kathryn Pearcy at
the Wharton School, who took the various bits of paper we gave her
and turned them into a manuscript.

Contents

Contributors

Peter Cappelli
Chair, The Wharton School Management Department
University of Pennsylvania

Laurie Bassi
American Society for Training and Development

Harry Katz
School of Industrial and Labor Relations
Cornell University

David Knoke
Department of Sociology
University of Minnesota

Paul Osterman
Sloan School of Management
Massachusetts Institute of Technology

Michael Useem
The Wharton School and Department of Sociology
University of Pennsylvania

**This study was commissioned by the National Planning
Association's Committee on New American Realities**

Change at Work

Introduction

Change at Work began as a conversation with the members of the National Planning Association's New American Realities Committee about changes under way in the workplace. We were all interested in stories appearing in the media about how relations among employee and employer and workplace practices were changing, but, when pressed, we discovered that our evidence about what was happening was just anecdotal. And the anecdotes about change in the workplace seemed to repeat the same examples over and over—Motorola as the example of rising skill requirements and more intensive training programs, General Electric as the example of restructuring, Saturn as an example of empowered workers. We realized that we did not have a good sense about what really was happening in the typical workplace. Yet much of the policy debate, which was becoming increasingly elaborate, was based on assumptions about these changes in the workplace. Arguments like the following were common: Skill requirements were rising, the educational performance of students was falling, and education and training had to be given massive pushes in order to make up for the growing "skills gap." Or employers were failing to introduce more effective "high-performance" work systems and needed somehow to be pushed into doing so for the national interest.

We decided that a first step in our research project should be to document the situation in the workplace. Our original focus on studying work organization and estimating the extent of high-performance systems soon broadened to include other issues, such as employment security, training, and labor market outcomes. The notion of taking a "snapshot" of the extent of workplace practices soon gave way to thinking about changes in those practices over time.

What began as a simple effort to assess the state of the workplace soon became a considerable undertaking directed at both estimating and understanding the wide-ranging changes that seem to be under way in the U.S. workplace. Many of the assumptions used as the basis of policy, like those just described, turned out to be simply untrue.

We found that the traditional methods of managing employees and developing skilled workers inside companies are breaking down. What we see in their place is a new employment relationship where pressures from product and labor markets are brought inside the organization and used to mediate the relationship between workers and management. Employees now bear many more of the risks of doing business through reduced job security and contingent pay. Jobs demand more of workers but seem to offer them less. Employees are pressed to manage their own career development in work settings that may be reducing the incentives for employers to provide training, especially for entry-level jobs. At the same time, sharp declines in employee commitment have forced employers to rethink how to manage employees in ways that do not rely on traditional commitments to the organization.

The extent of change and the departure from more traditional systems of employment that we as academics had become used to seeing as the model, especially for large organizations, call into question some of our traditional notions about what the employment relationship should do for employers and employees.

A Tale of Restructuring

The place to begin a story about change in the workplace is with the traditional system of employment that has been associated with large organizations, a system that developed skills inside the organization and then worked to keep them there. In its most stylized form, the internalized arrangements involved hiring unskilled workers and management trainees with no experience and then insulating them—especially management—from variations in both product and labor markets. These arrangements placed a premium on planning and predictability.

Perhaps the first point to note about these "traditional arrangements" is that they are in fact rather modern, having first appeared in the early part of the 1900s but taking hold in most large companies somewhat later, in the middle of the century. Before that, employment relationships were much more at arm's length and were mediated by market forces. (The more contingent nature of work in the earlier period in fact resembles nothing so much as the "new" arrangements with leased employees and pay at risk that we describe in subsequent chapters.) By the 1980s, the apparent success of Japanese management practices, with their paternalistic employment relationships and long-term attachments, seemed to suggest that U.S. employers had not gone far enough in providing job security, training, and career development and generally in protecting employees from outside market pressures. The business literature argued with depressing regularity that the United States was behind Japan in developing effective management practices and that U.S. businesses needed to emulate Japanese practices in order to catch up.

Even a casual observer of the business world is aware that the accepted wisdom in business seems to have changed 180 degrees in the past five years. Talk of protecting workers seems to have reversed as employers are encouraged on a variety of fronts to cut workers loose and use the outside market to restructure organizations and jobs.

The contemporary changes in the workplace begin in our study with the pressures on employers to restructure their operations in a search for better performance. These pressures came from divergent sources—from competitors, especially foreign producers whose techniques were different and whose own improved operations forced U.S. companies to cut costs and improve products, and from investors and threats of hostile takeovers, both spurring companies to raise profits. Surprisingly, public policy also played a role in the transformation. Employment law and the various pieces of legislation designed to protect workers like the Fair Labor Standards Act were aimed at traditional employment relationships, and employers have worked hard to change those relationships in order to avoid the requirements of the legislation.

Two additional factors were especially important in pressuring employers to restructure. The first is the perception that product markets and consumer demand had changed in ways that placed a premium on flexibility—on the ability to produce a wider range of products that responded faster to changing consumer demand. The need for flexibility often went beyond developing additional models or variations of the same basic product to produce altogether new products requiring substantially different production skills and techniques.

The other related development was a series of new ideas about how to manage organizations, particularly those in competitive product markets. These included making executive compensation heavily contingent on performance, which aligned the interests of managers with those of stockholders and responded to the long-standing criticism that traditional models of management paid too much attention to the interests of managers (such as job security) and not enough to maximizing profits. New models of organizing work that included total quality management programs and worker empowerment were also widespread. Perhaps the most important new management argument from the perspective of restructuring was the notion that companies' competitiveness depended not so much on their business strategy or positioning in the market relative to competitors but on their "core competencies." These competencies were aspects of business that a particular company did better than its competitors, such as marketing or responding to changing consumer demand. If some function is not central to a company's core competency, the argument went, it is simply a distraction that should be sold off or outsourced.

Together, these pressures began to push employers in a very different direction. Conglomerates began to disassemble, selling off divisions, often in response to pressures from the investment community. Under pressure to cut costs and improve profits, companies squeezed costs and reengineered tasks in order to cut out "fat." In most cases, the "fat" was mainly workers. Companies subcontracted functions that had always been peripheral, such as cleaning and security services, and, increasingly, functions that had been traditionally viewed as integral to an organization, such as human resources and clerical work.

The organizations that emerged from this restructuring process were flatter in terms of organizational structure and often much more profitable, and they had very different relationships with their employees.

The most obvious aspect of the new employment relationship was the sharp reduction in job security. Under the more traditional arrangement, it was typical in large organizations for virtually all white-collar employees to have something close to jobs for life, subject to adequate performance. Even production workers had something quite similar through union contracts and efforts to mimic those contracts in the nonunion sector that provided income protection and seniority recall rights for temporary layoffs.

Layoffs in the face of declining business were always common in the United States. The concept of "downsizing," reducing staffing levels when business was not declining, was not. Except for isolated instances where union workers traded work rules—and ultimately jobs—for wage increases, there are almost no accounts of anything like downsizing before the 1980s. Since then, as chapter 2 documents, there has been a tidal wave of downsizing that has hit virtually every industry and occupation. Downsizings actually increased even as the economy pulled out of recent recessions and continue to increase through the mid-1990s. The vast majority of companies seem to have experienced at least one wave of downsizing, and many have experienced several. As the evidence in chapters 2 and 5 makes clear, the more recent waves of downsizing seem to be different from those of even ten years ago in that they cut much more deeply into management jobs, affect older workers holding more seniority, and hit the service sector harder. And the evidence from employee data in chapter 5—data on both tenure and employee attitudes—seems consistent with the argument that the attachment between employees and employers has declined.

There is a natural inclination to view downsizing as a manifestation of a one-time adjustment inside organizations. After all, the argument goes, companies cannot keep cutting forever. Once these new methods of doing business are incorporated, companies and jobs will settle back down to something like the traditional model. The problem with this view is that the downsizing wave has now gone on for more than a decade, increasing in size and scope along the way. There is no evidence yet of a settling down in the downsizing trend. If this is a one-time adjustment, it is taking a long time to complete.

The alternative view is that downsizing may be part of a more permanent change in employment relations. Certainly companies cannot keep cutting forever without disappearing. But they can cut and hire new workers, then cut again if their markets or their core competencies change, treating labor much like their "just-in-time" procurement of other factors. The important question is whether the pressures on companies to restructure are continuous. Is business simply undergoing a transition to a new model, where employers adopt a new, more efficient mode of operating and then settle down? Or are the pressures such that companies will have to keep changing, keep rearranging their competencies in response to changing markets and competitors? If it is the latter, and much of the evidence we review suggests as much, then the odds are that employment relationships will not settle back into the traditional model.

A piece of evidence arguing for systematic change is the growth of the contingent workforce, described in chapter 2. Part-time and temporary help jobs are no longer confined to clerical agencies. They cover every position up to and including chief executive offi-

cers. (There are several agencies that now supply "temporary" executives.) Contingent workers reduce the fixed costs of operating,
avoid some of the requirements of protective labor legislation, and
give employers considerable flexibility in responding to changes in
their situation. It is difficult to estimate the extent of contingent
work in the United States, largely because there are disagreements
as to how it should be defined. But however it is defined, there is
agreement that it has been growing at an explosive rate. Even more
clearly than downsizing, contingent work represents a permanent
change in the nature of the employment relationship. The expectations between employers and contingent workers, especially those
under contract from agencies, are perhaps the most obvious manifestation of the change.

The one piece of uniformly good news in the restructuring of
employers concerns work organization. As described in chapter 3,
the rise of new ways of organizing work has been rapid, and these
new models are now reasonably widespread. They have the common theme of a reaction against traditional systems of management
control where decision making was based on formal rules and bureaucratic structures. The new arrangements, in contrast, rely
heavily on transferring decision making to individual employees—
empowerment—and on using teams as substitutes for management
structures. Supporting practices like job rotation have helped
broaden substantially the tasks performed by individual workers
and break down the narrow job titles associated with scientific management practices.

The good news about work organization is, first, that these new
arrangements appear to be more effective for organizations. They
make it possible to reduce expensive supervision as well as the
middle-management structures required to monitor supervisors
and ensure compliance with bureaucratic procedures. They also
allow organizations to be more flexible, to adapt more quickly to
change, and to tap the knowledge and ideas of employees. The
second bit of cheer is that, as the behavioral research has suggested
for decades, employees like the greater autonomy and variety associated with these new work systems and seem to respond with better
performance.

Internal Contradictions Inherent in the Changes at Work

The changes in work organization described in chapter 3 are also at
the heart of a series of contradictions and internal problems facing
the evolving model of work organization. These new work systems
demand substantially more from employees than did traditional

arrangements. Employees need more skills, particularly team-related behavioral skills, to succeed in these new systems. And many of these skills can be provided only on the job, by the employer. These new work systems are also more "fragile" on a number of dimensions. The greater autonomy they provide makes far greater demands on the conscientiousness of employees. With less supervision, employees who decide not to do a good job—or worse, to be disruptive—can now be much more damaging to the organization. In order to function, team-based systems rely on interpersonal relationships and networks that are severely disrupted if employees are rearranged.

The contradictions associated with these new systems for organizing work turn on the fact that the needs they generate seem to go in the opposite direction from the trends being introduced in the employment relationship. Thus, while new work systems seem to require greater job security, the reality seems to be that job security has declined. In addition, the new ways of organizing work require more employer training, but the incentives for employers to provide that training are reduced. As described in chapter 4, employers pay for the investment in company-specific skills of the kind required by teams through the improved performance of team members following that training. Because reductions in the length of time that employees stay with a company reduce the period of time over which the employer can capture the benefits of that improved performance, they greatly limit the company's ability to provide that training in the first place.

Changes in the organizational structure of the workplace that are driven in large part by these new work systems also create problems in developing employee skills. More traditional work systems had steep promotion or job ladders that typically began at the entry level with unskilled jobs—pushing a broom in production work, or the management trainee equivalent. A worker with no job skills or work experience could enter this system, make a contribution, and gradually learn enough to progress to the next level. Production workers who were ambitious and hard-working could expect to move into supervisory jobs and then even into higher management.

Employee development of unskilled workers is much more difficult and may be impossible with many of the new work systems. The unskilled, entry-level jobs have been eliminated, employee teams supervise themselves, and the simplest blue-collar jobs, like housekeeping and quality control, have been rolled into existing jobs. Nor is it obvious where the workers will come from to replace the existing skilled workers in team-based systems. It is one thing to take a group of skilled workers and rearrange their production process into a team-based system, eliminating the traditional job ladders where skills were learned. That process is difficult but one that organizational consultants now have mastered. But figuring out how to introduce new, unskilled workers into these team-based systems has yet to be thought through. Truly unskilled workers would flounder, so replacement workers will probably have to be hired from someplace where they have received at least basically similar work experience. That is likely to be other employers, possibly those who still have traditional job ladders, reducing employee attachment further. As more and more companies abandon traditional work systems, it becomes harder to see where the work-based skills will come from to fill the new, team-based jobs. Perhaps more to the point, it is difficult to see how unskilled school leavers will make the transition to skilled jobs.

Perhaps the most important contradictions associated with the change at work concern the employee outcomes described in chapter 5. Labor market outcomes in particular are a product of a great many macroeconomic factors as well as the work-related decisions of individual employers. But some of these outcomes seem directly linked to employment decisions. We see, for example, employees taking on many more of the risks of business as job security and compensation become increasingly contingent on organizational performance; the attachment to employers seems to have declined and the returns associated with staying with the same employer have fallen; morale has declined and work-related stress has increased as more is expected of employees while less is offered to them; employees are now told to manage their own development and careers with the expectation that the process will take them on to jobs elsewhere.

A simple way to think about these changes is that pressures from both the product market and the labor market are now taken inside the company and brought to bear on individual employees. If the more traditional employee relationship buffered employees from market forces, the new relationship is mediated much more powerfully by the market. For workers, these developments represent a new psychological contract at work, a new set of implicit expectations between employer and employee.

Perhaps the most important part of the traditional psychological contract at work was employee commitment to the organization, which developed in part in return for employer offerings such as job security and other protections from the variability of employment associated with outside markets. When employers backed away from their traditional obligations and offered nothing new in return, employee commitment collapsed, as suggested in chapter 6. How employers will operate with sharply lower employee commitment is an important issue, especially given that they have moved toward work systems that demand greater commitment through greater autonomy and reduced supervision.

At the moment, organizational performance does not appear to have suffered from declining employee commitment and morale, in large part because threats of continued layoffs and comparisons with other workers who have lost their jobs have restrained employees from acting out their frustrations. And the fact that most large organizations in particular are going through similar transformations makes it difficult to pursue the most common reaction to perceived inequity, quitting to go work someplace else. At the moment, then, the psychological contract at work is something like a spot market where workers are encouraged to focus on their immediate self-interest, and employers promise to do the same. Longer-run efforts to develop a new psychological contract include making relations with employees more contractual, with contingent pay and more clearly defined performance outcomes. These efforts will come with their own costs, however, including the inevitable increase in litigation associated with any contractual relationship.

Costs for Society

The discussion so far has focused on employers and their interests in the new employment relationships. The interests of individual employees and of the society as a whole may ultimately be more compelling. For employees, perhaps most of the short-term effects have been negative, with the exception of increased opportunities for more satisfying work associated with new work systems. How employees will deal with arrangements that force them to accept more risk and variability in their lives, for example, is an important issue. Will workers still be able to make long-term investments, contracting for home mortgages or college educations for children, when both jobs and pay become more variable? When career development takes place outside a given company, what kind of demands for continuing education and retraining will the workforce make on our postsecondary education system?

Perhaps the most important implications of the new employment relationships concern increased inequality in the workplace and, ultimately, in society as a whole. The traditional employment system essentially redistributed rewards in ways that reduced inequality. Wages, for example, tended to be held somewhat higher than average productivity for new entrants, lower than average productivity for prime-age workers, and higher than average productivity for older workers, smoothing out an individual's earnings profile over time. The new arrangements, with their market and performance orientation, are eliminating those redistribution aspects and increasing inequality. We might well expect the trend toward greater economic inequality associated with differences in education levels to accelerate as the move toward more market-mediated arrangements makes academic credentials one of the only clear measures of general skills.

Nowhere is the rise in inequality more obvious than in the growing gap between the treatment of executives and that of other employees. The traditional point of division within most workplaces between supervisors on the one hand and supervisees and exempt and nonexempt workers on the other has largely disappeared. Supervisors have in many ways been hit harder by restructuring efforts in terms of job losses than have their subordinates. And as some companies are pushed by their unions to provide somewhat greater protections for blue-collar workers, we are seeing something like a convergence in the structure of blue-collar and most white-collar jobs. Among other things, this convergence calls into question the underlying structure of most labor law, which assumes that blue-collar workers require greater protection from employers than do their white-collar supervisors.

The more important division in the workplace is now between executives and all other employees. The growing use of employment contracts for executives gives them special protections from restructuring not enjoyed by other employees, and the huge contingent compensation packages they receive make it clear that they have a very different stake in the organization than do their subordinates. While these arrangements seem to have secured the commitment of executives, they may have reduced executives' ability to lead, in part because of resentment among nonexecutives.

The final aspect of inequality relates to the division of rewards between employees and their employers, who are ultimately the owners. While organizational performance seems to be up sharply as a result of restructuring efforts, the employees have not shared in those rewards. Real wages continue to decline in the economy as a whole and, as noted earlier, most of the nonpecuniary aspects of work seem to have gotten worse.

What Are the Options?

What we would all like to see, of course, are the performance benefits of restructuring without the need for employees to bear the costs. Unfortunately, there are some zero-sum aspects to this relationship. Employers benefit, for example, when wages are held down and working time increased. Even beyond that relationship, it is not obvious how employees can be protected from the costs of restructuring. The response that has been popular in Europe, for example, is to use legislative regulations to prohibit employers from pushing adjustment costs onto employees (by imposing restrictions on layoffs and limiting the use of contingent employees, for example). These restrictions appear to be at least in part successful at protecting current employees from many of the problems we have outlined, but they also appear to have come at the considerable cost of reducing employment opportunities for new hires.

At present, individual employers who try to protect workers from the costs of restructuring are seen, particularly by the investment community, as paying a large price for doing so in terms of overall organizational performance. Employers clearly have some discretion in their employment strategies and can certainly do some things to protect employees—use attrition instead of layoffs or retrain instead of firing and then hiring new skills, for example. The strategies that employers choose to restructure clearly do matter, and it is certainly not clear that the "slash-and-burn" approach is best for organizational performance, let alone for employees and society, in all cases. But if we believe that the pressures to change are long term and continuous, it is probably too much to expect employers and their unions to resist the pressures to restructure. At best, they appear to be able only to soften the costs to employees.

Among the most promising avenues for dealing with the problems of restructuring are to be found in public policy efforts to assist change rather than to block it. Efforts are under way in some states, for example, to help companies that are restructuring avoid the pattern of layoffs and hiring in new skills by subsidizing the retraining of their current workers. And if employment relationships are in fact moving toward a more market-mediated form, then perhaps what we need are efforts that make it easier for employees to operate in that new environment. These might include making pensions and health care more portable, as well as creating systems of credentials that help signal a worker's relevant skills to potential employers.

The more difficult problems are associated with the reduction in unskilled, entry-level jobs. As noted earlier, new entrants to the workforce may find it increasingly difficult to make the transition to good jobs in team-based work systems as employers find that they no longer have a good way of providing work-based learning for new hires. Schools may help provide opportunities for work-based learning as part of a general effort to improve the transition from school to work. As such, they, rather than government training programs, may become the most important instrument for employment policy, since the schools are widely seen as a legitimate avenue for public policy intervention. And as workers are pressed to manage their own career development, they may well look to the schools for help. Access to training opportunities through public postsecondary institutions may be an important part of an effort to reverse the growing inequality in workforce outcomes.

It is difficult at this point to be sure how far the restructuring of employment will go, whether as a society the United States will push further out toward more market-mediated arrangements or pull back somewhat toward more traditional arrangements with greater attachment to an individual employer. There will certainly be increasing variance in employment practices across employers and, indeed, within the same employer over time as companies search for the best way to manage their changing environment. The evidence assembled here suggests that the traditional relationship between employer and employee has eroded and, at least for the foreseeable future, may well continue to do so. The debate about how to protect employees and society as a whole from the costs of restructuring efforts has just begun.

Outline and Authorship of the Book

The authors worked together to outline the book, and individual authors then took responsibility for each chapter.

- Chapter 1 describes the pressures on organizations to restructure employment and was prepared by Michael Useem and Peter Cappelli.

- Chapter 2 documents trends in downsizing and in the use of contingent workforces and was produced by Harry Katz.

- Chapter 3 discusses the changes in work organization within organizations and was prepared by Paul Osterman.

- Chapter 4 describes arrangements for employer-provided training and the changing incentives associated with it and was prepared by David Knoke.

- Chapter 5 describes how the shift toward a different employment relationship affects the demand for skills in society and was the work of Peter Cappelli and Laurie Bassi.

- Chapter 6 considers the consequences of the changing employee relationships for employees and was prepared by Peter Cappelli.

The authors made extensive comments on each other's chapters along the way. The introduction and conclusion were put together by Peter Cappelli based on the ideas assembled by all of the authors.

1

The Pressures to Restructure Employment

Relationships between employers and employees in the United States are undergoing a transformation that begins with the pressures on companies to restructure the way they operate. These pressures go beyond the desire to cut costs to more fundamental changes that increase companies' flexibility as they respond to changing markets.

Since the turn of the century, employers in the United States have sought to rationalize and control their labor supply by bringing the development of skills inside their organizations. Good employee management meant hiring raw talent at the entry level into an "internal labor market" that not only developed workers' skills over time but also insulated jobs and employees from developments in the outside labor market.

The challenge to these arrangements began in the mid-1980s and has accelerated in the 1990s. One might think of these challenges as a kind of "deregulation" of employment where at least some of the insulation that the internal labor markets provided is giving way. Under these new arrangements, employees share much more in the risks of doing business, take on more of the responsibility for managing their own careers, and find that their relationship with management is governed to a greater extent than in recent decades by market forces.

This chapter and those that follow explore the pressures that led to the changes in the old system, what the new developments in employee management look like, and the implications of these changes for employees, organizations, and society.

The Employment System That Died

The changes in employment relations that began in the 1980s appear dramatic because they represent a sharp contrast to the practices that had developed in the United States over the past fifty years. While these practices were never uniform across the entire economy, they were both relatively stable over time and consistent across large sections of industry.

These "traditional" employment practices, in turn, themselves represented a sharp contrast to the dominant system of industrial employment at the turn of the century in which power was essentially devolved to the foreman, who had virtually complete authority to hire, fire, and pay employees. Training occurred informally, on the job; there was no job security, except for some skilled craft workers, and the fear of being fired provided one of the main sources of worker control. A central element of this system was its variability; work rules, norms concerning effort, and employment practices varied across foremen, even in the same factory. Indeed, they could vary over time for the same foreman. For the workers themselves, the terms and conditions of employment appeared both uncertain and arbitrary.

One of the first attempts to rationalize employment relations was made by employers who applied the principles of scientific management to work organization. The pressures to increase production and to reduce its variability during World War I led to some scarcity of labor and put pressure on businesses to pay more attention to employment practices. The government created a series of labor agencies that attempted to impose standard procedures and institutions on employment. The government's General Order 13, for example, imposed regulations on hours and standards for safety and wages on all ordinance contractors. The "Washington Agreement" between employers and the government set employment standards for the entire railroad industry. In both cases, standardization contributed to a rationalization of rules and procedures.

The military acted as a kind of model for industry through its use of selection tests to screen entrants and place them into jobs and its rational models for manpower planning. The government developed programs and course work to extend professional systems of personnel to industry. These training programs spread to the major universities, and their graduates went into leading companies like

DuPont and General Electric. The increasing size and scale of industrial operations also helped foster the rationalization of employment practices by requiring a level of predictability and control that the more casual, foreman-dominated system could not deliver. This was particularly the case during the 1920s, when industry began making massive investments in new equipment that led to the development of more integrated assembly operations.

The most important pressures for rationalizing and standardizing employment practices across the economy, however, came from trade unions, and the first responses were associated with management efforts to resist union organizing. Employer groups such as the Special Conference Committee brought together executives of the largest corporations to coordinate their resistance to unions. The best-known approach to union avoidance was "the American Plan," a systematic program of employment practices that attempted to counter much of the interest in union organizing by addressing worker complaints. A common theme throughout these efforts was the imposition of a system of rules on employment practices that reduced management's arbitrary authority and established standardized practices. And employer organizations like the American Management Association helped to spread these practices across companies.[1]

Not only did the rise of industrial unions in the 1930s revolutionize employment practices, but the union principle of imposing common practices on competitors in the same industry in order to eliminate competition based on labor costs created common systems within industries. Comparisons—and implicit competition—between unions in different industries spread the common system across much of the economy. A great many of the employers who resisted the tide of union organizing did so in part by adopting some of the practices that the unions had secured. Typically they accepted the concept of formal rules governing employment that trade unions put forth but lowered costs by retaining greater flexibility, particularly in the rules governing work allocation.

Characteristics of the Internal System

Among the central principles of what we might now call the traditional system was, first, an implicit distinction between the interests of shareholders and those of management. Shareholders were seen as the group that shouldered the risks associated with business, while management acted to reduce uncertainty. A large part of the interest in forming conglomerates, for example, has been traced to management's interest in diversifying its portfolio of operations in order to smooth out revenues and the overall performance of the corporation.[2] The fact that these actions also smoothed out perceptions of their own performance was not coincidental.

Second, there was a sharp division in both responsibilities and practices between management and labor. Following the model suggested by scientific management, managers made all of the important decisions—did the "thinking" work—while nonmanagement did the physical or mechanical work involved in carrying out those decisions. As a result, employment policies treated managers as the essence of the organization, therefore worthy of substantially greater protection than was offered to other employees.

Third, the criteria governing employment decisions, in contrast to those in earlier systems, tended to be objective characteristics such as seniority rather than individual merit and other factors that involve subjective judgments by supervisors. Seniority was explicitly the criterion for nonmanagement workers, although time served was implicitly an important factor for managers as well.

In addition to these general themes, the traditional employment arrangements had these more specific characteristics:

- *Selection:* Companies often hired unskilled, inexperienced recruits for entry-level, nonexempt work. For management positions, recruits were typically straight out of college or university. While specialized backgrounds were needed for professional positions such as corporate counsel, entry-level positions for most management jobs required only general education.

- *Training and development:* Companies could take in workers without industry experience or even basic business skills because there were opportunities to learn those skills on the job. It was not uncommon to have formal apprenticeship programs for craft work, especially in unionized operations. For production work, employees would begin with the simplest unskilled tasks, such as housekeeping, as entry-level jobs and learn a little about the business and about other jobs by observing. After some period of time—a year or perhaps more—they would bid for a more demanding, higher-paid job.

  Management jobs, in contrast, were likely to involve formal training programs that provided classroom instruction and rotation through jobs in order to allow the trainee to gain practical experience. Larger companies often had extensive training departments that utilized both assessment centers that evaluated the skill needs and development of managers and off-site training centers where skills were taught.

- *Promotion:* Because much of the training was on the job and informal, the promotion structure was closely related to training and development. For nonexempt workers, promotion or transfer to more desirable jobs was based either entirely on seniority or on seniority subject first to a minimum-skills test. Promotion for managers had explicit performance or merit criteria, but the need to rotate through jobs for experience often gave it a "time served" aspect not unlike seniority (Mills, 1985). Larger companies often had an independent, "fast-track" career path that took especially promising candidates from entry-level jobs to the top of the organization.

- *Organizational structure:* The organizational charts of companies were structured according to functional areas, with a separate management hierarchy corresponding to each function (e.g., finance, accounting, production, industrial relations/human resources). Decision-making power was concentrated at the top, at corporate headquarters. It was common for a company's organizational chart to have fourteen or more different levels of hierarchy between production workers and the chief executive officer.

- *Work organization:* As noted earlier, work tended to be organized around the principles of scientific management, with each job having a clearly specified job description and tasks being sharply differentiated across jobs. An assembly operation, for example, might have 100 distinct job titles for production work. The tasks that workers performed were broken down into their simplest components. Industrial engineers designed those tasks, and individual workers had very little autonomy or variety in how they performed their jobs.

  Within management, the functional orientation of tasks produced a similar fragmentation of work; for example, marketing managers assigned to a given product would know only about the marketing issues associated with that product. Above the supervisory jobs and below the executive suite where strategy decisions were made lay a vast "middle management" whose tasks were largely associated with the control function of management. They collected information on performance of a function, compiled it, and passed it up the organizational chart. More important, they ensured that company procedures and policies were followed in the areas they monitored.

- *Job security:* The distinction between employment practices for managers and those for nonmanagers was nowhere as sharp as it was for job security. For practical purposes, managers had jobs for life, subject to minimally acceptable performance. Production workers, on the other hand, were subject to temporary layoffs associated with business cycles. Union contracts helped reduce the costs of layoffs in several ways. First, they often included supplemental unemployment benefit plans that allowed workers to receive some substantial portion of their wage from the company when they were laid off. Second, layoffs were allocated inversely with seniority—the most junior were laid off first—so older, more senior workers were essentially insulated from most layoffs. And workers were recalled from layoffs according to seniority, the most senior first.

One consequence of these procedures was that the laid-off workers remained tied to the company; if they accepted other jobs, they were willing to quit them and come back because they had something very much like a property right invested in their jobs. Wages, promotion prospects, and job security all got better the longer one stayed. As a result, the workforce tended to stay together even in the wake of layoffs. Permanent layoffs associated with productivity improvements or structural change were rare.

- *Wages:* A theme that governed wages for managers and nonmanagers was that the shareholders, not the employees, were the ones taking the risk with respect to business outcomes. For production workers, the only variability in pay concerned overtime work. While managers often had bonus plans, the bonuses tended to be paid on the basis of overall corporate performance (over which the individual manager had little control) and were associated with achieving targets that were not typically missed. There was relatively little association between company performance—including layoffs—and employee compensation. Indeed, the lack of association between pay and company performance became such a "stylized fact" of economic life that a special theory was developed to explain it.[3]

  Pay varied according to job title and by seniority (Medoff and Abraham, 1980), but not according to individual performance. While many organizations had merit pay for managers, in practice, performance evaluations tended not to differentiate employees, and differences in merit-based pay were often trivial (see Foulkes, 1980).[4]

Taken together, these various arrangements helped constitute internal labor markets that internalized employment and insulated it somewhat from the pressures of competitive product and labor markets. Internal labor markets benefited employees, protecting them from the changes that buffeted the organization. But they also aided employers by making the supply of labor and its quality much more predictable. Corporate efforts to rationalize employment can be seen as part of a more general effort to increase predictability and, ultimately, to reduce costs by internalizing functions and vertically integrating operations.

Arguments for the Internal System

It is essential to understand the forces that brought this system together in order to get some idea about what is causing it to fall apart. Why the management of employment was brought inside the company is part of a larger question about why *anything* is produced within the company when there is an option of getting it on the open market. Specifically, why do companies decide to manage functions or tasks that could be subcontracted or purchased directly from the market—why do they have their own legal departments when representation can easily be purchased outside, why do manufacturers produce components themselves instead of buying them from subcontractors, and why do employers develop skilled workers themselves instead of hiring them from the outside? In short, why are there companies at all?

Perhaps the main argument for integration of functions within the company is that it reduces the costs—mainly, the uncertainty—of transactions made in the open market. These arguments were first made by Ronald Coase (1953) and have been developed and expanded by Williamson (1975, 1980). Arm's-length, contractual relationships on the open market can make it difficult to ensure a predictable, high-quality supply of parts from a subcontractor who may, for example, get a better offer from one's competitors for the same parts. While it is possible to sue the subcontractor for breach of contract, in the meantime one's company may be out of business. In addition, the incentives for both employers and employees to try to cheat each other on issues like payment and delivery are increased in short-term, casual relationships.

For employers, the incentives for workers to break agreements on issues such as effort and work quality create a need to monitor carefully the performance of individual employees, a costly undertaking. Employees have had fewer alternatives for addressing the incentives for management to break their side of these agreements unless they could form unions. Then they traditionally responded to these low-trust relationships with highly specific and restrictive contracts that used the threat of legal sanctions to enforce compliance.

Managing the supply of skilled workers presents employers with some additional problems. As Becker (1964) noted, some of the skills that an employer needs from its workforce are unique to that employer. The employer has to pay the training costs for learning those skills, and it is generally inefficient to have the training done elsewhere, especially for skills that are best learned on the job. Employers recoup training costs through the improved performance of employees following training, and it is therefore difficult to provide training unless arrangements are available to tie employees to their employer. Systems of internal promotion and job security that bind workers to the organization help make such training possible.

A final problem related to the basic transaction cost issue noted earlier is that a contractual relationship with employees implies the ability to reopen and renegotiate contracts on an almost continuous basis. The early "drive" system of employment, which relied on the external market both for labor and for discipline (fear of layoff), required virtually continuous negotiations between management and foremen and then again between foremen and workers to make sure that enough bodies showed up with the right skills and performed at the desired level of effort. The transactions involved in this system were time-consuming, and the outcome was very uncertain. As transaction and coordination costs rose, the need to internalize employment increased.

While these arguments turn on the economic efficiency of internalizing employment, other arguments suggest that management may have had additional reasons for bringing control of employment within the company. One set of arguments focuses on management's own needs with respect to the organization of work. Marglin (1974), Edwards et al. (1979), and others suggest that management's interest in taking responsibility and authority away from employees through scientific management derived from the fact that doing so made the jobs of managers simpler and easier, even if it was not necessarily more efficient for the enterprise; it is easier as a manager to give orders than to negotiate and coordinate with empowered employees.

For many companies, then, the decision to introduce internalized employment structures may not have been based entirely on productive efficiency but rested on external pressures such as union demands, comparisons with other companies, and an interest in simplifying the job of managers. If those external pressures were to erode, there might be little commitment inside the company to maintaining these arrangements.

So apparently successful and entrenched were the efforts to internalize employment that the models for "best practices" in personnel and human resources were basically arguments about internalizing these relationships even further. Through the 1980s and even into the 1990s, scholars and practitioners argued that job security would improve commitment and performance (Dyer et al., 1985) and that management should extend its internal labor markets further with formal succession systems going up to the top of the organization. And companies that actually adjusted their business strategies to smooth out production and protect the internal labor markets from change, such as Hewlett-Packard, were held up as models to emulate. IBM was especially praised for its virtually lifetime employment security and career development (see Mercer, 1987).

The many books and articles describing the factors that seemed to be associated with the superior performance of Japanese businesses had a particularly powerful effect on management thinking in the 1980s. A central theme in this research was that Japanese companies were more able to tap the resources of their workers by training and developing their skills over a lifetime at work and by keeping employees committed to the company with offers of lifetime job security. In short, they succeeded by internalizing employment even further.[5] U.S. employers were encouraged to adopt the central concepts of Japanese employment management—essentially lifetime job security for at least a core of workers, extensive on-the-job training, and seniority-based promotions that took workers from the shop floor all the way up to the executive suite.

An obvious question, but one difficult to answer, is the extent to which this internalized system was really optimal for the organizations and the economy as a whole and not just for the managers who administered it. The fact that it became dominant does not necessarily suggest that it was superior to other, perhaps untested alternatives. The internalized employment contracts reduced uncertainty, helped develop firm-specific skills and employee commitment, and helped keep those skills from competitors. But they also locked in culture, kept new ideas out (promoting "group-think"), were inflexible in the short run, and may have contributed to complacency associated with too much insulation from the consequences of actions. A more manageable related question concerns the factors that are changing employment relationships. Perhaps the world has changed in ways that no longer allow the internalized arrangements to function as effectively, or perhaps it has changed in ways that simply reveal the drawbacks that always existed with the old arrangements.

How the World Began to Change

A series of pressures and new challenges came to a head in the 1980s and created enormous incentives for companies to restructure both the way they operated and their relationships with employees. While most of these pressures were associated with developments in the world economy, some were home grown.

Labor Law and Public Policy

An important and underexplored influence on the changing employment system is the legal framework for employment, an influence that plays out primarily through its effects on the fixed costs of different approaches to employment. The common law, case-driven basis of much of the U.S. legal system is much more reactive to changes in the economic system than are civil law systems such as those in Japan and in continental Europe where the presumption is that legislation will impose a particular order on the economy and society. (In Germany, for example, labor law has basically prohibited the expansion of the use of temporary workers.) Nevertheless, the United States has important labor legislation as well, and the order it imposes on the economy is driven by a 1930s view of the industrial workplace. As the economy evolved, new arrangements developed that made it possible to avoid the mandates and costs associated with these laws. And as the mandates increased, so did the incentives to avoid them. The consequence—and the irony—is that the workplace may have been transformed even faster, in ways that reduced employee protections, because of the incentives created by labor legislation designed to protect employees.

The array of federal legislation directed at employment is vast and has made the U.S. Department of Labor the largest enforcement agency in the federal government. Among the main pieces of legislation are the National Labor Relations Act governing employee representation, the Civil Rights Acts on equal opportunity in employment, the Fair Labor Standards Act governing wages and hours, the Occupational Safety and Health Act on workplace conditions, the Employee Retirement and Income Security Act on pensions, the Worker Adjustment and Retraining Notification Act affecting plant closings, the Family and Medical Leave Act providing unpaid leaves, the Americans with Disabilities Act, and a series of executive orders on similar issues whose mandates work in much the same way as legislation. Important state legislation—workers' compensation in particular—and private lawsuits under common law concerning violations of employment contracts also put pressure on the employment relationship.

These laws provide important protections for employees. They also constrain the actions of employers and impose significant administrative costs associated with documenting compliance. Most of the legislation has as its model a very traditional notion of industrial employment in which an "employee" is on site in a long-term relationship where the arrangements look much like those we have described. Arrangements that differ from that traditional model can lead to situations where "employees" are no longer covered by the legislation. Consider the following examples.

Among the most important labor laws is the 1938 Fair Labor Standards Act (FLSA), which was designed to protect employees from being required to work excessive hours and other management abuses. The FLSA was driven by the assumption that workplaces were divided into two parts, regular employees and management, and that those in management were "committed career employees" who did not need to be protected from the employer; management would look after its own. The expressions "exempt" and "nonexempt" employees are ubiquitous in dividing the U.S. workplace and come from this act. They distinguish supervisors and management, who are exempt from the act, from other workers. A key criterion used to differentiate exempt from nonexempt employees is whether an employee is paid on a monthly (exempt) or an hourly (nonexempt) basis.

As one of its mandates, the FLSA requires that an employer pay nonexempt workers a 50 percent overtime wage premium for weekly hours worked beyond a general norm of forty hours and that they receive at least the national minimum wage. An employer can avoid these requirements and become exempt from the FLSA if the nature of the employment relationship changes and moves away from the traditional model; for example, hourly workers can change to being paid monthly or move to commissions or contingent pay and become exempt from many aspects of the act.

The National Labor Relations Act (NLRA) as amended in 1947 deals with employee representation in most of the private sector. This act also divides the workplace into two camps—workers and managers—and does not extend the right to be represented by labor organizations to supervisory employees. In a famous case involving Bell Aerospace, the Supreme Court in 1974 extended this exclusion from coverage to purchasing agents who had no supervisory responsibilities. The argument for excluding them was that they were seen as part of a management group—as being more like managers than hourly workers. The key characteristic that defined their work for the purposes of the NLRA was that they carried out their tasks with considerable autonomy. In other words, they were not themselves supervised.[6] An employer who redesigned jobs to give workers autonomy would effectively take those positions away from union representation and would remove those workers from the protections of the act.

The most important exemptions concern the use of leased or temporary employees, an issue discussed at greater length in chapter 2. Most of the important labor laws allow some exemptions for small employers, as measured by the number of workers they employ, to help reduce the administrative burden on them. And while the arrangements differ for each piece of legislation, most of the laws do not count workers who are truly temporary or leased as employees of the organization. Small but growing employers can shift jobs to these contingent workers in order to retain their small-employer exemptions.

More to the point, employers can avoid the requirements of these laws, and the administrative burdens associated with them, if their workers meet the test of being leased employees (that is, leased from an agency such as a temporary help agency). The considerable compliance burdens and threats of litigation associated with hiring and firing workers are removed from an establishment when its workers are in fact the direct employees of an outside agency. The establishment's management can simply cancel the contracts of leased employees that they do not find acceptable, for whatever reason. As we note in chapter 5, they can also use the leasing or temporary agencies to screen employees, hiring the temporaries they like onto the establishment's permanent payroll.[7]

Another incentive to use leased employees and outsourcing of jobs comes from the 1975 Employee Retirement Income Security Act (ERISA). As Baron and Pfeffer (1988) note, the act requires employers to provide pension arrangements equally to all "employees," so generous retirement programs for management have to be offered proportionately to lower-level employees as well. Employers who take low-level jobs off their own payroll and place them on to a contractor's reduce substantially the burden of providing more generous pensions for management.

Changes like reduced supervision and greater autonomy for employees, the increasing use of contingent pay that varies with performance, and the growing popularity of contingent and leased employment are central parts of the restructuring of employment in the United States. And while there are many other factors pressing for these developments, they are also consistent with efforts to avoid the substantial requirements of existing labor legislation. The industrial model of employment that underpins these laws, most of which were enacted in the 1930s, seems less and less applicable and raises the question of whether the entire system governing employment law needs to be rethought.

Increased Competitiveness

The most important factors helping to change the employment relationship in the United States began with developments in the world economy. A series of unique economic conditions helped make the old system possible. First among these were stable, protected product markets. Many industries, such as transportation, had explicit product market regulations that restricted competition both in services and in price. Heavy industries like autos and steel were effectively oligopolies where prices were administered informally rather than competitively. Industries that were competitive, such as meatpacking, had standardized union contracts that prevented competitive pressures from impinging on labor costs.

The simultaneous appearance of inflation and low growth—"stagflation"—that began during the Nixon administration may have been the first indication that things had changed in the economy. But in terms of employment, the big changes began following the price increases imposed by the Organization of Petroleum Exporting Countries (OPEC), especially the second round of increases in 1979. Fuel-efficient Japanese cars began taking market share from the U.S. auto producers, and as U.S. auto sales scaled back, so did the related demand for steel and for components such as tires. U.S. consumers also particularly noticed the rising market share of imports in electronics and consumer appliances, although foreign products were equally as competitive in other areas.

The relative salience of the competitive fray is evident in the survey of 531 corporations on their experience in 1992. When asked to identify the factors motivating their restructuring, three quarters of the companies cited economic pressure from competitors (Wyatt Company, 1993). Within the United States, the deregulation of airlines in 1978 and of trucking and railroads in 1980 and the gradual easing of regulations in financial services and telecommunications produced the most obvious and dramatic increases in competition. In industries that had always been highly competitive, such as meatpacking and tire production, the rise of lower-wage, nonunion operations inside the United States provided yet another form of competitive pressure. One immediate effect of this competition was a sharp increase in business failures and the job losses associated with it (see Fig. 1.1). Plant closings and other reductions in capacity in companies that survived was a related outcome.

An interesting study of the economy of Dallas, Texas, suggests the magnitude of the turbulence in the corporate world and in employment. In 1970, about 6.8 percent of all the businesses operating in Dallas failed. By the mid-1980s, about 21 percent of the businesses in the city were failing each year. Twenty-seven percent of all the private-sector jobs that existed in Dallas in 1986 were gone three years later, replaced by new ones (Tully, 1993).

Much of the competitive pressure for restructuring came from

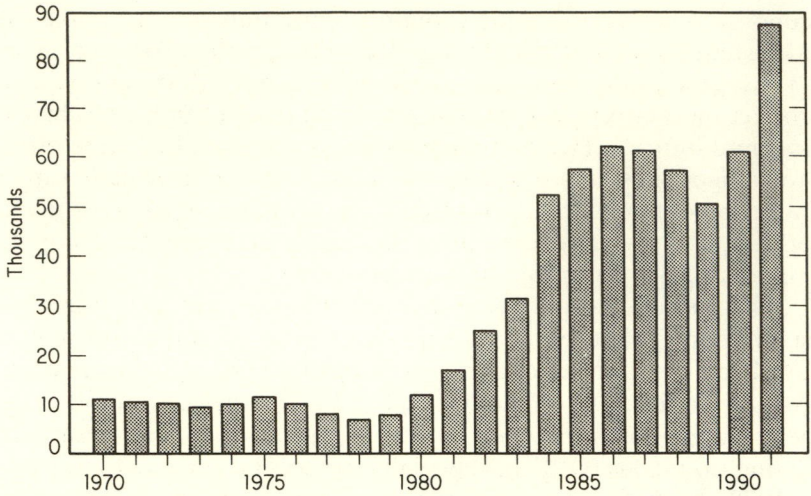

Figure 1.1. Number of Company Failures, 1970–1991. *Note:* Because of statistical revision, data prior to 1984 are not directly comparable to the new series. Data for 1991 are preliminary. *Source: Business Failure Record* (New York: Dun & Bradstreet, 1992).

international competitors who often operated with substantially lower labor costs, especially in the 1970s and early 1980s before the slow growth in real wages in the United States had its cumulative effect. A simple measure of the growing importance of international competition for businesses in the United States during the 1980s is the share of imports as a proportion of gross domestic product (GDP). That figure rose only about one percentage point per decade from 1960 through 1980, when imports averaged just under 8 percent of GDP. But by 1994, imports had risen sharply to more than 14 percent of GDP (*Economic Report,* 1995).

Evidence for the influence of international competitive pressures at the corporate level comes from a 1991 Lou Harris survey of 406 large companies. The researchers' analysis reveals that the larger the proportion of the company's workforce outside the United States, the more likely the company was to have downsized its employment ranks and redesigned its work system.[8] Companies with more of their workforce outside the United States face greater international competitive pressures and have more exposure to alternative models for organizing work from which to learn than do companies whose operations are located largely within the United States.

The importance of international lessons for organizational restructuring can be seen in a comparative study of productivity during the early 1990s in the United States, Japan, and Germany. Using intensive case analysis, the study focused on nine industries, among them food, steel, automobiles, soaps and detergents, consumer electronics, and computers. It found that many of the national differences in productivity could be traced to differences in the companies' manufacturing and organizational designs. Manufacturing design included the extent to which companies used standardized components, minimized parts, and streamlined process. Organizational design included the degree of decentralization in authority, distribution of information, and provision of incentives for performance. In contrast, differences in workforce skills, capacity utilization, and other factors played little role in explaining the productivity differences. Many of the differences in the organizational systems were traced in turn to international competition. Companies that faced highly productive international transplants in their home market, for instance, were far more likely to adopt the improved organizational designs pioneered by the transplants (McKinsey and Co., 1993).

During the 1980s, U.S. companies were especially likely both to feel the global pressures for improved performance and to see the new production systems and organizational designs that were developed elsewhere. The rising importance of international competitors within the United States can be seen in trends on the investment of non–U.S. companies in U.S. facilities and operations. From 1981 to 1986, new foreign direct investment in the United States averaged $21.4 billion annually. From 1987 to 1990, in contrast, it more than doubled, averaging $57.1 billion annually. Similarly, the total stock of direct foreign investment by non–U.S. companies in the United States in 1980 stood at $83.0 billion; by 1990 it had reached $403.7 billion. Direct investment by U.S. companies in ongoing and new operations abroad also rose during the 1990s, although not as rapidly. The stock of direct foreign investment by U.S. companies outside the United States in 1980 stood at $220.2 billion; by 1994 it had reached $610.1 billion (United Nations, 1995).

Changing Markets

Perhaps because they now faced more real competitors in the marketplace, companies began searching for new ways to be competitive in addition to cutting costs and prices. A promising route was to track changes in consumer demand more closely and to adjust products to those changes. Reducing the lag between assessing consumer needs and getting products out the door is the best way to do that.

Making this reduction requires becoming more flexible, and, as a practical matter, becoming more flexible means replacing dedicated equipment and procedures with ones that can be rearranged more easily.

The pressures to achieve flexibility in the face of changing consumer demands is one of the most important factors driving the restructuring of employment because it makes fixed investments obsolete more quickly. Internalized employment structures and the long-term commitments associated with them (hiring essentially unskilled employees, investing in their training, gradually recouping the investment, then maintaining compensation after performance deteriorates) are one of the most substantial aspects of fixed costs.

Much of the pressure for quicker response to markets came from Japanese competitors. Within Japan, the epic battle for market share in the motorcycle industry between Honda and the smaller but more aggressive Yamaha taught a lesson that spread throughout Japanese industry. After being initially caught out of position by Yamaha's new product lines, Honda reorganized its product delivery and introduced a staggering 113 new models over the next eighteen months, making the Yamaha lines look old and dated and effectively burying Yamaha's challenge (Stalk, 1988). Womack et al. (1990) observed that Japanese car models in the 1980s were replaced by new ones twice as quickly as U.S. and European models. In the 1970s, new products accounted for one fifth of corporate profits, but by the 1980s that figure had risen to one third (Slater, 1993). These were lessons that would soon be adopted by U.S. companies.

One source of the pressure to cut development time is the fact that new products no longer enjoy their novelty for long. One factor reducing the life of new products, especially those where matters of taste are important, such as fashion, has been the globalization of consumer preferences. It was common in previous decades for U.S. producers to transfer products to consumer markets in developing countries for a few years once they had fallen out of fashion in the United States, significantly extending the life and the production runs of those products. As television and other media became increasingly global, however, advertising campaigns followed, and trends in tastes became much more common across borders. Designs now fall out of fashion in Mexico City at about the same time as they do in Chicago, making it much more difficult for companies to extend product lives by shipping them abroad. Another factor reducing the novelty of new products is the increasing ability of competitors to copy them. Studies of "reverse engineering" find that for about 70 percent of all new products, modern competitors can learn just about everything they need in order to produce it themselves within one year. Even about 40 percent of the idiosyncratic "process learning" associated with production is eventually acquired by competitors (Ghemawat, 1986).

The time from conceiving to producing and marketing a product has dropped dramatically across a wide range of products—by half for products like cars and telephones (Griffen, 1993). Reducing time delays in production, for example, not only cuts time to market but also reduces costly excessive production that occurs when product demand is changing but output has not yet been adjusted (Stalk, 1988). In addition, as producers find that they benefit significantly in terms of market share and profitability by having broader product lines (Kekre and Srinivasan, 1990), they are forced to develop "flexible factories" where costs do not rise when variety expands.

These developments have affected employee relations in several ways. Empirical studies find that an important way to cut development time is to change traditional, functionally oriented systems of work organization and replace them with cross-functional teams (Stalk, 1988; Morris, 1993). Another important technique is to rely on external sourcing and subcontractors, especially where product markets are uncertain (Rosenau, 1988).

The most important impact on employees, however, arises from the fact that the competencies and skills needed change when products change and the old skills become obsolete. Companies look outside for the new skills, utilizing subcontractors, joint ventures, and outside hiring, in part because it takes too long to develop them inside. And they drop employees with the obsolete skills to avoid carrying the associated costs.

How do these arguments square with the assertions presented earlier that companies like IBM found flexibility within through internal labor markets and employment security? These arrangements helped reduce resistance to what might be considered low-level restructuring associated with rearranging existing workers and skill sets. Piore and Sabel (1984) take this argument a step further and assert that in order to react quickly to changing markets, to produce new products that can be tailored to market niches, companies need a highly skilled and committed group of employees that can be redeployed quickly and flexibly. This seems especially sensible in large-scale manufacturing when contrasted with the massive dedicated systems of assembly-line operations and the huge production runs needed to make them efficient.

Innovations in auto manufacturing, however, have demonstrated that high levels of flexibility and product variety can be achieved in assembly-line operations that do not fit the flexible-specialized model (MacDuffie et al., 1996). The workers in these operations are basically the same mix of the unskilled and the semiskilled as in traditional assembly, not skilled crafts as in flexible-specialization, and the work organization is still an assembly line.[9]

Further, the flexible-specialized model does not fit situations that go beyond variations on the same product. In the pharmaceutical industry, for example, the shift from physical chemistry to biochemistry as a basis for new drugs meant that the old research and development competencies based on physical chemistry were largely obsolete. Particularly in the service industries, where competencies reside more clearly within individual employees as opposed to within an organizational system (e.g., software development, accounting, or legal services), rearranging competencies may require rearranging employees, and market opportunities may disappear long before an employer can develop these new skills among its current employees.

Financial Restructuring

The changes that have occurred in competition in product markets appear to have occurred gradually when compared to the pressures brewing in the financial markets. These pressures were driven by changes in ownership structure and in ideas about how corporations should be structured, and their influence on restructuring was both immediate and dramatic.

The United States has experienced several waves of financial restructuring. The first, between 1896 and 1902, was driven by horizontal mergers and acquisitions that led to concerns about monopoly power in the marketplace. The second, between 1926 and 1933, involved mergers and acquisitions based on vertical integrations of the kind discussed earlier that reduced transaction costs and uncertainty. The third wave, concentrated between 1965 and 1969, was the creation of conglomerates, putting together unrelated businesses in order to achieve financial synergies by smoothing out variations in corporate revenue. All of these trends were driven by the notion that bigger is better and that there were scale economies to be achieved by putting organizations and functions together.

The most recent wave of restructuring, which began around 1981 and is continuing in the mid-1990s, represents an entirely different development. In essence, it is driven by the opposite notion, the belief that there are gains to "unbundling" existing operations. An important component of this restructuring trend began with innovations in debt financing, "junk bonds" in particular, that made it possible to raise large amounts of cash for speculation. The availability of this cash, in turn, made it possible for even small groups of investors to purchase publicly held companies and to take them private through "leveraged buyouts." It was then necessary to operate the acquired company in ways that would generate higher profits in order to pay off the high interest on the junk bonds and make the transaction financially feasible. Jensen (1989) and others argue that higher debt forces companies to run more efficiently. One reason why so many of the leveraged buyouts were led by the companies' existing managements was that they knew how to make the companies more profitable. Of the 500 companies on the *Fortune* list of top manufacturers in 1980, one third had experienced a hostile takeover threat by the end of the decade, and one third no longer existed as an independent entity by 1990 (see Table 1.1).

Many of the changes installed by corporate raiders in the 1980s and 1990s were simple and stemmed from the notion that management in earlier periods had operated the companies with more complicated goals than simply maximizing profits. The changes centered on efforts to increase profits by cutting costs. Reducing management perks such as expensive offices and facilities and corporate jets was an obvious place to start. Cutting jobs was another. The empirical research on companies acquired by leveraged buyout suggests that they cut substantially more jobs—12 percent more—than did other companies (Kaplan, 1989).

A related development stemmed from research on conglomerates that found that diversification that took corporations away from their "core" or basic business interests hurt overall performance. For companies that acquired new businesses, the closer the new operation was to their existing operations, the better the overall corporate performance; for corporations selling off businesses, the more unrelated the sold operation was to their core functions, the better the corporations' subsequent performance (Markides, 1993). These results helped persuade conglomerates to spin off divisions that were not related to their core functions.

By the end of the 1980s, corporations were selling off divisions and companies and buying new ones at a rapid rate. In order to make an operation attractive to buyers, it was important to raise its profitability, and the easiest way to do that was to cut costs. Similarly, the best way to avoid being sold off or, for publicly held companies, being acquired through a hostile takeover was to show that it would be difficult to raise profitability—that there would be no

Table 1.1.   A Decade of Restructuring of Large Companies

Of the Fortune 500 largest manufacturers, between 1980 and 1990
- 1 in 3 received a takeover bid
- 1 in 3 ceased to exist as an independent business
- Employment dropped from 15.9 million to 12.4 million
- Product sector diversity declined by half

obvious gain for the acquiring company. And the best way to do that was to cut costs in advance of a takeover.

Investor Pressures

A related pressure for change came from the growing concentration of ownership among large institutional holders. Pension funds, bank trusts, insurance companies, and investment managers acquired steadily increasing fractions of company stock (Fig. 1.2). Traditionally, they had followed the "Wall Street rule" and expressed their disappointment with a company's performance by selling their holdings. But by the 1990s the largest institutions were no longer able to dispose so readily of their undesirable stocks, in part because a portion of many large holdings were indexed, a practice in which funds are invested among stock according to a preset formula and not actively managed. In total, about one sixth (15.9 percent) of all institutional stock holdings is indexed, much of it allocated among the widely used Standard and Poor's 500. Mutual fund managers rarely use indexing, but about one third of the equity managed by banks (33.4 percent) and corporate pension funds (35.9 percent) is indexed, and more than half (51.7 percent) of the equity managed by public pension funds is indexed (Riverside Economic Research, 1994). The value of index-based investments changes when the overall index changes, not just when an individual company's performance plummets, and it is difficult to sell off the shares of the individual companies without breaking the indexing rule.

For the nation's largest holders, even an actively managed, non-

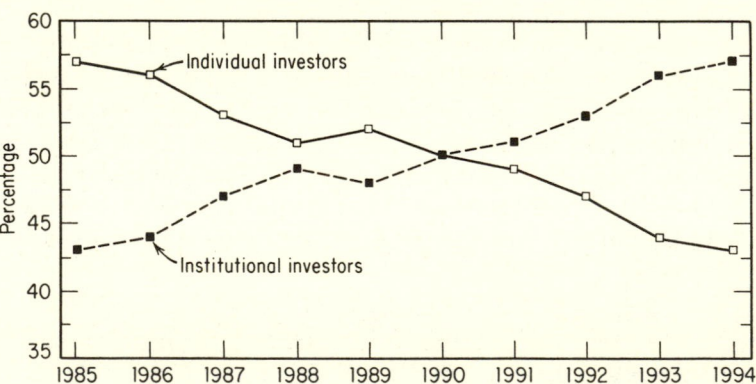

Figure 1.2. Percentage of Shares of 1,000 U.S. Largest Companies Held by Individual and Institutional Investors, 1985–1994. *Source: Business Week,* 1994.

Table 1.2. Influence of Institutional Investors on U.S. Companies

Insitutional investors press companies to . . .
- Redesign the company to become more competitive
- Improve short-term and long-term performance

Institutional investors press companies by . . .
- Occasionally voting against company directors
- Sometimes voting against management proposals
- Sometimes asking for better managers
- Often urging companies to alter structure, and improve performance
- Frequently meeting with company executives
- Frequently asking for quarterly performance of units and products
- Almost always seeking more information on company plans

indexed investment in a downwardly spiraling company cannot be disposed of readily. To do so requires finding buyers willing to acquire the shares, which often run in the millions. Other prospective buyers large enough to absorb such a position, unfortunately for the would-be seller, are already familiar with the same bad news. Investors do, of course, continually trade their shares (Riverside Economic Research, 1994). Still, for investors with very large holdings, an alternative to disposing of ever larger blocks of a declining stock (see Table 1.2) is to pressure management for company changes to improve performance.

The largest investors, as a result, increasingly turned to pressing troubled companies to change and develop new ways to express their concerns, including voting against a company's directors, supporting unfriendly acquisitions, and directly negotiating with management. During the late 1980s, for instance, large institutions expanded their support for shareholder proxy resolutions calling for changes in governance, whether to rescind a poison pill provision, introduce confidential voting, or establish a shareholder advisory committee. (A poison pill is a financial device intended to discourage unwanted takeovers; confidential voting is a process device designed to protect institutions against undue pressure by management to vote favorably on proxy resolutions; and a shareholder advisory committee is a board device intended to facilitate direct communication among large investors, company directors, and top management.) Rarely did the antimanagement resolutions gain shareholder majority, but they did gain management attention (Bethel and Liebeskind, 1993; Hoskisson et al., 1993; Useem, 1996). Studies found, for example, that job cuts resulting from restructuring were greater when shareholders were organized into large blocs, such as in institutional holdings (Bethel and Liebeskind, 1993).

The specific mix of the outside demands for restructuring has evolved since the mid-1980s. At that time, frontal assaults on owner-ship and control, both actual and threatened, served as a major impetus for financial restructuring, with organizational change coming in its wake. This way of forcing restructuring rapidly ta-pered off at the end of the 1980s, as seen in Figure 1.3; after peaking during the 1987–1988 period, corporate acquisitions (including mergers) and leveraged buyouts dropped substantially in value.

Takeovers—and attempted takeovers—had a powerful effect on employment. About 27 percent of the stock price premium associ-ated with takeovers has been attributed to the cost savings of layoffs (Bhagat, Schleifer, and Vishay, 1990), and the cuts were especially deep in white-collar jobs (Lichtenberg and Siegel, 1987).

A sharp sell-off in the stock market in October 1987 contributed to the decline in the number of takeovers, as did a drop in the quality of available deals. Another factor was a sharp drop in the high-yield bond market following the bankruptcy of firms that had been at the forefront of acquisitions during the 1980s, including Drexel Burnham Lambert. Some acquisition and buy-out activities had been driven by dynamics of their own, and the demise in the late 1980s may have also derived from a loss of confidence little related to any underlying financial trends (Kaplan and Stein, 1992; Yago 1991; Blair and Schary, 1993).

In the active market for corporate control that began to decline during the early 1990s, boards of directors more often intervened directly to force changes in top management. Citing lackluster fi-nancial results, in 1992 and 1993 governing boards replaced the chief executives of American Express, Borden, Digital Equipment, Eastman Kodak, IBM, and General Motors. All of the boards had been under criticism from shareholders angered by languishing stock prices. None had forced out a CEO in recent memory (GM had

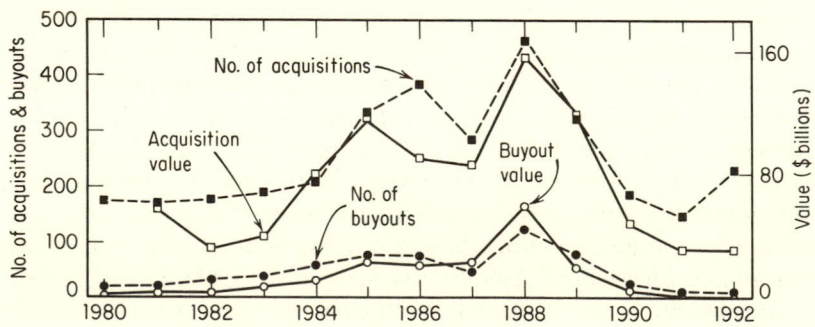

Figure 1.3. Acquisitions and Buyouts of Publicly Traded Companies, 1980–1992. *Source:* Merrill Lynch, 1993.

not done so since 1920), and some had never done so (the Digital ax fell on its founder). The boards brought in new CEOs committed to corporate change, and, in the aftermath of the resulting organizational upheavals, the companies often pushed through extensive financial changes. IBM's new CEO, for instance, brought in a new chief financial officer in 1993 whose financial controls over inventories, process, and research were far more stringent than those of his predecessor. The new financial regime at IBM in the 1990s was akin to what often followed hostile takeovers at other companies during the 1980s (Hays, 1994).

The stronger shareholder presence pointed in a single direction. Investors gauged their own success by the improved market value of their shares plus dividends over a quarter, year, or perhaps several years. How companies produced that outcome was of little direct interest so long as it was delivered. When companies faltered, however, institutional holders were now quicker to insist that the company find new strategies and structures to produce. Making that all the more difficult was the increased competition faced by large businesses, something that was viewed by investors as management's problem, not their own. Companies would simply have to become more competitive. To do so would no doubt require cutting costs, improving productivity, and raising quality. It would be up to management to find the organizational formula.

And the formulas they found concentrated on restructuring the companies and slashing jobs. One study of share price reactions to company layoff announcements from 1979 to 1987 illustrates the thrust of the investors' message for would-be restructurers. In the days immediately following layoffs announced as part of general restructurings, stock prices rose an average 4 percent. Downsizing announced simply as a cost-cutting measure, however, depressed stock prices an average 6 percent. Wall Street appeared to like restructuring *and* job shedding but disdained cutbacks shorn of broader plans for improved results. Although some investors seek quick returns and expect to gain from immediate cost cutting, more investors seek enduring returns from restructurings that may entail layoffs but must also include organizational change (Worrell et al., 1991).

Illustrating the Wall Street applause for layoffs that are symptomatic of a larger restructuring strategy, investors generally cheered the Xerox Corporation's announcement in late 1993 of its plans to slash its workforce by 10,000 employees, or about a tenth. Many investors recognized the action as only the latest component of a prolonged and extensive remaking of the Xerox organization dating back to the early 1980s. Said an analyst with First Boston on learning of the layoff announcement. "We are just starting to see these types of restructurings. These guys are ahead of the curve."

Xerox had been decentralizing its divisions and streamlining its work for several years, and the downsizing was but the latest piece of the puzzle. In announcing the cutbacks, Xerox CEO Paul Allaire asserted that "we are going to make the company more productive, more customer-oriented, and bring products to market more quickly." By day's end, Xerox stock had soared by 7 percent (Hays and Naik, 1993; Holusha, 1993).

Many companies, of course, restructured well before they were directly affected by competition or pressures from investors. Some changed in anticipation of a more market-competitive and investor-accountable future; others started the process simply because top management decided it was an act of good management. Still, for many businesses, the perception of a demanding world of more vigorous competitors and more vigilant investors constituted an important catalyst for change (Useem, 1993; Donaldson, 1994).

An accounting technique called "economic value added" (EVA) played a central role in shaping the way that companies restructured. This technique takes into account the opportunity cost of capital and related fixed assets when calculating after-tax operating profits. So, for example, a division with large profits that sits on expensive real estate would find its performance looking much worse under the EVA calculations after the investment value of its real estate and capital equipment was deducted from its performance. EVA techniques and their various derivations are used widely in industry, where they are thought to predict accurately future movements in stock prices.[10] The effect has been to create incentives for managers to cut fixed investments of all kinds.

In addition to acting as an incentive to cut jobs, the various financial pressures we have described have other important effects on employment. Perhaps the most important of these is to inject uncertainty and change into all aspects of the employment relationship. The relentless pressure for improved performance creates a continuing need to experiment and restructure in the face of changing opportunities. Further, the pressure to increase profits by cutting costs focuses special attention on fixed investments, especially where the long-term payoff is difficult to quantify. As we discuss in chapter 6, the psychological contract with employees, in which an employer's investment in employee development and job security is repaid by employee loyalty and performance, is an example of such a long-term investment. The financial pressures to cut back on the employer's end of the contract with employees are enormous.

New Management Techniques

Developments associated with the practice of management also contributed to important changes in employment relationships by providing a vehicle for pursuing the greater pressure for financial performance. Some of these were driven in part by academic research.

Incentives Benchmarked on Shareholder Value

Studies of executive compensation during the 1970s and early 1980s documented the lack of a relationship between corporate performance and executive pay. Indeed, several studies indicated that existing arrangements for compensating executives in fact created perverse incentives for them to take actions that were not in the interests of stockholders, such as diversifying the portfolio of the company (Lambert, Larker, and Verrecchia, 1991).

These results helped fuel stockholder pressure for better performance. The managerial decisions of executives were more explicitly tied to their anticipated worth to stockholders by making the incentives that affect promotion, compensation, and dismissal—especially for executives—more contingent on changes in shareholder value. Top management compensation became increasingly linked to shareholder value through expanded use of stock options. Between 1984 and 1995, the variable fraction of total compensation received by the top seven employees at forty-five large firms (as tracked by a consulting firm) rose from 37 percent to 61 percent. Virtually all of the drop in the fixed fraction had been filled by long-term incentive pay, up from 19 to 40 percent of the compensation pie. Long-term incentive compensation is generally based on company stock options, a compensation device closely aligned with shareholder value (see Figure 1.4). As a new chief executive assumed office at Eastman Kodak in 1993, for example, he received options to purchase more than 750,000 shares of Kodak stock, options that had little or no value unless the stock price increased substantially but whose potential worth was between $13 million and $17 million if the stock price did rise (Bounds, 1993). Detailed analysis of incentive packages for large-company chief executives for 1988, 1991, and 1992 reveals a sharp increase in the extent to which CEO compensation is linked to the production of greater wealth for stockholders (Jensen and Murphy, 1990; United Shareholders Association, 1993; Hewitt Associates, 1994; Useem, 1996).

These arrangements had the added feature for executives of apparently justifying much higher overall compensation because it appeared to be paid for out of additional performance—that is, the additional compensation appeared to be "free" in the sense that it came from new earnings. Contingent pay plans accelerated rapidly through the 1980s and soon worked their way down into the middle management ranks as well, albeit at substantially lower amounts, increasing the incentives for managers to maximize profits by cutting costs (see Figure 1.5).

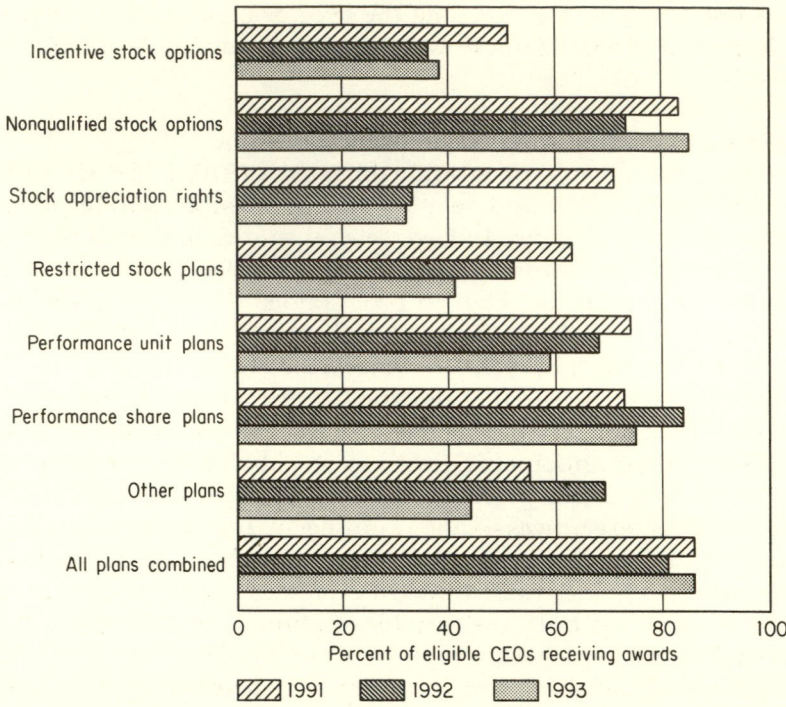

Figure 1.4. Long-Term Incentive Plans, 1991–1993. *Source:* 1993 Hay Executive Compensation Report—Industrial (Philadelphia: Hay Group, 1993).

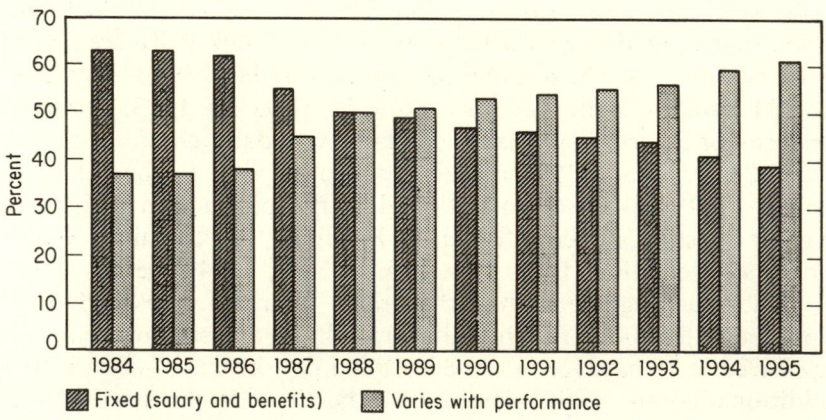

Figure 1.5. Percentage of Senior Management Compensation That Is Fixed or Variable, 1984–1995. Data are for top seven to eight executives at 45 large companies. *Source:* Hewitt Associates surveys (unpublished).

Efforts to reform compensation structures and to tie them to performance, combined with the push toward autonomous work groups, led to a substantial move toward decentralizing control over options. Entire divisions could become "profit centers" that were held accountable to a single standard, profit and loss, and that had more or less complete autonomy over how they achieved that standard. One consequence of this development was that the need for corporate-level control and oversight, and, along with it, the need for corporate staff, diminished dramatically. A second consequence relates to the need to cut fixed costs noted earlier. As each unit became accountable for meeting overall performance targets, it also bore the risks of failure when markets changed. Efforts to minimize that risk led to a strong preference for variable costs that could be adjusted to changing markets over fixed costs. With respect to employment issues, that pressure played itself out especially in a preference for contracting out and using contingent workers in place of full-time employees and for contingent pay.

MIS Systems

A second contributor to the restructuring of employment was new management information and control systems made possible by cheaper computer power. Spreadsheets and financial planning software took over tasks that in the past had been performed by lower- and mid-level accounting managers and now were available to virtually every employee of the company. Sophisticated management information systems kept track of financial performance, material flows, and intermediate transactions throughout the company, tracking and identifying trends. This information was available, often in real time, to everyone on the network, taking over the important control function previously performed by middle management. Research by Osterman (1986) shows how the introduction of computers affected the distribution of employment across jobs inside organizations, leading to a net reduction in management jobs.

TQM Movement

Efforts to reform the way work is organized—the way tasks are designed and the authority structure—go back at least fifty years in the United States (see chapter 3). These efforts stagnated until the 1980s, when they received a boost from an unlikely source: the quality revolution that was imported from Japan. The attention to Japanese management practices accelerated during the 1980s, but the lessons that had the most impact in the United States concerned programs for improving production quality in areas where Japanese companies had an obvious and undeniable edge. Quality control techniques like Statistical Process Control became standard concepts in U.S. companies, but it was the quality circles—teams of workers empowered to address and solve shop-floor quality problems—that may ultimately have had the biggest impact.

Some estimates suggest that as many as 85 percent of U.S. companies now have total quality management (TQM) programs, with larger and more industrial operations being more likely to have them (Conference Board, 1993). One interesting difference between U.S. programs and those in Japan is that while the Japanese plans rely more on skilled lower-level workers to run them, those in the United States rely more on management (Rogers, 1993). TQM programs have recently received a great deal of attention for their failures, in part because they have often been introduced as a "quick fix." But while they may have failed to meet expectations in some companies, they almost always opened the door to employee involvement and teamwork as a general approach to solving problems. Where they succeeded, the appetite for autonomy and problem solving grew, leading in many cases to work arrangements that freed employees to make decisions on their own. The direct implementation of employee ideas is one manifestation of this development (Fig. 1.6) and is explored in detail in chapter 3. Where employees are given more authority to manage themselves, fewer supervisors are needed. And when the number of supervisors is

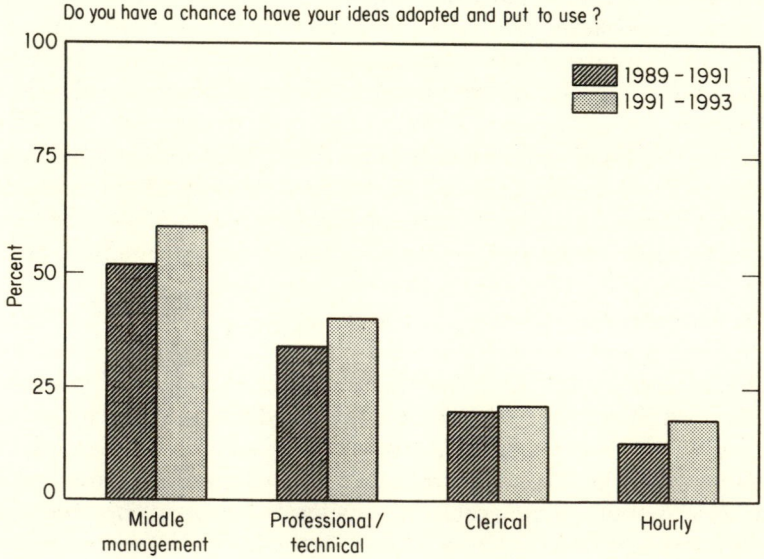

Figure 1.6. Use of Employee Ideas. *Source:* Hay Research for Management database.

reduced, so is the need for the middle managers who supervise the supervisors. The consequences for restructuring organizations include sharp cuts in the management structure and in management jobs.

Movement to "Core Competencies"
The arguments, noted earlier, that conglomerates should concentrate on related businesses in order to become more successful have their parallel within the management of individual operations. Here the argument is that successful businesses have a "core competence" or distinctive capability that differentiates them from competitors and drives their competitiveness (Prahalad and Hamel, 1990). Such competencies might include superior product design abilities or better marketing skills, competencies that cut across individual product lines. To become more successful, companies need to nurture and develop those competencies. Efforts directed at aspects of the business that do not make use of those core competencies are essentially wasted; a company whose competency lies in product design, for example, should not be devoting a great deal of its time and energy to managing extensive real estate holdings.

One implication of these arguments is that businesses should not only get out of business lines that do not exploit their competencies but should find other ways to perform necessary functions that are not among their core competencies. For many companies, outsourcing basic administrative functions such as payroll and benefits management might be one example. What makes this argument especially important for restructuring is that it creates a virtually continuous pressure for change: A business's "core competency" changes when consumer tastes and preferences change. If the demand for high-volume/low-cost products erodes, for example, companies with that competency have to find something else on which to rely.

In addition, whether a competency creates a competitive advantage depends on what one's competitors are doing. Product development was a core competency for Japanese auto companies selling in the United States precisely because they were much faster to market than U.S. companies. But now that Chrysler is able to get new models out even faster than the Japanese auto makers, those companies may have to look for a different competency, just as they shifted from their original reliance on cost as a source of competitive advantage (as the yen appreciated) toward product development and quality in the 1980s.

Companies that follow the core competency notion have to restructure in significant ways when those competencies change. In the banking industry, for example, some banks have decided that their competency is not in back-office administration. They outsource the processing of checks to other banks that have decided that such administrative work is in their competency. The banks that decide to outsource drop entire departments and the staff that goes with them, while the banks taking in the work add staff and expand departments. When the price of check clearing on the outside market begins to rise, however, or when the outsourcing banks redevelop their own competencies, they start to rethink their outsourcing decision. Some bring check clearing back inside, adding new departments and staff, while the banks that lost their business cut staff.[11] In short, because competencies change, restructuring never ends.

The Restructuring of Organizations

The pressures noted in the previous section and the new ideas about how organizations should be managed have led to widespread and profound changes in the structure of companies, changes that have had immediate effects on the employment relationship.

Corporate restructuring generally refers to substantial change in a company's financial structure, organizational form, or both (Bowman and Singh, 1990, 1993). Financial restructuring includes changes in ownership, management buyouts, and divestitures. Organizational restructuring includes decentralization of authority, development of teams, and downsizing of employment. Although separate in principle, the two components are more frequently intertwined than not. At times, the financial component can drive the organizational changes; at other times the organizational component drives the financial changes. The leveraged buyout of RJR Nabisco in 1987 by Kohlberg Kravis Roberts entailed not only a transfer of ownership but also a wholesale redesign of the company's operations. The restructuring of Eastman Kodak, Westinghouse, and General Motors in the wake of the dismissal of their chief executives in between 1992 and 1993 involved not only internal reorganizations but also reconfigurations of their relations with the major owners.

By almost any measure, the period from the mid-1980s to the mid-1990s constituted a watershed in the structure of U.S. business. While employment among the 500 largest service companies grew from 9.3 to 11.3 million from 1982 to 1993, employment among the manufacturing 500 dropped from 14.4 to 11.5 million. In 1982 manufacturing jobs constituted 61 percent of the *Fortune* 1,000 employment ranks; by 1993, their share had declined to 50 percent. The number of different markets in which large manufacturing companies attempted to compete also declined. In 1990 companies on the

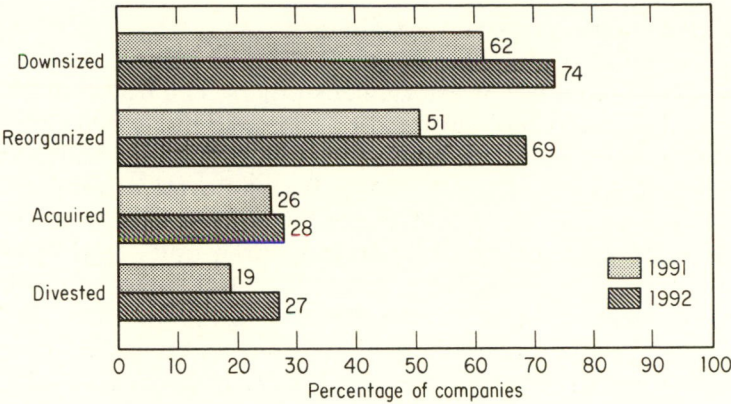

Figure 1.7. Percentage of Large Companies That Restructured in 1991 and 1992. *Source:* Wyatt Co., 1993.

Fortune 500 industrial list were active in only half as many product sectors as their 1980 counterparts had been (Doeringer et al., 1991; Davis and Stout, 1992; Lawler et al., 1992; Davis et al., 1994).

The breadth of restructuring among large companies can be seen in two surveys of large companies on their 1991 and 1992 restructuring experiences (see Figure 1.7). Three quarters of the 531 companies surveyed had downsized in 1992, nearly the same proportion had reorganized, and one quarter had divested, merged, or been acquired.

The Redesigned Organization

The new approaches to management that we have described, combined with the pressures from competition and shareholders, led companies toward new ways of organizing themselves. Organizational redesign can be seen as an encompassing effort to build a more productive mechanism. The paths of organizational restructuring include downsizing and work redesign, which we discuss in chapters 2 and 3, and fresh principles of organizational design, changes that in combined form have attracted such labels as the "horizontal corporation" (Bryne, 1993) to describe the associated reduction in management structures.

An assessment of various studies suggests that four main principles have guided much of the organizational redesign. These are briefly described as (1) customer-focused operating units; (2) devolved decision-making authority; (3) streamlined management but tighter financial control; and (4) reengineered business process.

Customer-Focused Operating Units

Company building blocks are increasingly defined around products or services for internal or external customers. The traditional large functional divisions built around development, manufacturing, and marketing are giving way to numerous smaller divisions built around discrete product or services. ABB Asea Brown Boveri, a multinational manufacturer, groups its workforce of 240,000 into some 4,500 profit centers (Barnevik, 1991). The output-focused units tend to stress teamwork and downplay hierarchy. A thrust of the organizational restructuring at the Xerox Corporation during the early 1990s was to move away from strong functional divisions and toward nine units focused around distinct products and markets. More generally, the working concept was one of "market in," of bringing the market inside the organization through a host of organizational devices ranging from focusing operating units on specific market to placing customer representatives on management-appointment committees (Howard, 1992; Cole, Bacdayan, and White, 1993). Bringing product and supplier market pressures inside the organization helps bring pressures from the labor market inside as well.

Devolved Decision-Making Authority

Authority to succeed and fail is pushed lower in most restructured companies, giving their operating units greater autonomy. Business units acquire more responsibility for setting strategy and other policies, but they are also held more accountable for results. Strategic business units (SBUs), with full profit and loss responsibilities, are increasingly becoming the dominant form, and these in turn are divided and subdivided on much the same principles. SBUs and their equivalent subunits are typically focused around distinct products or services for internal or external customers. Each of the units and subunits incorporates as many company functions as possible, including planning, production, and marketing. With relationships to customers more clearly established, managers and units acquire stronger incentives to respond; with responsibility for decision making more clearly delegated, they acquire a greater power to act. And with accountability for results more clearly pinpointed, they acquire stronger reason to perform.

At the same time, a greater premium is placed on cross-boundary management, on massaging relations among the units that are now more autonomous and independent of one another. A detailed study of the Hewlett-Packard Company reveals, for example, that, in the wake of its continuing restructuring, managers have less authoritative power of office and must rely more on their powers of persuasion and on mutual cooperation (Beckman, 1996). These developments help break down the functional orientation of jobs, substantially broaden the nature of individual jobs, and focus responsibility—and risk—on individual employees.

Streamlined Management Control, Tighter Financial Control

In restructured companies, central offices are scaled back, headquarters staffs are reduced, and management layers are thinned. Operating units receive fewer policy directives from the corporate office but stronger financial directives. During its 1993–1994 restructuring, IBM reduced its corporate staff from 5,100 to 3,900. "Our view of corporate headquarters," offered its senior vice president for human resources and administration, "is that there should be as little of it as possible" (Lohr, 1994). The corporate office of a large electrical equipment manufacturer that underwent extensive restructuring during the 1980s is illustrative (see Figure 1.8): The number of both senior managers and headquarters staff steadily declined over a decade of restructuring.

In thinning their management ranks, companies also expanded managers' spans of control. Seven main layers in the organizational pyramid and seven direct subordinates for each boss had been the historic norm for many corporations. Now the thrust is to reduce layers, expand spans, and move organizational form from tall and narrow to flat and wide. Consistent with such trends, comparison of the organization form of eleven insurance companies in 1992 with

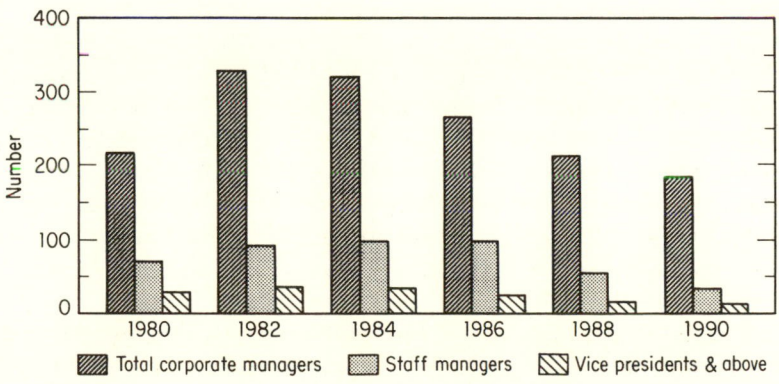

Figure 1.8. General Corporate Management of Large Electrical Products Company, 1980–1990. Includes division directors and presidents, corporate vice presidents and above. *Source:* Company records.

that of 1986 revealed substantial leveling of hierarchies and widening of the span of control (Janger, 1989; Scott, O'Shaughnessy, and Cappelli, 1996).

Reengineered Business Process

Some of the efforts to reduce costs and improve operating efficiencies have focused on rethinking which tasks need to be performed in organizations and how they are carried out. The term "reengineering" refers to the systematic effort to redesign specific organizational tasks, usually white-collar functions. One way to think of reengineering is as the equivalent of restructuring at the level of specific work processes and functions. Some observers suggest that it is to white-collar functions what industrial engineering was to production tasks. Reengineering has become such a popular phrase in contemporary management that it merits an example to illustrate exactly how it changes organizations and jobs. Consider the typical function of processing claims in the insurance industry.[12] A customer who has an accident or fire calls his insurance agent to file a claim. The agent sends the claim into the company headquarters, where it is assigned to a claims representative, who verifies whether the customer's policy is paid and in effect. If it is, the claim may be passed on to a company investigator, who determines whether the claim is fraudulent and, if not, whether the insurance company or some other party is liable for the damages. The claim then goes to an adjustor, who determines the total damages and attempts to settle with the claimant. In all, the claim has passed through at least four offices and may take as long as six weeks to complete. Ten to fifteen percent of the total costs of insurance claims are associated with the administrative costs of processing claims.

The reengineering of this process relies heavily on new MIS technology. The most important changes begin right when the claim is filed with the agent. In the new system, the agent calls up an information system on her computer that immediately verifies whether the customer's coverage is valid. She then calls up an expert system that looks at the customer's previous claims, assesses the nature of the current claim, including the dollar value, and estimates the likelihood that the claim is valid and should not be contested by the company. If it passes that threshold, then the agent simply pays the claim. If not, the claim goes to headquarters for more traditional process. The cost and overall time required to process claims falls dramatically.

Several important changes have occurred in the company because of the reengineering of this one process. First, the job of claims representative disappears because coverage is now verified by the agents using their computer information systems. Second, the number of investigator jobs falls precipitously, as does the number of adjustor positions, because the expert system now decides whether claims should be investigated and pays most without a fight. The organization structure or "chart" gets dramatically flatter as these administrative functions, which constitute the middle of the organization, are cut out.

In addition, the job of the agent now becomes significantly broader, somewhat more demanding, and considerably more important to the company. In many insurance companies, however, the agents are not employees of the company at all but are independent contractors who deal with several insurance companies. The dilemma for the companies is how to monitor and control the actions of these agents, over whom they have no direct supervisory control. One way is through the MIS system that the agents use. This system not only provides the agents with information, structuring their decisions; it also keeps track of the decisions that the agents make and reports them back to the company.

No expert systems are so perfectly automated that they leave employees with no judgment decisions, and the companies need to find ways to shape the judgment of the agents without being able to supervise them directly. They do it with financial incentives— contingent compensation—that, in this case, reward agents for reducing errors and catching fraud. And the agents are made directly accountable for all issues associated with claims.

The reengineering of this one organizational task has shifted responsibility and decision making down in the organization (in the case of independent agents, shifting it out of the company altogether), flattened the overall structure of its division, and substituted incentives and accounting measures for direct supervision of employees.

Reengineering produces dramatic changes in work systems. Procedures for producing products or reviewing paperwork are pared to reduce cost and increase quality, service, and speed. Job titles are broadened, information systems are improved, incumbents acquire greater power to make decisions, short-term checks and controls are reduced, the work process is streamlined, and accountability for results is increased. Some of the work, and occasionally entire functions such as information processing, are outsourced to specialist providers. The Ford Motor Company, for example, reduced its accounts payable staff by three quarters by eliminating most paperwork from the process of ordering and receiving products from suppliers and by redesigning the process to reduce radically redundant and inconsistent information. Although business process reengineering often fails to produce anticipated gains, when it is effectively implemented, cost and time reductions of 50 percent or more are frequently reported (Hall et al., 1993; Hammer and Champy, 1993).

Together, these four principles are leading organizations to develop stronger relationships with outside markets and stronger market relationships within the company. In the name of improved information flows and response times, company boundaries with the outside world are becoming less opaque and more permeable. As market relations increasingly infuse the business, control can be exercised less through hierarchic authority and is more dependent on the application of financial measures and incentives tied to the market.

Organizational form looks different as well, with hierarchies flatter and spans broader; divisions less functionally divided and more self-contained; authority more decentralized and less authoritative; and accountability better gauged and more tightly linked to owners' interests. The form itself becomes more flexible and more responsive to market whims and customer demands. Vertical charts yield to more horizontal networks.[13]

A description of these changes in organizational design comes from a study of 140 major companies from 1986 to 1992 (Cappelli and O'Shaughnessy, 1995). The exempt, white-collar jobs in these companies were grouped into four main management categories, with the lowest level those with no supervisory responsibilities, the next level supervisors, the third-level managers who direct supervisors (e.g., directors of divisions), and the highest-level executives with strategic decision-making responsibilities (vice presidents and above). The change in the distribution of jobs across these four levels of hierarchy, as illustrated in Figure 1.9, is dramatic and demonstrates a major flattening of the organizations.

Figure 1.10 represents a vivid example of how the organizational chart for senior management has changed over time at one company. The total number of corporate managers, defined by the company to include the heads of all major divisions and functions, fell from more than 300 in 1984 to fewer than 200 by 1990. General managers with staff functions dropped from 31 percent of the total in 1984 to 18 percent by 1990. In 1984 this corporation employed about one general manager for every 400 employees, but by 1990 this ratio had declined to one general manager for every 600 employees. In 1984 the general managers of the company's twenty-three business units (divisions that carried profit-and-loss responsibilities) faced thirty-seven managers between themselves and the chief executive. By 1990, following the elimination of almost an entire layer of management, heads of the company's sixteen business units faced only eighteen managers between themselves and the CEO's office.

The most extreme change in the design of organizations is what

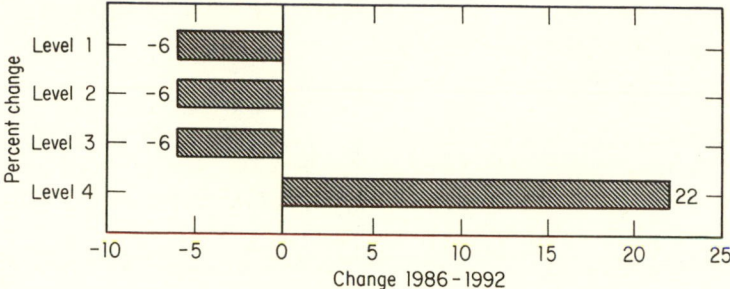

Figure 1.9. Flattening of Hierarchies, 1986–1992. Level 1 = top executives; level 2 = middle managers; level 3 = supervisors; level 4 = nonsupervisory exempt for 160 large employers. *Source:* Hay Associates database.

is sometimes referred to as the "virtual" organization. The idea behind the virtual organization is simply to bring together resources only when they are needed and to eliminate fixed investments in permanent structures. The core competency notion and the general arguments about using subcontractors are taken to the limit in the virtual organization, where the permanent, core components of the company are reduced to almost nothing, perhaps just an executive team. The reduction in the physical facilities of virtual companies have received the most attention—contractors faxing work into the company from their office at home or renting office space when face-to-face meetings are required—but the forces that are driving this development are present in some degree in almost all companies.

Not surprisingly, employment systems also become less demarcated by company boundaries. As the internal operations of companies become more closely aligned with outside markets, so too do employment relations. Internal labor markets are weakened as organizational capacities are strengthened; employees now come into much greater contact not only with the product market but also with the outside labor market and find that their circumstances are governed more by it. As more employees flow in and out of a company, they begin to identify themselves more with their function as defined by the outside labor market than with the company—"I am a marketing manager" rather than "I am an Acme employee." Companies and employees display reduced commitment to each other, and the use of temporary contracting and contingent workers makes careers less secure, exacerbating these trends.

Who Restructures?

A number of companies have adopted one or more of these redesign components as part of a restructuring agenda. A number have also

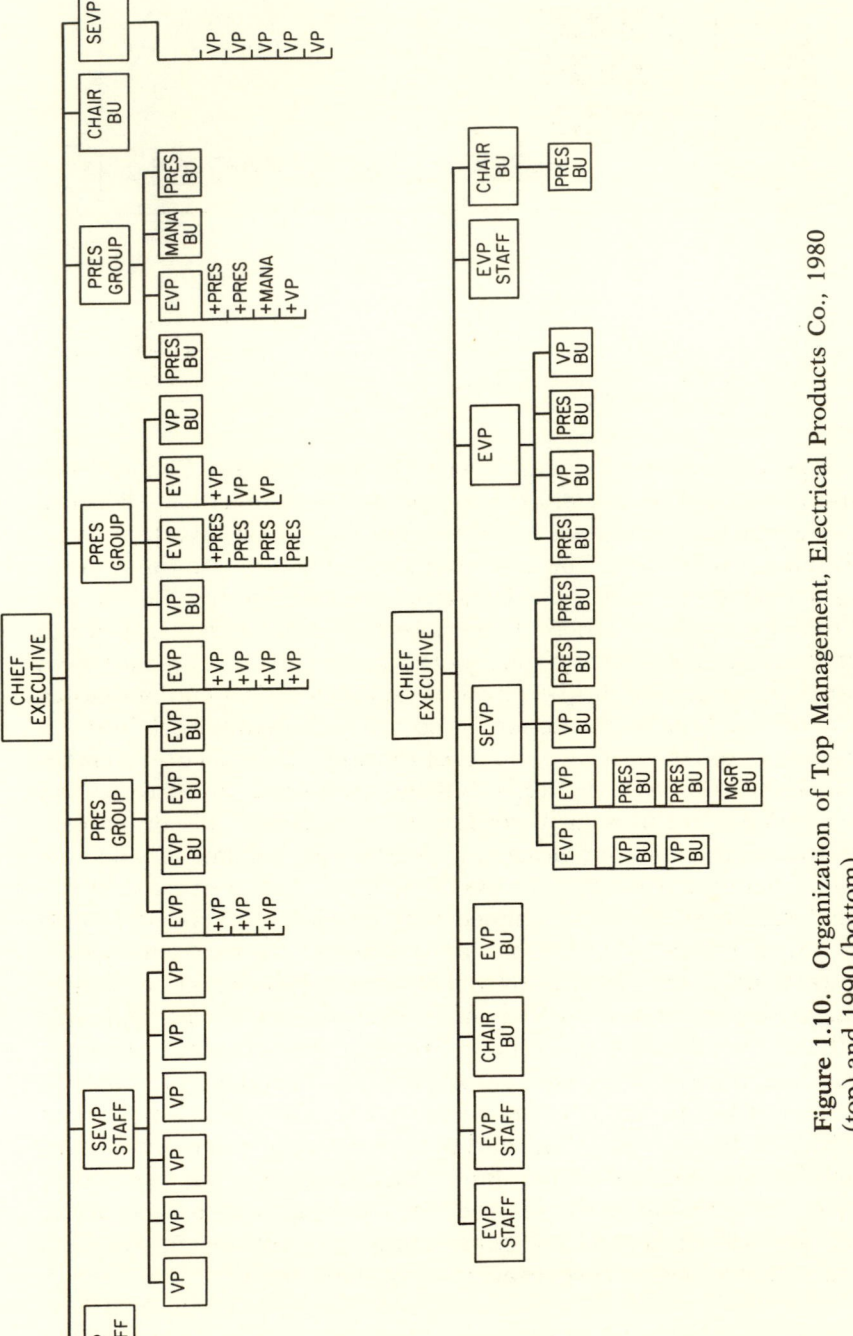

Figure 1.10. Organization of Top Management, Electrical Products Co., 1980 (top) and 1990 (bottom).
SEVP = senior executive vice president; Chair = chairman; BU and + designate business units.

introduced new work designs and have downsized their workforces. More than half of the nation's largest corporations downsized in 1991 and 1992, and a majority or near-majority introduced fresh work designs, such as team building. Seen from the vantage point of the employee, the incident rates appear high as well. A national survey of 2,958 employees in 1992, for example, confirms widespread workplace change (see chapter 5). Two in five employees experienced a downsizing of their companies or a permanent cutback of the workforce. A fifth to a quarter had experienced a merger or acquisition, a reduction in the number of managers at their companies, or turnover in the organization's leadership (Galinsky et al., 1993).

Since international competitive pressures and domestic investor pressures have been most intense at larger companies, the most extensive restructuring is likely to have been felt there. Foreign direct investments both into and out of the United States are disproportionately the province of large corporations, as are domestic investor holdings and the pressures accompanying them (United Nations, 1995). And in fact, company size has been found to be a good predictor of both financial and organizational restructuring. The relevance of size is evident again in the 1992 survey of 2,958 employees. Data from this survey reveal that, compared with workers at smaller companies (fewer than fifty employees), workers at larger companies (500 or more employees) were two to three times more likely to experience a merger or acquisition, a cutback in the managerial ranks, turnover in top leadership, and a downsizing of the workforce. The more widespread impact of restructuring among larger companies is probably a product of the urge to "unbundle" operations, which is driven by competitive and investor pressures. It may also derive from the tendency of major companies to track one another's policies and to adopt newly defined cutting-edge practices, such as total quality management, business process reengineering, and high performance systems, more quickly than their smaller counterparts.

Performance Effects of Restructuring

Restructuring actions taken singly, research studies suggest, tend to achieve few enduring gains. In the absence of a broader plan, downsizing the workforce can generate short-term cost savings, but often at the expense of long-term cost increases. Similarly, the introduction of a total quality initiative or a reforming of a company into strategic business units without a host of associated changes may yield little enduring gain. Studies of the introduction of new information technologies, lean manufacturing methods, and employee stock ownership plans, for example, reveal that alterations in each of these areas without parallel changes in the culture, compensation, and reporting structure of the company tend to leave the intended effects largely stillborn (Conte and Svejnar, 1990; Scott Morton, 1991; MacDuffie and Krafcik, 1992; Cameron et al., 1993).

Similar conclusions emerge from a 1993 reanalysis of 131 studies of companies done between 1961 and 1991. The companies had set out to refashion their organizations in ways akin to the corporate restructuring of the past decade. They applied a wide array of devices to improve their performance, including the formation of strategic business units, creation of cross-functional teams, and decentralization of decision making. In synthesizing the many studies' findings, the researchers found that the largest and most sustained improvements in company performance came when two conditions prevailed: (1) the company pressed integrated, systemic changes in both organizational design and human resources practices; and (2) the company fostered changes at the corporate and at the business unit levels, not just at the group or individual level (Macy and Izumi, 1993).

A study of process reengineering efforts at more than 100 companies during the early 1990s corroborates these conclusions. The redesign efforts ranged from improved processing of accounts payable to product development. The study reported that translating short-term process improvements into long-term gains for business units depended on two factors: (1) whether the change process was designed to yield improvements across the entire unit, and (2) whether the changes extended deep into the unit's performance measures, compensation incentives, information technologies, shared culture, employee skills, and organizational structure (Hall et al., 1993).

These findings are corroborated by other research and case studies and by consultants who often advocate an integrated application of a host of change drivers throughout a company. Systemic change is required, it seems, if performance is to be improved. If only one component is changed, its effects are likely to be washed out as other unchanged components undermine the intended impact. Giving more authority to operating units without simultaneously reducing the oversight by headquarters staff is likely to defeat the decentralizing effort. Devolving authority without also tightening financial controls around shareholder value is likely to undermine any efforts to improve stock price and dividend payout (Nadler and Tushman, 1988; Nadler et al., 1992; Auerbach and Barrett, 1993; Garone, 1993; Hiam, 1993; Berger and Sikora, 1994). These conclusions focus on the benefits of restructuring for the organization, of course, and the effects on employees (described in chapter 5) are considerably less positive.

Despite the uneven and sometimes limited applications of the restructuring elements, the research evidence indicates that comprehensive, integrated changes are generally required to make an enduring difference. With the accumulating experience from a decade of restructuring initiatives, with successes and failures to mull over, many executives have reached much the same conclusion. Although exceptions still abound, corporate restructuring with lasting effects tends to comprise a host of related changes within a company rather than a singular focus on one element, be it workforce downsizing, workplace team building, or organizational redesign. The many paths of restructuring are thus likely to be interconnected and the changes interrelated.

Choices and Leadership in Restructuring

Whatever the pressures on a company, it still has choices to make in managing how restructuring takes place and how the company's competitive position and its relationship with investors are assayed and translated into strategies for change. Top management is, of course, constrained by the organization over which it presides and the environment within with it competes. It nonetheless has choices for addressing these pressures for improved performance and retains considerable discretion in the strategy it chooses. Moreover, the preferred direction for the company's strategy and organizational redesign is rarely clear. Facing frequent choices and enjoying discretionary power, executives not surprisingly rely on their values and visions in shaping the directions that companies take during the restructuring process. Here is where leadership can play a critical role.

Evidence from several of the previously cited studies confirms the importance of company leadership for the restructuring agenda. A 1992 study of 875 work establishments, for instance, finds that managerial values were powerful predictors of which companies adopted work teams, quality circles, job rotation, and total quality management. Establishments led by executives who believe they carry a responsibility for employee welfare are significantly more likely to institute each of these workplace practices (Osterman, 1994). Similarly, in an analysis of company investment in education, training, and collaboration with local school systems using a 1991 Lou Harris survey of 406 large companies, management commitment to innovation and change was found to be an independent predictor of which companies invest in education and training (Useem, 1993). (The cross-sectional nature of such studies dictate caution in inferring causal direction, however.) Other studies repeatedly confirm the importance of top management in effectively guiding the restructuring process. The study of reengineering at some 100 companies finds, for example, that tenacious support by the chief executive for the redesign proved a key ingredient for realizing expected cost savings (Hall et al., 1993).

To see the difference that company leadership can make for restructuring, we draw again on the 1991 survey of 406 companies to focus on two facets of top management's attitudes toward its workforce. The first concerns management's commitment to innovation in human resources practices. The second is management's resistance to strategic change in the human resources arena. For the first factor, companies were asked to classify their human resources practices during the past five years into four categories. The categories reflect the degree to which a company and its management are committed to applying new human resources practices. The distribution of the 406 companies among the categories was:

10.8%	At the cutting edge; usually trying to lead in this area
38.7	Advanced; adopting policies to stay ahead of other companies
37.2	Thoughtful; adopting policies when an industry consensus is developed
10.6	Prudent; adopting policies only after they are already proven effective

Companies with management cultures that stress innovation were observed to be twice as likely to have embraced several of the work redesign measures. Conversely, companies with resistant management cultures were found to be substantially more likely to have downsized their operations. Differences remained even when each company's size, degree of workforce globalization, and other factors were taken into account.

The study of 531 companies surveyed for 1992, cited earlier, yields other evidence suggesting the importance of executive leadership. The companies were asked to evaluate retrospectively the factors that accounted for their effective restructuring initiatives. As they reflected on their recent experience, half of the companies stressed a clear executive articulation and communication of a vision underlying the restructuring. Three fifths of the companies also saw as critical the active and visible involvement of senior management in the restructuring process (Wyatt Company, 1993).

Although the specific impetus for company restructuring has changed since the mid-1980s, the general forces for change had abated little by the mid-1990s. The challenge from abroad is likely to redouble as businesses globalize further. The challenge from shareholders is also likely to strengthen as investors further master the art of pressure politics. Other developments in U.S. business,

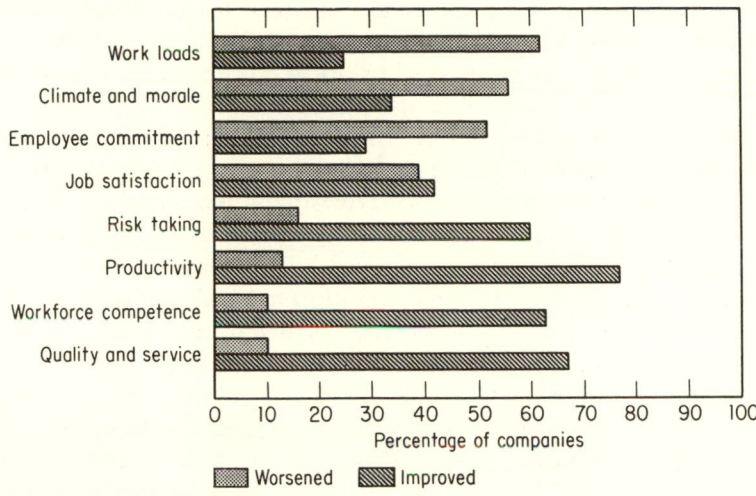

Figure 1.11. Changes in Workforce Features in Large Companies That Restructure. Restructuring among 530 large companies, 1992. *Source:* Wyatt Co., 1993.

such as the quality movement, are likely to add their own impetus as well. The picture is thus a dynamic one. Still, it is already clear that companies of the late 1990s will look significantly different from those of the early 1980s. To those who work in them, the world will appear far different, as well.

The Two Faces of Organizational Restructuring

The restructuring of companies has clear benefits for employers. It also has profound and direct effects on the employment relationship, effects that are explored at length in the chapters that follow. The experience of 531 corporations with restructuring in 1992 illustrates what many believe is the typical outcome. As seen in Figure 1.11, their restructuring enhanced quality and customer service, risk taking, workforce competence, and productivity. It also heightened work loads, diminished morale, and undercut employee commitment.

In fact, restructuring has a two-edged effect on company employees. In addition to the negative effects, it includes some changes that may actually improve the work experience for employees. The negative experiences are easier to see, however. The restructuring of Combustion Engineering in 1989–1991 following its acquisition by ABB, for example, included the reduction of its headquarters staff from 600 to 100, with about a third of the employees forced to leave the company (the others were moved into business units or stand-alone operations offering fee-based services to the units). To the extent that the belt-tightening is concentrated in certain facilities and regions, company suppliers and local communities can also be hard hit (Barnevik, 1991; Newman, 1989).

As explained in chapter 5, the lasting effects for employees whose jobs are terminated can included prolonged periods of unemployment, lowered income upon reemployment, and even withdrawal from the labor force. For those who do survive, the aftermath can bring long work weeks and high stress levels, and these effects can spill over to the organization as a whole. In one study, researchers surveyed 597 employees of a national chain of small retail stores in the early 1990s that had closed many of its outlets during the previous twelve months. Those experiencing the most intense distress from the restructuring saw their work performance taper off, especially among those most financially insecure (Brockner et al., 1992, 1993). Other research confirms that restructuring undermines employee attachments to the company and makes recruiting and retaining employees more difficult. One early 1990s study of managers at 17 *Fortune* 500 companies, for example, reported that managers who had survived a restructuring process focused more on their own careers and less on organization goals (Reilly et al., 1993). Another study revealed that downsized companies reported greater difficulty in recruiting new employees, especially college-educated employees (Useem, 1993).

While the costs of restructuring for employees and organizations may be considerable, changes in work organization as described in detail in chapter 3 may lead to fresh benefits for employees as well as for companies. A journalist's account of a downsized General Electric plant is illustrative of what is more widely reported. The employment ranks at the jet-engine plant had been cut by half in recent years, and those still on the payroll feared additional rounds of layoffs and the associated problems we have described. At the same time, they found the reorganized work system more engaging, more collegial, and more flexible. Employees acquired more responsibility for the work they performed; more of the work was conducted through relatively autonomous teams that made decisions formerly reserved for supervisors; and all were freer to redesign the work flow to reduce costs and errors. Though the GE employees were "working scared," reported the observer, they were also "working smarter, harder, more flexibly and more cooperatively" (Kilborn, 1993).

The two facets were also evident in a study of managers at one of the seven regional Bell operating companies. Because of competitive market pressures, this company had undertaken extensive restructuring, including substantial downsizing of its managerial ranks. An early 1990s survey found that a majority of its middle managers reported that their work loads had intensified during the past several years. Three fifths now had more overtime or take-home work than they desired. Spans of control had also considerably broadened; two fifths supervised three to five additional employees, and another third oversaw an additional six to fifteen. Moreover, three quarters or more of the middle managers reported reduced job security, fewer promotion opportunities, and less job mobility. Fewer than two in ten now expressed satisfaction with their job security or career opportunities.

At the same time, many of the company's middle managers affirmed that other features of their work had improved. A majority reported, for example, that they had more discretion to meet customer needs, that they participated in cross-functional or problem-solving teams, and that they had substantial control over their work tasks, procedures, and pace. Consistent with these dual aspects of corporate restructuring, seven in ten expressed satisfaction with their jobs and the work they did, while at the same time a similar proportion expressed *dis*satisfaction with their employment and career prospects (Batt, 1996).

More generally, those who remain with or newly join a restructured business often experience more challenging work and greater autonomy. This can be seen through reanalysis of data collected on the 406 companies in 1991. The companies reported the extent to which they had taken eight downsizing actions during the past five years. The companies also reported whether they had invested a substantial amount of time and money during the past decade to create "significant changes in their office and production areas" in three areas of work design: work process, job involvement, and quality management (Table 1.3).

Downsizing clearly has negative effects on employees, whereas the changing organizational structures and work systems seem to have some positive effects. The question is whether the two necessarily go together. Companies that had taken downsizing steps, thereby increasing employee insecurity and stress, were also found to have introduced the work redesign measures, which increased employee attachment and productivity. For this analysis, companies were classified into four groupings according to the number of downsizing actions they had taken. Companies that had applied six to eight of the downsizing measures were most likely to have restructured the work systems as well.

The dual impact of corporate restructuring on those who experience it accounts for much of the schizophrenic attitude toward restructuring. Devastated communities and ruined careers abound. So too do environments filled with high anxiety and low morale. In

Table 1.3.   Percentage of 406 Large Companies that
Had Taken Downsizing Actions During Past Five Years
and Had Invested Significant Time and Money in Work
Redesign During the Past Decade

	% of companies
Downsizing action	
Shut down some operations	64.3
Combined operating units	62.3
Imposed hiring freeze	57.1
Sold any business units	51.0
Laid off a substantial number of workers	47.3
Offered early retirement incentives	40.4
Reduced management staff significantly	38.4
Used substantial no. of part-time workers	10.1
Work redesign	
Redesigned work methods and processes	44.1
Promoted employee involvement	38.7
Operated a total quality program	37.4

Source: Reanalysis of the 1991 company survey. The study's methodology is
described in Johnson and Linden (1992) and Mirvis (1993). The percentages are based on 406 companies.

the same company settings, however, the organizational quality is
often improved, introducing a sense of variety, responsibility, and
collegiality that survivors had never before experienced or had expected to see in their future. "People are working smarter, harder,
more flexibly, and more cooperatively," concluded the journalist
covering the downsized GE engine plant, although he also warned
that "they're working scared" (Kilborn, 1993).

The effects of organizational restructuring may not be distrib-
uted equally across the labor force. We examined the incidence of
restructuring on six groups in society: older workers, women, African American workers, and college-educated, white-collar, and
unionized employees. The 1991 survey of 406 large companies
found that companies with higher-than-average proportions of older
workers were also those that were more likely to have taken some
downsizing and redesign measures, as seen in Table 1.4. Of those
businesses that had laid off a substantial number of workers, for
example, in 28 percent at least three out of every ten employees were
over age 50, while only 13 percent of those companies that had not
downsized reported this high a proportion of older workers. Similarly, in 28 percent of companies with total quality management
programs, at least three employees in ten were age 50 or older, but
only 16 percent of the other businesses had this high a percentage.
The explanation may be that establishments with an older workforce are themselves older and more in need of change.

Table 1.4. Percentage of Employees Age 50 and Over at Companies that Had Taken Eight Downsizing Actions and Introduced Three Work Redesigns

	% of companies with 30%+ employees age 50 and over among . . .	
	% Companies that did not downsize	% Companies that downsized
Sold any business units	15.4	23.3
Laid off a substantial number of workers	13.3	27.8
Offered early retirement incentives	17.1	23.9
Reduced management staff significantly	14.2	28.9
Imposed hiring freeze	17.4	21.1
Shutdown some operations	24.7	17.5
Combined operating units	24.6	17.7
Used substantial no. of part-time workers	20.8	12.5
Redesigned work methods and processes	20.3	19.6
Promoted employee involvement	18.9	21.8
Operated a total quality program	15.6	28.0

Source: Reanalysis of the 1991 company survey. The percentages in the two columns in the upper panel are based on 69 to 127 and 83 to 137 companies respectively. The column percentage in the lower panel are based on 118 to 134 and 75 to 92 companies respectively.

For the five other subgroups, we combined both the downsizing actions and the redesign actions into one category. We compared the demographics of companies that had taken six or more downsizing actions with those that had taken five or fewer; and we compared those that had introduced two or three work redesign measures with those that had one or none. Table 1.5 reveals that women and African Americans are slightly less likely to be employed by companies that have introduced innovative work programs. Greater differences appear for college-educated, white-collar, and unionized employees. Smaller concentrations of college-educated and white-

Table 1.5. Average Percentage of Employee Groups by Company Downsizing and Work Redesign

Group	% Downsizing		% Work redesign	
	Little	Much	Little	Much
Women	46.5	42.6	46.5	41.6+
African American	11.3	11.7	12.1	10.1+
College-educated	48.4	36.8**	47.4	37.8**
White-collar	53.9	46.4*	54.2	44.5**
Unionized	45.1	62.4**	48.3	61.0*

Source: Reanalysis of 1991 company survey. The number of companies on which the percentages are based ranged from 213 to 406. The levels of statistical significance for comparison of the group percentages are: ** = < .01; * = < .05; + = < .10.

METHODIST COLLEGE LIBRARY
Fayetteville, N.C.

collar employees are found in companies that have downsized or redesigned their work systems; larger concentrations of union employees are found in both.

Corporate restructuring thus brings its costs and benefits in different measure to various groups in the U.S. workforce. Older, non-college, blue-collar, and unionized employees bear more of the downsizing brunt. They find themselves disproportionately located in companies that have cut their workforces through a host of actions. At the same time, these same groups experience more of the redesign benefits. They find themselves overrepresented in companies that have increased employee involvement, introduced quality programs, and redesigned the work process.

Resistance to Change

Despite the fact that the changes in employment associated with restructuring seem to make employees substantially worse off, at least in the short run, resistance by employees seems to have been virtually nonexistent. One reason is that the ability of unions to counter management efforts to change practices declined sharply in the 1980s. The overall weakness of many organized companies left unions with little option but to acquiesce in restructuring efforts or see the enterprise fold. In other situations, management's ability to move jobs away from union representation seriously weakened union power and forced the union to accept concessions. In the past, union gains have spilled over to nonunion facilities where management adopted practices that protected workers as a way of buying out some of the interest in unions. But as the threat of union organizing declines, nonunion companies are increasingly abandoning those practices in a kind of reverse spill-over.

A second factor undermining employee resistance is the ubiquitousness of these changes. An employer that adopted practices that ran counter to employee interests might expect to find itself losing workers and unable to hire new ones as applicants flocked to competitors. But because most companies in the 1990s are engaged in similar restructurings, no company is at a relative disadvantage for doing so. And the fact that the changes tend to shed labor helps create an excess supply of skilled labor on the outside market that, in turn, makes it easier for companies to adopt these new strategies. It is relatively easy to obtain skills from the outside labor market, making it costless to abandon internal development practices. And the visibility of so much job loss appears to reduce the complaints of those who still have jobs.

Whether there were alternatives to having the employees bear as much of the costs of this restructuring as they have, whether organizational flexibility of this level had to be achieved by making the employees bend, is an open question. And whether these new practices represent a transition phase or a stable system in themselves also remains an open question that turns on the level of change to which organizations will need to adapt in the future. At present, the level of corporate restructuring is so great that it is difficult to imagine how it could be accomplished within an internalized model of employment.

Conclusion

Restructuring was initially viewed by some as a passing phenomenon, a kind of overdue corporate correction. The continuing opening of the U.S. economy to international competition and the further involvement of U.S. companies in other economies, however, can be expected only to intensify the pressure for change. So too should the continuing concentration of corporate ownership in a small number of very large hands. The pressures inside companies for increased flexibility and for reduced fixed costs, as well as the continuous redefinition of competencies, should keep the need to restructure on the agenda for years to come. Organizational structures and work systems are therefore likely to be further reconfigured in the years ahead. Moreover, since integrated, systemic change is required if restructuring it to achieve its ends, the reshaping is also likely to press more deeply into more facets of organizational and work systems. In short, restructuring means more than a one-time adaptation to a new organizational model. It means adapting to a model in which changes are likely to continue.

As the following chapters make clear, the connected paths of restructuring can leave a swath of destruction in their wake. Some employees find that they have lost all, or are on the precipice of losing all. Job security, pension income, and health insurance may be at risk or gone altogether. At the same time, for workers who survive their companies' workforce resizings, the reorganized office or plant has often come to be a more challenging, more creative, more engaging place. Virtually all workers have been expected to do more with less. Yet at least with respect to the work they perform, many also have found the new organizational environments an improvement over the old.

Although managements are driven to consider restructuring by external forces not of their own making, they still must make their own way in response to the forces. There are choices to be made. As organizational restructuring continues its uneven but seemingly unrelenting course, managers and unions must take their organizations in one of two directions. If the leadership has resisted change and is forced to confront its competitive decline at the eleventh hour, Draconian downsizing and restructuring measures may be the only feasible course. In that case, the costs to employees and the company may be high as workplace insecurity and short-term pressures override long-term commitments. On the other hand, if the leadership has built a culture that accommodates change and is ready for organizational innovation before the eleventh hour, it may be possible to address the pressures earlier and with less disruption. If so, the benefits to employees and companies may be high as workplace empowerment and long-term planning dominate the agenda.

Notes

1. See Jacoby (1985) for an excellent overall guide to these developments. Other arguments about the pressures on management to development human resource practices can be found in Kochan and Cappelli (1984) and especially Baron et al. (1986) for arguments about government pressures in particular.

2. See Lambert, Larker, and Verrecchia (1991). Stockholders with an interest in diversifying their investment portfolios can purchase share in many different companies. They do not need to invest in a single corporation with diversified holdings.

3. The theory of "implicit contracts" asserts that companies are better able to absorb risk than are individuals, and employees basically pay a premium (by accepting lower wages) in order to have the employer absorb the risk of product market variations on compensation.

4. An encyclopedic guide to employment practices during this period, especially for nonexempt workers, can be found in Slichter, Healy, and Livernash (1960).

5. These books include Ouchi (1981) and Abegglen and Stalk (1985).

6. *NLRB v. Supreme Court*, 416 U.S. 267 (1974).

7. Not all of the requirements of labor law are so easily eliminated with contract workers. Safety and health legislation applies equally to contract workers, for example. Although the requirements for coverage differ from act to act, in general, contractors are required to comply when they directly supervise contract workers (see Dennard and Northrup, 1994).

8. Reanalysis of the data reported in Johnson and Linden (1992) and Useem (1993).

9. Where Piore and Sable's (1984) flexible-specialization model seems to apply best is to what is now referred to as "quick-response" manufacturing where reasonably standardized products are customized to the needs of individual consumers. Perhaps the best-known example is Japan's National Bicycle Company, where bicycles are assembled at the factory to the precise measurements of each individual customer. The "lean production" methods of auto assembly may eventually push out "flexible-specialization" in these markets if volume gets big enough to justify setting up the system.

10. See "The Real Key to Creating Wealth," *Fortune* (September 20, 1993), p. 83.

11. We are indebted to the Wharton School's Financial Institutions Center project on productivity for this example.

12. This example comes from a study of productivity in financial services under way at the Wharton School.

13. Descriptions of many of these features can be found in Byrne (1993), Donaldson (1994), Garone (1993), Nadler et al. (1992), and Useem (1993).

2

Downsizing and Employment Insecurity

Since the early 1980s, U.S. employers have been downsizing their organizations in an effort to make them more competitive. Most alarming, particularly for employees' job security concerns, is the fact that downsizing has occurred even among blue-chip companies such as IBM, Xerox, Procter and Gamble, Kodak, and Citicorp. Everyone, worker and manager alike, appears to be vulnerable to the risk of downsizing, regardless of industrial sector or the size of the company. While companies clearly cannot keep cutting their workforces forever, the restructuring trends noted in chapter 1 and the expansion of contingent work and other trends described in this chapter portend long-term changes in the concept of job security in the United States.

This chapter reviews how downsizing has extended its reach beyond the traditional blue-collar and manufacturing workforces. What has not changed are the large income losses that are suffered by many who are downsized, and so we also examine the extent of those losses.

With the heavy and often repeated experience of downsizing that has occurred in many businesses, it now becomes possible to trace the longer-term consequences of downsizing for employees (including those who are not downsized) and for organizations. Here, as this chapter shows, the role of corporate strategy plays a key role as a determinant of both the reaction of retained employees to downsizing and the corporate economic returns to downsizing.

The accumulating evidence reveals widespread morale declines among employees who remain in downsized organizations, which may have long-term consequences.

The Nature, Depth, and Breadth of Downsizing

Before we examine the consequences of downsizing, it is important to clarify what downsizing is and what it is not. "Downsizing is not something that happens *to* an organization, but it is something that organizations undertake purposely" (Cameron, Freeman, and Mishra, 1993). We should carefully distinguish between temporary layoffs that are a response to cyclical recessionary forces of the kind historically associated with heavy manufacturing and permanent layoffs that result from changes in the size and/or structure of companies. It is the latter employment reductions that constitute downsizing and contribute to the observation that "an increasing share of workforce reductions are strategic or structural in nature, and are not a reflection of short-term market conditions" (American Management Association, 1994).

Hard data verify the breadth and depth of corporate downsizing. Surveys routinely find that most companies had downsizing programs in the early 1990s. In the Louis Harris survey (Harris and Associates, 1991) summarized in Table 2.1, 64.3 percent of managers reported that during the previous five years their organization had shut down some operations, and 47.3 percent had laid off a substantial number of workers (although it is important to note that these figures, like many others, confound recession-induced layoffs and layoffs due to permanent changes in corporate size and structure). The Wyatt Company's survey (Wyatt, 1993) found that 72 percent of companies had layoffs between 1990 and 1993, and 44 percent introduced some kind of early or voluntary retirement programs to reduce employment.

Table 2.1. Extent of Downsizing

Percentage of firms during the past five years that:	
a. Shut down some operations	64.3%
b. Sold any business units	51.0
c. Imposed a hiring freeze	57.1
d. Laid off a substantial number of workers	47.3
e. Allowed substantial numbers of workers to shift to part-time schedules	10.1
f. Offered early-retirement incentives	40.4
g. Reduced management staff significantly	38.4
h. Combined operating units	62.3

Source: Louis Harris and Associates (1991) Question B1.

Since the early 1980s, job displacements have continued at many companies even in periods when there was sizable employment growth in the economy as a whole. For example, although from 1985 to 1989 total employment expanded by 11.7 million, during this period 4.3 million workers who had been with their employers for at least three years lost their jobs because their plants or businesses closed down or moved, their position or shifts were abolished, or not enough work was available for them to do (Herz, 1991). Roughly one in five workers saw his or her job disappear permanently during the 1980s. The rate of job loss among older and more educated workers was actually higher in 1990–1991 than it was in the depths of the recession of 1982–1983.

The data from the American Management Association (AMA) survey reported in Table 2.2 reveal no letup in the pace or scale of downsizing, even in the midst of the strong national economic growth that occurred in 1993 and 1994 (the recession that started in 1989 ended in most industries by early 1993). The percentage of companies planning to downsize actually rose slightly in 1994.

Downsizing displacements have been unusual in their breadth as well as in their depth. One reflection of the broadening of downsizing is the fact that the industrial focus of job displacements spread after 1980 as job displacements increased markedly in the service and retail trades sectors, moving beyond their earlier concentration in manufacturing industries (Podgursky, 1992). At the same time, even in the face of this broadening, job displacement did remain disproportionately concentrated in manufacturing and goods-producing industries.

Another reflection of the broadening of downsizing was the movement along the occupational axis away from an earlier heavy concentration on blue-collar workers. News accounts of the layoff of large numbers of white-collar managerial employees at companies such as General Motors, Kodak, IBM, Exxon, and Merrill Lynch illustrated this development. Salaried employees had held 62.4 percent of the jobs eliminated in 1993–1994, which is significantly larger than salaried employees' share (40 percent) of all jobs (Ameri-

Table 2.2. **Trends in Downsizing**

	1993–94	1989–90
Companies reporting any workforce reductions (%)*	47.3	35.7
Average reduction of workforce (%)	10.2	10.9

*These figures include companies that experienced *any* elimination of jobs during the surveyed period and not necessarily a net reduction in their work forces.

Source: American Management Association (1994).

Table 2.3. Occupational Distribution of Downsizing

Percentage of jobs eliminated that were:	1993–94	1990–91
Hourly	37.6%	55.8%
Supervisory	25.5	13.8
Middle Management	18.5	17.2
Professional/Technical	18.2	13.2

Source: American Management Association (1994).

can Management Association, 1994). The figures in Table 2.3 document the recent increases in the share of job cuts borne by middle management, supervisors, and professional/technical employees.

Detailed statistical analysis documents that by the mid-1980s, managers were actually more vulnerable to displacement due to downsizing and plant closings than were lower-level employees after controlling for industry and individual characteristics (e.g., education, experience, race, and sex) (Cappelli, 1992). This contrasts with earlier periods when downsizing was relatively concentrated among blue-collar employees and is consistent with the data reported earlier showing the disproportionate job cutting borne by salaried employees in the 1990s.

Perhaps the most striking change in the pattern of displacement is that toward the end of the 1980s, job loss was actually higher among older and more educated workers (Farber, 1993). This is in contrast to the historical influence of seniority-based layoffs that concentrated job loss on the youngest, entry-level workers. The shift toward older and more educated workers is consistent with the restructuring arguments given in chapter 1, suggesting that jobs are being cut in the top rungs of the corporate hierarchy.

Why do corporations downsize so abruptly and discharge so many employees all at once? That might at first seem like a silly question, but it is justified by the fact that corporate growth, the opposite of downsizing, tends to occur in a very gradual manner. New employees are typically hired after deliberate screening in an incremental fashion. Why, then, do companies let go thousands of employees with so little notice? One reason for the abrupt character of downsizing is the fact that corporate executives commonly turn to downsizing in an effort to respond to severe financial pressures and as a result of the need to show quick results. A slow reduction in force wouldn't do the job. In addition, since there is often resistance to change, companies often wait until financial conditions deteriorate substantially before making large-scale layoffs. Furthermore, the fear that disgruntled employees will turn to equal employment opportunity or age discrimination suits to challenge layoffs appears to lead organizations to carry out reductions in mass, which offer some defense for their actions, since it is more difficult to make a charge of discrimination stand when so many other people (and many others with similar demographic or personal attributes) are simultaneously being laid off.

The Consequences of Downsizing
on the Displaced

The high costs that downsizing imposes on those laid off has been as alarming in recent years as the scale of downsizing. It has been very difficult for displaced workers to find new jobs since the mid-1980s. Displaced workers had seven times the unemployment rate of others as long as two years after their job loss; for men, the chances of finding a new job were even worse in the 1990s than during the 1982–1983 recession; displaced workers who did find a job were more likely to be working only part-time, and, on average, their wages were about 15 percent less than those of equivalent workers who had not been displaced (Farber, 1993).

Roughly one quarter of the workers displaced in the 1980s suffered annual earnings losses of 20 percent or more relative to their earnings on their previous jobs. A similar percentage of workers who had been previously covered by some form of health insurance on their lost jobs no longer were covered by any group plan when surveyed a few years after their job displacement. Income losses continued for displaced workers even as the economic climate improved from 1993 on. Of the workers displaced between 1991 and 1993 and reemployed by February 1994, 47 percent experienced declines in pay (Bureau of National Affairs, 1994).[1]

Many displaced employees have to move or change occupations to find new work. The proportion reemployed in work similar to the jobs they had lost varies by industry. Six of every ten workers displaced from the service industry were reemployed in new service industry jobs, while, in contrast, only 43 percent of displaced durable goods manufacturing workers found new jobs in that sector (Bureau of National Affairs, 1994).

The press picked up on the fact that minorities, particularly blacks, suffered disproportionately from downsizing. In a headline story, Rochelle Sharpe of the *Wall Street Journal* reported that "Blacks were the only racial group to suffer a net job loss during the 1990–91 economic downturn at companies with 100 or more workers" (Sharpe, 1993). Statistics collected by the Equal Employment Opportunity Commission reveal that some of the nation's largest corporations shed black employees at a high rate. Aggregate data show that blacks and Hispanics are more likely than whites to be displaced; they are less likely to be reemployed and experience greater income losses from job displacement (Herz, 1991; Kletzer, 1991).

Minorities are disproportionately displaced, in part due to the fact that they more frequently have low seniority and as result are affected disproportionately by last-in–first-out layoff rules.

Does the large number of layoffs and plant closings mean that few workers are likely to enjoy long spells of employment with any one employer during their work career? Are we in the midst of a transition to a world in which nearly everyone will have to change employers frequently over his or her working life? The evidence on these matters suggests that job tenure (and long spells of employment with one employer) declined *somewhat* in recent years, but not as much as some of the dire accounts that appeared in the popular press would suggest (Rose 1995). Swinnerton and Wial (1995), for instance, calculated that the proportion of workers with eight or more years of tenure on their jobs fell from .541 in 1979–1983 to .527 in 1987–91.

Analysts cannot yet tell, however, whether working careers have permanently shortened for a large segment of the population, because it is not clear if recent job displacements were one-time events resulting from the shock of international competition or corporate reorganization or if they represent the start of a broad deterioration in job security and job quality. Farber (1993), for instance, concludes that the *costs* of job loss to displaced workers (such as forgone income and earnings changes) were not unusually high in the 1980s.

Given the confusion that exists in the ranks of economists regarding what is in store for American blue- and white-collar employees in the way of future job security, it is not surprising that employee fears were stirred by the near daily news headlines reporting further downsizing. Employees' fears that downsizing will continue and may even grow coincide with managers' expectations that downsizing will continue in the future.

It is also interesting to note that managers do not always endorse the downsizing occurring within their own organizations. In the Harris (1991) survey, 42.1 percent of managers thought that periodic downsizing by their companies was *not* necessary.

Corporate Policies to Ease the Burdens of Downsizing

Adjustment Policies

Corporations used a number of policies to avoid layoffs or soften the effects of downsizing. As revealed in the National Survey of Estab-

Table 2.4.   Strategies that Firms Use in an Effort to Avoid Layoffs

Percentage of firms that, to avoid layoffs of core employees, use a strategy of:
    a. Buffering with temporary workers   22.4%
    b. Withdrawing subcontracting   19.9
    c. Smoothing product demand   24.7
    d. Multiskilling workers so that they can switch to other jobs   24.7
    e. Reducing overtime to avoid layoffs   79.2
    f. Work-sharing (e.g., putting workers on reduced hours)   51.2
    g. Finding innovative activities for otherwise underutilized workers   59.7
    h. Using early-retirement programs   48.8

Source: National Survey of Establishments (1992), Questions E27–29.

lishments (1992) (NES) summarized in Table 2.4, corporate adjust-ment policies included hiring freezes, salary reductions or freezes, mandatory short workweeks or workdays, and job sharing.[2] A sub-stantial number of businesses (48.8 percent of those in the NES survey described in Table 2.4) used early retirement programs to generate voluntary severance as an alternative to involuntary layoffs.[3]

The variety of strategies used to try to avoid layoffs of "core" employees is described in Table 2.4. The figures show that reduc-tions in overtime and work sharing are particularly popular. The use of these procedures as alternatives to layoffs, however, is not a re-cent development. What is striking about recent trends is the extent to which these workforce adjustment policies have not been suffi-cient. As a result, companies feel compelled frequently to turn to involuntary severance. One reason is that these alternative arrange-ments are typically aimed at temporary downturns in business where the assumption is that the jobs will eventually return.

Although many companies took steps to cushion the impacts of downsizing on displaced employees, managers often received better treatment than did workers. As shown in Table 2.5, businesses were

Table 2.5.   Outplacement Assistance Received by Managers vs. Hourly Workers

	Managers	Workers*
Received *some* outplacement assistance	51%	37%
Received larger severance payments for downsizing-induced layoffs	30%	24%
Offered job retraining opportunities	17%	13%

*This category refers to nonexempt employees.

Source: American Management Association (1990), as reported in Greenberg (1991).

more likely to offer outplacement assistance to departing managers than to workers. Similarly, managers more frequently than workers received larger severance payments for downsizing-induced layoffs as compared to the payments they would have received if laid off for other reasons.

Layoffs have often been heaviest in smokestack industries where unions are heavily concentrated. As a result, collective bargaining frequently has been utilized to expand workforce adjustment policies. Among large unionized businesses, the use of early-retirement incentives to facilitate workforce reductions is mandated in nearly one fifth of all collective bargaining agreements, and fully 10 percent of the workforce in large unionized companies was offered early retirement incentives at some point during the 1980s, with 4 percent actually taking advantage of early-retirement programs. (Katz and Keefe, 1993).

Unions and their employees also introduced a host of innovative programs to provide outplacement counseling and relocation financial assistance. The AT&T/CWA & IBEW Alliance described in Box 1 is a noteworthy example of the joint efforts that appeared in unionized settings in recent years to cushion the effects of displacement.

The Growth of Contingent Employment

While downsizing was severing employment relationships altogether, the growth of contingent employment offered employment with substantially less attachment and commitment by either side. A small percentage of companies retrained or transferred employees when business conditions deteriorated, but more took advantage of part-time or temporary employees or workers employed by suppliers or help agencies (i.e., external to the company).[4] Contingent work represents an alternative to full-time employment and includes temporary, part-time, and contract labor.

How widespread has contingent work become? It is difficult to acquire an accurate assessment of contingent work because government statistics do not track its many forms, yet indicative data are available. Belous (1989) estimates that the number of contingent workers in 1988 was between 29.9 million and 36.6 million, representing 25 to 30 percent of the civilian labor force. Part-time employment grew from 16.4 percent of all nonagricultural workers in 1970 to 18.0 percent in 1990. Nearly 90 percent of this increase was due to the growth in involuntary part-time employment (an involuntary part-time worker is defined as someone who works fewer than thirty-five hours a week because she or he cannot find a full-time job) (Callaghan and Hartmann, 1991).

As Callaghan and Hartmann (1991) reported, "It is important to

---

Box 1
The Alliance

The CWA/IBEW/AT&T Alliance for Employee Growth and Development is a joint labor-management training fund established under contract in 1986 to fund a wide variety of opportunities for members, both to upgrade skills for jobs within the corporation as well as to pursue new occupations on the outside. The fund serves workers displaced by corporate restructuring and downsizing as well as those that continue in the active work force. While members gain from increased employment security, the firm benefits from improved employee morale and commitment to corporate productivity.

The Alliance funds training over and above that provided by AT&T as a normal part of doing business. The company, for example, routinely trains employees in the jobs for which they were hired and provides retraining in relation to technology change. The Alliance, by contrast, provides training to meet entry-level requirements for employees who wish to change jobs within AT&T or find new jobs outside of the firm. It also finances educational programs for personal growth and skill development.

The fund generates resources through a formula, initially set at $3.75 per employee per month and gradually raised to $9.50 in 1991. In its first four-and-a-half years in operation, the Alliance allocated $80 million to training programs, including $6 million generated from external sources. There were approximately 108,000 union members at AT&T, and there were 122,000 enrollments in a variety of programs from 59,000 workers. Approximately 60% of the trainees have been part of the active AT&T work force, and the remainder have been displaced workers.

The Alliance, then, serves as a bridge between jobs—either inside or outside of AT&T—for displaced and "at-risk" employees. Given the intense and on-going reorganization at AT&T, however, most employees can not dismiss the possibility of job loss or of new skill demands to remain employed. For displaced workers, the Alliance provides tuition assistance for up to one year following lay-off, plus additional time based on seniority. For displaced or at-risk workers who wish to stay at AT&T, the Alliance fills an important training gap: it funds courses in basic skills and preparation for qualifying exams that AT&T administers for all new hires.

Source: Osterman and Batt, 1992.

---

note that some workers prefer part-time jobs and some part-time jobs provide wages, benefits, and advancement opportunities that are comparable to full-time jobs." Employers reduce the hours for these employees (what Tilly [1991] refers to as retention jobs) so as not to lose valuable full-time employees who desire part-time status.

Yet, the growth in involuntary part-time employment suggests that employer rather than employee preferences are the most significant factor driving the expansion in part-time employment (Callaghan and Hartmann, 1991).

Temporary employment (employment that is of limited duration) has also grown dramatically in recent years. Temporary employment has grown nearly three times as fast as overall employment since 1982 (Callaghan and Hartmann, 1991). Those employed in part-time work are disproportionately female, young, or old, while those employed in temporary work are disproportionately female, minority, and young (Callaghan and Hartmann, 1991). And as Callaghan and Hartmann (1991) noted, although some of these workers may prefer contingent employment status, the substantial growth in involuntary part-time employment and the fact that many temporary workers work every day suggest that worker preferences are not a good explanation for the demographic concentration of contingent labor.

The NES found significant, although somewhat less dramatic, increases in contingent work as compared to the aggregate statistics cited earlier. The NES survey asked about two patterns: temporary workers who work in the establishment but are on the payroll of another company (e.g., a "temp" agency) and contingent workers, who are on the payroll of the host company but are not "regular" employees and are seen as temporary. As shown in Table 2.6, the NES found that 10 percent of all regular employees worked part-time, while another 7 percent of employees were temporary or "contingent" employees.

The NES revealed that managers expect the use of contingent employees to grow significantly.[5] Furthermore, the use of tempor-

Table 2.6. Use of Temporary and Contingent Workers

	Expectations about future use of employees	
	Temporary[a]	Contingent[b]
Decline a lot	5.1%	6.0%
Decline a little	13.0	7.6
Stay the same	51.0	48.0
Grow a little	21.4	31.5
Grow a lot	9.2	6.5

[a]Percentage of employees counted as temporary workers = 2%.

[b]Percentage of employees counted as contingent workers = 2%.

Source: National Survey of Establishments (1992), Questions B1aa and B3a.

ary and contingent labor is expected to be greater in large businesses (in establishments with 500 or more employees surveyed by the NES, 49.2 percent expect the use of temporaries to grow a little or a lot, compared to 40.6 percent for all establishments).

The increase in temporary help accounts for a significant share of the rise in contingent work. Employment in temporary-help agencies has risen 240 percent since 1984 and accounts for 20 percent of all new jobs created since then. The largest employer in the United States is now Manpower Temporary Help Agency, with more than 600,000 employees.

Contingent employees work at all skill levels. Temporaries are not limited to clerical workers but include engineers, computer programmers, and draftsmen. Imcor, a Stamford, Connecticut, temporary agency, for example, limits its business to executive positions. There are now more than 100 law firms aimed at provided temporary legal work for lawyers. Furthermore, the use of part-time work schedules now extends even into managerial ranks. A majority (52.7 percent) of companies report that they already utilize some part-time managers (Harris and Associates, 1991).

Why has the use of contingent labor, especially involuntary part-time and temporary workers, increased so dramatically in recent years? One reason is the shift in the composition of economic activity toward trade and service industries. Contingent work is a relatively large share of work in these expanding sectors.

The growing use of contingent employees also may reflect the "disassembling" of internal work structures as corporations seek to reduce job security and implied commitments to incumbent employees in order to either lower costs or respond to increased economic uncertainty. It is interesting to note that the relative wages of contingent workers have not fallen in recent years. Employers get their greatest savings through the limited fringe benefits provided to employees who are employed on contingent status. Consistent with the latter is survey evidence showing that contingent employees are much less likely than others to receive health benefits or pensions (National Establishment Survey, 1992; Callaghan and Hartmann, 1991).

Unionized companies use fewer temporary employees but more contracting out and subcontracting (Abraham, 1990). Temporary employee use tends to be either banned or limited in union contracts. Yet, it appears that unionized companies make relatively high use of contracting out and subcontracting in response to the higher costs of union labor and the presence of other contractual constraints.

There may be factors other than cost and changes in industry composition that explain the growth in contingent labor. Many analysts, for example, argue that high-performance work organization requires increased employment security and suggest that one way companies may attempt to provide this is to surround a core labor force, which receives job security, with a buffer of peripheral employees. The Saturn contract (an exemplar of the transformed model), for example, permits General Motors to staff 20 percent of the labor force with workers who are not covered by security pledges. Companies also may be turning increasingly to outside suppliers or subcontractors because of the specialized skills held by these outsiders (Abraham, 1990).

A final factor concerns public policy. The U.S. workplace is governed by an array of legislation that protects employee rights. The costs to employers of complying with this legislation are considerable, as are the risks of litigation if they fail to comply. Part-time workers are generally covered by most of this legislation, as are employees hired on a temporary basis, but contract workers—temporary employees who are employed by an agency and who work under contract—are not.[6]

The ability to avoid compliance with this legislation by hiring staff through agencies has been limited considerably by various court rulings that essentially hold that if a contractor directs the performance of a contract worker and essentially supervises his or her work, the contractor is treated as if it is the employer and is governed by all relevant labor laws. On the other hand, most of this legislation is directed at employment decisions such as hiring and firing, wage, and promotion decisions. When an organization contracts with a temporary agency for workers, the typical organization does not make any of those decisions and is therefore substantially less affected by the legislation. An organization that is unhappy with a temporary worker, for example, simply fails to renew the contract for that worker with the temporary agency. It does not have to fire the worker and expose itself to potential litigation.

Because most litigation concerns decisions to fire workers, the costs and risks of hiring and firing workers have risen considerably. Using temporary-help agencies substantially reduces those costs. Organizations may use temporary agencies as a costless way to "shop" for permanent employees by trying out temporary workers. Many temporary agencies are attached to employment agencies precisely to facilitate this shopping function, charging organizations that hire away their temporary workers a finder's fee. There is a growing practice of organizations interviewing and selecting workers and then asking a temporary-help agency to place them on the agency's roster; in other words, the agency is simply acting as an employment "front" for the organization.

Some companies appear to be making increased use of contingent labor as part of their strategic decision to pursue a low-wage, low-skill, high-turnover path to profit making (Tilly, 1991). An indication of this trend is found in the fact that part-time employment has grown the most in the less skilled occupations (Tilly, 1991). Although the use of some temporary and part-time arrangements seem sensible, the danger is that an increasing number of businesses are using these arrangements "to avoid the human resource investments that would guarantee flexibility and adaptability in the long run" (Callaghan and Hartmann, 1991). And while it may make sense to make greater use of contingent labor to adjust to fluctuations in the demand for labor, the bothersome tendency is that companies are using contingent labor as part of their regular staffing arrangements.

Not all businesses make great use of contingent employees or expect their use to increase in the future.[7] Here, as with other human resource policies, companies differ in their strategic responses to economic pressures.

Internal Flexibility and Training as Alternatives to Displacement and the Use of Contingent Labor

It may be impossible to avoid the economic fluctuations and cost pressures that are features of the modern economy. But companies do have strategic alternatives for responding to these economic forces. A number of labor market analysts argue that employers and the workforce would benefit by the creation of greater "internal flexibility" in job and work structures. Internal flexibility would broaden job definitions, generate the capacity to move employees more frequently inside an organization in response to market pressures, and induce companies to rely *somewhat* less frequently on "external flexibility" (downsizing) when product demand falls or shifts.

A number of the measures described in Table 2.4 (finding innovative activities for otherwise underutilized workers or multiskilling workers so that they can switch to other jobs) would promote greater internal flexibility. As the figures in this table indicate, there already is some use of these measures.

Yet, other data suggest that U.S. businesses remain relatively inflexible in their internal structures. The survey of union companies mentioned earlier found that while internal flexibility was enhanced by reductions in the number of job classifications during the 1980s, as of 1990 the average company still had sixty-nine job classifications for production and skilled workers (in 1980 the average company had ninety-four job classifications). Thus, the internal flexibility of U.S. corporations continues to be limited by the persistence of numerous job demarcations.

The same survey found that while 10 percent of the workforce was offered early retirement during the 1980s, only 4 percent accepted retraining to avoid layoffs (Katz and Keefe, 1992). This figure is consistent with evidence from the AMA survey reported in Table 2.5 showing the limited availability of job retraining opportunities to departing hourly workers or higher-level employees. These percentages are much lower than those for the percentage of companies offering outplacement services or severance payments. Not only was the use of training infrequent as an alternative to layoff; it was also the case that those companies fearing that an economic crisis would threaten their survival invested less in training than did companies that did not face such a crisis (Katz and Keefe, 1993). Furthermore, international data suggest that U.S. corporate and labor policies make external flexibility relatively easy and more attractive than internal flexibility, especially compared to policies common in Japan and German (Katz and Sabel, 1985; Osterman, 1988).

Although many businesses recognize the need for greater internal flexibility, their drive for flexibility often clashes with downsizing and other cost-cutting strategies. Useem (1993), for example, found that companies that downsized were less likely to have introduced changes in the work process, job involvement, or quality involvement.

Although more internal flexibility would be beneficial, greater internal flexibility is unlikely to avoid the occurrence of downsizing. When there are major shifts in competitive pressures and companies find that their previous products or market strategies need major restructuring, large-scale employment reductions may be unavoidable. Yet, greater internal flexibility could be used to reduce the frequency and the scope of downsizing. Furthermore, enhancement of internal flexibility might stimulate greater employee acceptance of downsizing when no other alternative is possible.

Employer versus Employee Reactions to Downsizing

While employers appear to be generally satisfied with the outcomes produced by downsizing, employees are quite disturbed by these events. Employer satisfaction with downsizing is evident from survey responses as well as in the frequency with which companies have adopted downsizing. In the Harris survey data reported in Table 2.7, for example, 79 percent of the management respondents reported that they were either "very" or "somewhat" satisfied with the downsizing that had occurred in their organizations, while only 1 percent were not satisfied.

The harmful effects of downsizing on the income of laid-off

Table 2.7. Managers' Satisfaction With Downsizing

Survey question: Overall, how satisfied are you with the results of the downsizing?	
Very satisfied (fully met corporate objectives)	43.1%
Somewhat satisfied (met corporate objectives to some degree with some negative results)	36.0
Minimally satisfied	3.4
Not satisfied at all	0.7
Not sure*	3.7

*Another 13.1% of the responses to this question were missing.

Source: Louis Harris and Associates (1991), Question B8.

employees is clear from the evidence discussed earlier. Perhaps as troubling is the evidence that has surfaced in recent years showing that downsizing also brings severe morale problems among retained employees after a downsizing.

The organizational behavior literature has created a new term, "survivors' syndrome," to refer to morale problems among those who remain in the downsized organization. The evidence from this extensive research is that survivors "may feel a profound sense of job insecurity—i.e. wondering whether they are the next to go" (Brockner, 1988). Research shows that survivors' perceptions of the fairness involved in the downsizing process exert a strong influence on survivor attitudes and behavior. In particular, survivors appear to be heavily influenced by the extent to which they believe the laid off were treated fairly and in a caring manner by the company (Brockner, 1988).

Survivors are also affected by how their work conditions and work environment are altered by downsizing. A review of studies of survivors' reactions finds that "the postlayoff environment *has the potential* to be quite stressful for a variety of reasons (e.g., survivors' concerns about job insecurity). Stress, in turn, *has the potential* to affect adversely survivors' work attitudes and behaviors" (Brockner, 1988). Some individuals are driven to work harder after surviving a layoff, particularly those with low self-esteem who become worried about their own job security after watching layoffs.

In addition, downsizing can create job demands that employees are not prepared for or equipped to handle. "A common complaint among top managers was that downsizing created job demands that most of their managers were not qualified to fulfill" (Cameron, Freeman, and Mishra, 1993). Employees were asked, in the face of downsizing, to take on broader and unfamiliar responsibilities as part of efforts to cover the tasks previously performed by those who were let go. Because of such demands, burnout, frustration, and declines in organizational commitment follow many corporate downsizings.

Table 2.8. After-Effects of Downsizing

	Declined	Constant	Increased
Operating profits*	20%	29%	51%
Worker productivity	30	36	34
Employee morale	86	12	2

*These figures were reported by 713 human resources managers in relatively large companies that experienced one or more spells of downsizing between 1989 and 1994.

Source: American Management Association (1994).

Survivors' syndrome extends into the ranks of management and is not just a problem among blue-collar and other lower-level employees. Remember, as discussed earlier, managers report satisfaction from downsizing only with regard to the effects of downsizing *on their organizations* (also see Table 2.8). When managers are asked about how they feel about *their own career security,* they reveal substantial insecurities as a result of downsizing. Evidence of this appears in the fact that middle managers' ratings of their companies and corporate policies declined substantially during the 1980s in the midst of large-scale white-collar layoffs, as revealed in Table 2.9. Managers' job security fears are justified in the face of the evidence, discussed earlier in this chapter, showing that managers are now just as likely as other employees to face downsizing. Middle managers have become particularly suspicious of the ability of top management (the percentage expressing a favorable attitude toward top management's abilities declined from 54 percent in 1985–1987 to 38 percent in 1988–1990, as reported in Table 2.9).

Many managers appear to recognize the depth of these survivor morale problems. As shown in Table 2.8, 86 percent of the managers surveyed believed that employee morale had declined after a downsizing. Further evidence comes from a survey conducted by Right

Table 2.9. Middle Managers Rate Their Companies

Percent who expressed a favorable attitude about:	1985–87	1988–90
Information given to employees	85%	69%
The ability of top management	54	38
The company as a place to work	65	55
Companies who treat them with respect as individuals	51	43
Top management's willingness to listen to their problems and complaints	42	35

Source: Based on a survey of 750,000 managers by Hay Research for Management as reported in Fisher (1991). © 1991 Time Inc. All rights reserved.

Associates, a Philadelphia outplacement firm, of managers in companies that had experienced downsizing. Seventy-four percent of the senior managers said their workers had low morale, feared cutbacks, and distrusted management (Cascio, 1993).

While managers may be aware of the morale problems created by downsizing, they are less sure of what to do about these problems. As discussed earlier, many organizations have introduced early-retirement programs as a device to bring a more voluntary component to staff reductions. Furthermore, some progressive organizations have introduced wide-ranging employee counseling and relocation assistance to ease the hardships associated with layoffs. Yet, it is noteworthy that even in organizations that have introduced adjustment assistance programs, survivors' syndrome has appeared with full force. Keefe and Boroff (1995) surveyed surviving employees at AT&T, a company that has been noted in the press for the assistance it provides to downsized employees. Yet, survivors at AT&T are extremely angry about the layoffs, and many resent the company for violating its own principles by engaging in repeated large-scale downsizing.

It seems clear that many corporations have not convinced their employees of the justification for downsizing. Yet, coping with these matters is no easy matter, as there are no simple measures organizations can use to maintain the loyalty and commitment of the remaining workforce. As Brockner (1988) wrote, "It may be an overstatement to suggest that managers can implement layoffs in ways that have *positive* impact on survivors' work behaviors and attitudes (relative to prior to the onset of the layoff). However, it is not an exaggeration to assert that managers' handling of layoffs will have significant effect on the extent to which survivors exhibit *dysfunctional* work behaviors and/or attitudes."

While the research literature shows that morale declines often follow corporate downsizing, the research has not yet determined whether decreases in morale lead to declines in corporate performance. It is, of course, possible that while employees' morale is declining, these employees are working more productively in fear of further downsizing. Yet, it is instructive to note that Bassi (1993) found a positive correlation between improvements in morale and improvements in productivity, profits, and scrap/error rates in the small businesses she surveyed.

Does Downsizing Actually Lead to Improved Organizational Performance?

The goal of downsizing programs is to improve the performance of the organization, but does it really do so? The anecdotal evidence suggests a mixed picture. A Society of Human Resource Management survey of downsized companies found that 50 percent of the company respondents reported that productivity was either unchanged or dropped after downsizing. As reported in Table 2.8, less than a majority of middle managers believes that the aftereffects of downsizing include increases in profits.

The conventional wisdom claims that the rapid productivity growth experienced in the manufacturing sector in the United States has been caused in large part by the employment declines associated with corporate downsizing. However, recent analysis of company-level data shows that "there are in fact many manufacturing establishments where productivity growth accompanies increases in employment. Overall, plants that added workers contributed about the same to aggregate productivity as plants that downsized" (Baily, Bartelsman, and Haltiwanger, 1994).

Research also demonstrates that in many cases downsizing brings unanticipated harmful consequences to service quality and costs (Cascio, 1993). For one thing, the high performers that management wants to keep sometimes take advantage of early retirement or other severance options, and management ends up after downsizing with the wrong people. In the Harris survey, 17.2 percent of the respondents claimed that, as a result of downsizing, their organization had lost the wrong people (Harris and Associates, 1991).

Management's recent efforts to promote high-performance work teams may be harmed by downsizing. Managers and unionists often complain that layoffs (and associated seniority-based bumping) were extremely detrimental to the operation of work groups and teams.[8] The harmful effect of downsizing on teams illustrates the tension that exists between strategies that promote internal flexibility and those that promote external flexibility. Many companies try to mix these strategies, and that does not work well.

A study done at the Bureau of the Census on productivity growth in manufacturing highlights the fact that downsizing may improve performance in some establishments but not in others (see Figure 2.1). The study labeled plants according to whether they were successful at "upsizing" (increasing both employment and productivity) or not (increasing employment while productivity fell) and whether they were successful "downsizers" (productivity grew while employment shrank) or not (productivity fell while employment shrank). It found that the plants that were adding workers contributed about as much to overall productivity growth as did those that were cutting jobs.

While downsizing does not appear to work magic in all organizations, it clearly has been critical to the survival of some. It is hard

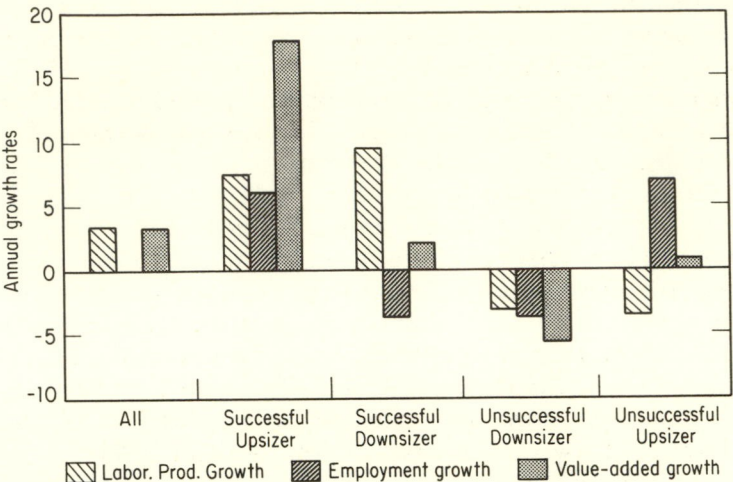

Figure 2.1. Decomposition of Manufacturing Productivity Growth (1977–1987). *Source:* Adapted from Baily, Bartleman, and Haltiwanger (May 1994), Figure 5.

to imagine that either IBM or General Motors, for example, would have been able to avoid bankruptcy without a heavy dose of downsizing, although that does not imply that downsizing was accomplished in the most effective manner in those companies. And for nearly all U.S. businesses, it seems clear that the heightened economic competition and volatility requires that corporations find a way to become "lean and flexible." How downsizing might best be accomplished is addressed in the next section.

Techniques for Promoting Constructive Downsizing

What can managers do to minimize survivors' guilt and other harmful consequences of downsizing? Here the research provides a number of suggestions, but to understand those recommendations, it is necessary first to clarify the various strategies organizations commonly use to implement downsizing.

The three strategies identified in a comprehensive review of U.S. companies' experience with downsizing are summarized in Table 2.10. The most common strategy, labeled *workforce reduction* in Table 2.9, focuses primarily on eliminating headcount or reducing the number of employees in the workforce. This strategy "consists of activities such as offering early retirements, transfers and outplacement, buyout packages, golden parachutes, attrition, job

Table 2.10. Three Types of Downsizing Strategies

	Downsizing Strategy		
	Workforce reduction	Organization redesign	Systemic
Focus:	Workers	Jobs and units	Culture
Eliminates:	People	Work	Status quo processes
Implementation time:	Quick	Moderate	Extended
Temporal target:	Short-term payoff	Moderate-term payoff	Long-term payoff
Inhibits:	Long-term adaptability	Quick payback	Short-term cost savings
Examples:	Attrition	Eliminate functions	Involve everyone
	Layoffs	Merge units	Simplify everything
	Early retirement	Redesign jobs	Change responsibility
	Buyout packages	Eliminate layers	Continuously improve

Source: Cameron, Freeman, and Mishra (1993).

banks, and in the extreme, layoffs and firings" (Cameron, Freeman, and Mishra, 1993). These policies are often implemented across the board, and they are designed to reduce headcount quickly. As Cameron, Freeman, and Mishra (1993) described it, the workforce reduction strategy is "similar to throwing a grenade into a crowded room, closing the door, and expecting the explosion to eliminate a certain percentage of the workforce."

Most companies that downsized used a version of the workforce reduction approach (Cameron, Freeman, and Mishra, 1993). They implemented sizable downsizing with little preparation and planning and limited forethought regarding how the organization would operate after the downsizing. Downsizing was a quick solution to financial pressures to lower costs. The evidence shows that this strategy is rarely effective, especially if it is not accompanied by other, more creative strategic endeavors (Cameron, Freeman, and Mishra, 1993; Cascio, 1993).

A second downsizing strategy described in Table 2.10 is an *organization redesign strategy*. "The primary focus of this strategy is to cut out work rather than workers. It often consists of activities such as eliminating functions, hierarchical levels, groups or divisions, and products. Other examples are redesigning tasks, consolidating and merging units, and reducing work hours. Because the redesign strategy is difficult to implement quickly, it is, by and large, a medium-term strategy" (Cameron, Freeman, and Mishra, 1993).

While the consequences of the redesign strategy are often better than those of the workforce reduction strategy, the redesign strategy's contributions can be increased if the strategy is broadened to incorporate the third approach, labeled the *systematic change* strategy in Table 2.10. A basic difference between the workforce reduction strategy and the systematic change approach is that the former is focused on producing a smaller organization while the latter focuses on creating a different organization. The systematic change approach "is fundamentally different from the other two strategies in that it focuses on changing the organization's culture and the attitudes and values of employees. It involves redefining downsizing as a way of life, as on ongoing process, rather than as a program or a target. Downsizing is equated with simplification of all aspects of the organization—the entire system. . . . Because this strategy takes a long-term perspective, it may not generate the immediate improvement in bottom-line numbers that a workforce reduction strategy will generate" (Cameron, Freeman, and Mishra, 1993).

Accumulating evidence suggests that systematic change strategies are more effective at leading to long-term improvements in organizational performance and at minimizing survivor problems.[9] The most effective downsizing has occurred at companies that "prepared for downsizing by conducting systematic analyses, involved employees, increased communication, and implemented change strategies incrementally" (Cameron, Freeman, and Mishra, 1993). Through this sort of incremental and participatory approach, lower-level employees are able to identify good targets for cost cutting as well as gain a better appreciation of the need for downsizing. Effective downsizing also "paid special attention to the transition experienced by employees who remained with the organization as well as those who exited" (Cameron, Freeman, and Mishra, 1993).

Summary

The depth and breadth of downsizing in recent years has been alarming. Employees of all occupational groups and economic sectors continue to fear that they may be next on the downsizing list. These fears are a rational response to the spread of downsizing and to the fact that there is no letup in sight in the pace of corporate downsizing.

When they downsize, corporations often try to ameliorate the harmful effects on both the laid off and the retained. Yet, even in the face of these efforts, downsized employees suffer substantial income losses, and for those who remain on the payroll, work often intensifies and morale plummets in the face of heightened insecurities.

In addition to this obvious dark side, downsizing has other costs as well. Corporate profits and employee productivity do not improve in many companies that travel the downsizing path. But for some companies, downsizing has been essential to their survival and has become an integral part of their renewal process.

Whether downsizing works well depends on the extent to which it is associated with wide and deep corporate and work reorganization. Corporate strategy, here as elsewhere in the U.S. economy, is a critical driving force. For some companies, downsizing is an end in itself, while other companies effectively mesh downsizing with internal reorganization.

U.S. corporations would be well advised to make greater use of the latter approach so as to increase the use of internal transfers and retraining and thereby lessen the frequency and scale of downsizing. As discussed in this and other chapters of this book, the effective use of these alternatives to downsizing can yield substantial long-term payouts and lessen the employee resentment and fears generated by downsizing. Yet, the evidence suggests that there is no one best way to reorganize, nor is it likely that the need for downsizing can be completely eliminated.

The consequences of downsizing depend on how it is accomplished and on the other corporate decisions that go along with the act of downsizing. Most critical is the degree to which companies are able to convince their employees of the rationale for downsizing and involve employees in the decision-making process.

Notes

1. Of the workers displaced between 1991 and 1993, as of February 1994, 19.1% remained unemployed and 12.9% were no longer in the labor force (Bureau of National Affairs [1994], B-7, Table 3).

2. See American Management Association (1994) for further and consistent survey evidence on the use of these techniques.

3. These data are similar to the responses in the Harris survey (1991) and in surveys by the American Management Association (1990, 1994).

4. Only 10.1% of firms did so as reported in the Harris survey (1991), Question B1e.

5. Similar growth predictions are contained in the responses to the Harris survey, in which 10 percent of managers predicted significant growth in temporary employees over next five years while 19 percent predicted significant growth in the use of part-time employees.

6. Legislation governing characteristics of the workplace, such as Occupational Safety and Health of the Americans with Disabilities Act, apply equally to contractees; legislation governing employment practices, such as wages and hours discrimination, do not. There is anecdotal evidence that part-time workers are less likely to sue their employers because they apparently do not perceive as strong a sense of obligation on the part of the employer as do full-time workers.

7. Of those managers surveyed by Harris and Associates (1991) 25.6% said they would *not* use part-time managers over the next five years.

8. This reaction was reported in field interviews conducted by the author.

9. A similar call for systematic change is made by Cascio (1993) in his review of the evidence concerning the effectiveness of downsizing.

3

Work Organization

Earlier chapters in this book have identified the pressures on U.S. businesses that are leading companies to reconsider their structure. These pressures have not only led to turmoil at the top; they have also led to efforts to reorganize how work is done throughout the organization. Giving impetus to this reconsideration are observations that much of the success of international competitors compared to U.S. businesses seems linked to how those competitors organize and motivate their workforce.

The need to respond to these pressures has led to both change and confusion. Many workers have been empowered to play a greater role in designing their jobs and in dealing with customers and suppliers. These employees are often better trained and more highly motivated than their peers in the past, but there is another side to these transformations.

In a number of respects, working conditions have worsened for many Americans, and this degradation often occurs at the same companies that are trying to restructure their workplaces. Wage levels have stagnated, companies are increasingly using contingent and temporary labor, and employment security is eroding. Since many of the new innovations in work organization require the cooperation of an active and committed labor force, it appears at the least problematical whether this cooperation can be attained, given the deterioration in working conditions.

In addition, many employers have not even begun to transform their workplaces. Sometimes they have made a judgment that reorganized work is not appropriate or necessary. In other cases, obstacles—an undertrained workforce, short-term performance pressures from investors, or recalcitrant middle management—block change.

In thinking about these often inconsistent tendencies, we must remember that in a large economy such as that of the United States we cannot be sure that we are not being misled by relatively few well publicized examples. In this chapter we seek to get behind the anecdotes and use national survey data to address several key questions. For example, we ask about the diffusion of specific practices such as quality circles and team production, which seem most closely associated with the new "high-performance" workplaces. We also take up the question of whether there is good evidence that new, flexible work practices are indeed more productive.

The Nature of High-Performance Work Organizations

Until a decade or so ago, the U.S. industrial relations system and work organization could be characterized by what might be termed a traditional model. In the traditional system, the workplace was organized around tight divisions of labor and narrowly designed specialized jobs. Decision making was in the hands of supervisors who decided how the jobs were to be performed, how work was scheduled, and how workers were judged. Employee participation was limited, and clear, detailed rules specified either in a personnel policy or a collective bargaining contact determined the criteria governing career progression from one job to another and the compensation associated with each individual job. Grievance procedures were the dominant voice mechanism for employees who believed that their job rights had been violated in some way by a supervisor or by some management decision. In the traditional model, employers were free to adjust employment levels as they wished, and hence hire-fire was the rule.

This system is under attack because it is increasingly perceived as less productive than the alternatives. The central problem lies in the internal rigidities associated with the traditional model. Consider, for example, the situation at General Motors under the traditional system. Among the job titles were "install front seats," "install rear seats," "install garnish moldings," and "install door trim panels." A "front seat installer" would not install rear seats (Katz, 1985).

It is important to see that this system was not irrational. In a world in which employers hired and fired at will, rigid job classifications arose to provide at least some level of protection to the labor force, so the system made some sense given the constraints under which it was created.

Although not irrational in its own terms, the traditional system has increasingly been seen as failing to meet the needs of both businesses and employees. The sources of failure are several. The efforts by companies to improve quality and to meet customer needs more effectively both have required a reorganization of production that puts more power in the hands of employees further down the organizational hierarchy. This tendency is given further impetus by efforts to cut costs, which also lead to elimination of bureaucratic layers and greater responsibility at lower levels. In order to "empower" these employees, their job definitions need to be flexible, they require greater levels of discretion, they often find themselves working in teams, and they require higher levels of skill and training. All of these imply a transformation in how work is organized.

In more specific terms, what do these reforms consist of? How might a reader concretely envision the content of these changes? The beginning to any answer to this question is to recognize (as the data presented later in this chapter demonstrate) that there is no single model that is being adopted everywhere. In some settings, such as the General Motors Saturn plant, joint union/employee/management activities extend from work teams on the shop floor to joint "management" committees at every level of the plant and in every area from product design to supplier relations. This, however, is only one model, and an unusual one at that. In other companies, change is being driven by the quality movement, and the transformation consists of a combination of work teams and off-line problem-solving groups.

A useful way of envisioning the nature of the new systems is to break them down into their component parts and examine the options for each component. As we work our way through these elements, it should become clear that the central principle is increased employee power and responsibility. However, the extent to which this occurs is not uniform across all employers that introduce elements of the new systems.

The Organization of Work

At the core of the new systems are changes in how employees do their jobs. Perhaps the most typical innovation is the introduction of work teams. In many instances, these teams are led by a management employee, but that person's role has changed from supervisor to coach or facilitator. In other instances, the teams are self-directed. In both cases, at the core of the idea of teams is the requirement that employees take responsibility for a group of tasks, that there be a sense of responsibility for the team's product, that the workers be broadly skilled, and that there be an element of job rotation.

In many cases, the teams can decide how best to do their job, but this is not always the case. For example, at the General Motors-Toyota joint venture, NUMMI, each task is rigidly prescribed. Employees, however, have considerable power to make suggestions as to how to alter these prescriptions. This brings us to the second point.

Involvement in Off-Line Activities

In many "transformed" companies, employees are involved in aspects other than direct work activities. The most common example is problem-solving groups in which employees work in groups, often consisting of a cross-section of employees and hence to some extent obviating traditional managerial/nonmanagerial distinctions. These groups address problems such as production techniques, quality issues, and health and safety. In the most extreme form these groups can take up topics that in the past have been seen as clearly "managerial" (e.g., outsourcing and supplier policy).

Link to Broader Objectives

It is frequently the case that organizations that implement the innovations described so far do so as part of broader efforts to transform themselves. These efforts include flattening organizational hierarchies and renewed emphasis on quality and customer satisfaction. Both of these objectives are consistent with empowering workers.

Link to Other Human Resources Policies

Organizations that implement these changes in work organization typically transform other aspects of their human resources systems as well. The two most consistent changes are increased use of performance-based compensation and higher levels of training. The importance of increased training is straightforward: To the extent that employees have more responsibilities and to the extent that they exercise greater discretion, they need to be prepared.

Performance-based compensation shifts risk from the employer to the workers and in this sense can be interpreted as a degradation of employment conditions. On the other hand, it also gives workers and teams that have new powers the opportunity to reap rewards from their efforts.

There is greater variation in other human resources policies. Some employers have linked work reorganization to higher levels of employment security. Examples include Saturn, NUMMI, and Xerox. These employers pursue this policy because they understand that the traditional system provided security in the form of rigid work rules; they believe that in order to induce employees to provide greater flexibility, they need to be compensated with some level of security commitment. However, the companies that undertake policies along these lines appear to be in the minority, as the evidence presented in this book on eroding job security demonstrates. A key question, to which we will return, is whether it will be possible to sustain new work systems in an environment of fear.

Companies also vary in their approaches toward unions. In some settings the new work systems are implemented in cooperation with unions. In other instances, however, the new systems are either part of a policy to avoid unionization or are implemented unilaterally without the cooperation of the existing union. Again, a difficult question is whether in the long run the more conflictual strategies are viable.

In order to get a sense of how these various policies fit together and of what is involved in implementing them, it is worthwhile to examine the case of one company in greater detail. A classic, and perhaps typical, example of work reform is Corning Glass. Corning,[1] with its headquarters in upstate New York, had closed nearly thirty-five plants in the 1970s and 1980s, with no end in sight. In 1986, however, the company decided to reverse its decline in manufacturing by dramatically altering work systems and internal labor market (ILM) rules. It built two greenfield factories, one in West Virginia and one in New York, which were organized around "high-performance work systems." These proved successful enough that the company began retrofitting existing plants. The retrofitting process typically involves establishing a joint union-management team that visits other companies, attends workshops, and develops a common vision of what new work systems might look like. This is followed by an "awareness program" in which all employees in the plant attend workshops. Subsequently, joint design teams, working with consultants, reorganize work flows, change job descriptions, organize and attend training, and establish training programs for the workforce. A typical result is a reduced number of job classifications and team production. These shifts in work rules and work flow are also linked to a new compensation system that puts substantial emphasis on performance pay. The performance targets are established by a joint union/management committee. Employees are promised that no layoffs will be implemented as a result of the reorganizations, but the company retains the right to implement layoffs resulting from product market developments.

This example is drawn from a large and prominent U.S. business, but a similar ferment is evident among the small and medium-size employers that are frequently the suppliers to the nation's industrial giants. Sometimes transformations occur when large companies impose quality standards and benchmarking and pass down new requirements. Other times smaller businesses fighting for a market niche find that they must reorganize work in order to meet the needs of their customers. An example is a small Massachusetts company, Brimfield Precision, which is a supplier to the medical industry (this case is developed in Mark, 1993). While Brimfield had a strong external reputation for quality, its rework rates and scrap rates were very high. In addition, it faced growing competition in its market and a considerably more volatile sales environment. In response, the company decentralized into small business units, established cross-functional work teams within each unit, trained its employees in various total quality management (TQM) techniques, and is moving toward a new compensation system that emphasizes pay for knowledge and pay for performance.

Documenting Changes in Work Organization

How much work reorganization is occurring in the United States, and what are the characteristics of employers that are undertaking these activities? To date, there has been relatively little information available to answer these questions, but recently several surveys have probed these issues. We begin with the National Survey of Establishments (see Osterman, 1994), which asked about a series of practices (all with respect to the "core" job family, defined as the largest group of nonsupervisory workers directly involved in the production of the good or service. This could be either blue- or white-collar.) In analyzing that survey, we focus on the four practices most often seen as most central to transformed organizations: self-directed work teams, job rotation, use of employee problem-solving groups (or quality circles), and use of total quality management.

For each practice, the respondent was asked whether or not the practice was employed in the establishment and, if so, what percentage of "core" employees was involved (the percentage involved is termed the "penetration rate"). The precise definitions given for each practice are shown in Appendix A.[2]

Table 3.1 shows the distribution of each practice for two levels of penetration: whether the practice is used at all and whether at least 50 percent of core employees are involved.

Table 3.1. Prevalence of Work Reorganization Practices

	All	Manufacturing
Percentage at any % level of penetration		
Teams	54.5%	50.1%
Rotation	43.4	55.6
TQM	33.5	44.9
QC	40.8	45.6
Nothing	21.8	16.0
Percentage at 50% level of penetration		
Teams	40.5	32.3
Rotation	26.6	37.4
TQM	24.5	32.1
QC	27.4	29.7
Nothing	36.0	33.2

Source: National Survey of Establishments (Osterman, 1994).

It is clear that if we simply ask whether or not a given practice is used among any fraction of core employees, we will conclude that the elements of flexible work are quite widespread. For example, more than half the establishments surveyed use teams, and 33.5 percent of the establishments employ TQM. The story becomes different, however, when we examine penetration. Looking at the intermediate category of 50 percent or more employees involved, the rates fall sharply. Each practice falls by roughly 15 percentage points. Even so, the distribution of self-directed work-teams is surprisingly widespread. There is clearly some discontinuity between the extent of usage of this practice and the others.

The manufacturing/blue-collar patterns, shown in the second column, are similar in that there is a substantial diffusion of the practices at any usage level, and there is a drop-off when one sets a 50 percent threshold for participation. Self-directed teams appear less widespread in manufacturing than elsewhere in the economy,[3] but the other practices are more common.

These data lead to the natural question of whether the practices form groups from which emerge identifiable patterns that might be thought of as the new systems discussed in the literature. Table 3.2 shows how the practices cluster together when a 50 percent penetration threshold is set (no conclusions are changed when other thresholds are imposed). It appears that there is no single major dominant cluster of practices. There is some representation for each of the possible combinations, and in most cases the distribution of clusters seems rather even.

Another source of information on the distribution of new work systems is the Harris survey (1991) (recall that this was limited to

Table 3.2. Clustering of Work Practices (50% or more penetration)

	Entire sample	Manufacturing/blue-collar
Nothing	36.0%	33.2%
All	4.8	5.0
Teams only	14.4	5.5
Rotation only	7.0	11.7
QC only	3.1	2.4
TQM only	2.6	4.5
Team/rotation	4.8	4.6
Team/QC	4.3	3.3
Team/TQM	4.6	4.2
Rotation/QC	3.0	3.3
Rotation/TQM	1.5	4.5
TQM/QC	4.4	4.9
Team/TQM/QC	3.6	4.2
Team/rotation/TQM	1.2	1.6
Team/rotation/QC	2.3	3.4
Rotation/TQM/QC	1.4	2.9

Source: National Survey of Establishments (Osterman, 1994).

Conference Board members and hence the largest companies). This survey asked how much effort each respondents' company had put into four practices: work redesign, employee involvement, total quality management, and introduction of advanced technologies. The survey also asked which of these four had received the greatest amount of effort and resources. The results are shown in Table 3.3.

Table 3.3. Employer Reorganization Efforts

	Work redesign	Employee involvement	Total Quality Management	Advanced computer technology
Amount of effort/ resources expended				
Significant	44.0%	38.6%	37.4%	72.9%
Some	46.5	43.6	33.2	24.8
Not much	9.1	16.7	26.6	1.9
Not sure	.2	.9	2.7	.2
Work practices receiving the most effort	10.2	6.1	14.8	65.4
Number of work practices receiving significant effort/ resources	36.0	25.6	18.4	19.2

Source: Louis Harris and Associates Survey (1991).

Consistent with the National Survey of Establishments, the Harris survey suggests that an important fraction of businesses have devoted resources to various forms of work reorganization (however, a caution is that the survey does not define the term "significant" and makes no effort to measure the fraction of employees involved). Two other notable findings are that companies value technology over work reform in their efforts to become more competitive and that only about 37 percent of companies report a significant level of commitment to two or more practices. This is consistent with the pattern found in the National Survey of Establishments.

Yet another source of data is a 1990 survey of *Fortune* 1000 companies conducted by the General Accounting Office. This survey repeated an earlier one conducted in 1987, and hence it is possible to get a sense of changes over time (the surveys were answered by corporate officials who were asked to provide data for their entire organizations. The response rate in 1987 was 51 percent and in 1990 was 32 percent). These data were analyzed by Lawler, Mohrman, and Ledford (1989, 1992).

Some of the relevant results of this survey are presented in Table 3.4. It is apparent that there was a considerable increase in the use of transformed work practices between 1987 and 1990. It also appears that the penetration rates are more modest than those derived from the National Survey of Establishments. However, it is important to recall that, in addition to other sampling differences, the National Survey of Establishments collected innovation and penetration data only on "core" employees, whereas the *Fortune* 1000 survey asked about all workers in the organization.

An additional source of data is the telephone survey of compa-

Table 3.4. Incidence of Transformed Work Practices (Based on Government Accounting Office Surveys)

	Penetration rate (percentage of employees involved)			
	None	1–20%	21–40%	41+%
Quality circles				
1987	39%	32%	18%	10%
1990	34	36	19	13
Job enrichment or redesign				
1987	40	38	12	11
1990	25	43	23	9
Self-managed work teams				
1987	72	20	6	1
1990	53	37	9	1

Source: Lawler, Mohrman, and Ledford (1992), pp. 27–28. Percentages may not add up to 100 but are taken from the original source.

nies conducted by Bassi. She found that 14.3 percent of non-manufacturing companies and 25.7 percent of manufacturing companies had implemented total quality management, 25.7 percent of nonmanufacturing and 39.5 percent of manufacturing companies had policies for increased employee empowerment, and 9.8 percent of nonmanufacturing and 20.3 percent of manufacturing companies used quality circles or work teams. The survey did not collect data on the penetration rate of these practices (Bassi, 1993).

The most recent source of information on work practices is the National Employer Survey's data from establishments with more than 25 employees (National Center on the Educational Quality of the Workforce, 1995), which found that 37 percent of establishments have adopted TQW programs and 54 percent of employees discuss work-related problems in regularly scheduled meetings. Eighteen percent of nonmanagerial employees participate in job rotation, and 13 percent are in self-managed teams. The questions in this survey covered all employees, not just those in "core" jobs. (Many of the employees not in core jobs are clerical and support staff, outside sales workers, and others for whom it is more difficult to introduce team-based systems. The extent of participation is therefore lower than for those in core jobs as measured by the National Establishment Survey.)

Looking within a single industry, the apparel industry has been traditionally a low-wage and low-technology industry, quite different from the automobile or steel sectors that are often studied in research of this kind. However, in recent years innovations that are analogous to high-performance work organizations—such as the bundle system and quick response—have emerged. These promise quicker times to market and better ability to meet customer needs. Bailey recently conducted a survey of a random sample of 480 production sites and examined six indicators of high-performance work organization: 50 percent of production workers receive training; regularly scheduled meetings are held with workers to discuss production problems; 50 percent of employees are paid through group incentives; plants use modules or other forms of team production; 50 percent of orders are handled via electronic data interchange; and the number of operations performed by a typical operator has increased in the last five years (Bailey, 1994). Among the plants surveyed, 25 percent used three or more of these practices, and for those with 50 or more employees, the figure was 28 percent. Thirty-six percent of all workers were in plants that used three or more practices. These findings are consistent with those of the National Survey of Establishments.

Additional evidence to support the patterns found in the National Survey of Establishments comes from a survey of U.S.-located

Japanese transplants in manufacturing. The survey, which was conducted by Richard Florida and Martin Kenney (unpublished) surveyed 1,150 transplants and had a 40 percent response rate. Of these establishments, 33.4 percent had self-managed work teams in place with 50 percent or more of the production workers involved, 63.2 percent had job rotation with a 50 percent penetration rate, 40.4 percent had quality circles or problem-solving groups with a 50 percent penetration rate, and 40.7 percent had TQM programs with 50 percent or more involvement. These results are very consistent with those presented earlier.

Finally, Ernst and Young, along with the American Quality Foundation, sponsored a survey of U.S., German, Canadian, and Japanese companies. The survey found that 49 percent of U.S. businesses involve more than one fourth of their workers in quality-related teams (Applebaum and Batt, 1994).

Whether these results suggest that the reform of work organization has been extensive or not may depend on one's expectations. In 1990, the *America's Choice!* report suggested that as few as 5 percent of U.S. establishments had the characteristics of high-performance work systems (National Center on Education and the Economy, 1990). By that standard, the results we have reported suggest a veritable explosion of workplace innovation over the past few years as the prevalence of these practices, by even the most conservative estimates, expands. On the other hand, the majority of workers—by some estimates, the vast majority—work without these innovations under traditional arrangements.

Discretion and Control

An alternative way of asking about work organization is to inquire about how much discretion employees have over how they do their job. The search for autonomy was at the heart of earlier concerns with the quality of working life, and it remains an important consideration.

The National Survey of Establishments asked three questions regarding control and supervision. On a scale of one to five, the respondent was asked how much control core workers had over the pace of their job and over the method for doing their job and how closely they were supervised. Table 3.5 shows the distribution of responses for all core employees and for core blue-collar and professional/technical workers.

A minority, but an important fraction, of core employees have substantial autonomy, with about 17 percent having little or no supervision, about 30 percent having complete or large amounts of discretion over the pace of their work, and about 45 percent enjoy-

Table 3.5.   Degree of Control over Work for "Core" Employees

	All core occupations	Blue-collar core workers	Professional/technical core workers
Closeness of supervision			
Complete	5.87%	5.88%	4.81%
Large	24.26	14.96	20.56
Moderate	53.02	61.95	43.08
Small	16.60	16.91	30.65
None	.25	.29	.90
Discretion over pace			
Complete	6.63	7.11	12.80
Large	24.31	16.80	37.55
Moderate	36.75	47.42	28.95
Small	19.98	15.75	9.19
None	12.32	12.91	11.52
Discretion over method			
Complete	4.81	3.13	8.97
Large	39.86	39.88	45.77
Moderate	37.04	39.70	32.59
Small	14.21	11.24	12.67
None	4.07	6.05	0.0

Source: National Survey of Establishments (Osterman, 1994).

ing complete or large amounts of discretion over how they do their work. It is also apparent (and not surprising) that professional/technical employees have much more autonomy than do blue-collar workers.

Discretion over method and pace, on the one hand, and degree of supervision, on the other hand, are two different concepts. In principle, employees may be able to decide how to do their work yet still be watched carefully and metered as they do it. In fact, to a surprising extent the two constructs move independently. In a two-by-two table, only 56.1 percent of the establishments are in the diagonal, i.e., take on the value of "one" for both variables or "zero" for both variables.

A useful way of testing the validity of these concepts is to see how well they correlate with work organization. One would expect that establishments that have low levels of supervision and high levels of discretion over method would be more likely to have high involvement in these flexible work practices.

Table 3.6 provides the relevant information, and these data support the validity of the measures. There is a clear relationship between both variables and work organization: Establishments that do not supervise closely and provide employees with substantial

Table 3.6. Relationship Between Control and Involvement in Work Practices

	Supervision = 0*	Supervision = 1*	Method = 0	Method = 1
Percentage of core employees in self-directed work teams	37%	51%	36%	43%
Percentage of core employees involved in quality circles	24	42	19	38
Percentage of core employees involved in Total Quality Management	24	31	21	30
Percentage of core employees involved in job rotation	—	—	23	30

*Supervision takes on the value of 1 if the establishment has little or no supervision of core employees. Method takes on the value of 1 if the establishment allows complete or large discretion for core employees in how they do their job.

Source: National Survey of Establishments (Osterman, 1994).

control over how they do their work are more likely to adopt "transformed" forms of work organization.

Supportive Human Resources Practices

Many students of human resources (HR) believe that reform in work organization needs to be accompanied by supportive human resources policies. For example, observers believe that many companies that have moved toward more flexible work organization have accompanied the shifts in work systems with comparable changes in internal labor market rules governing wages, on the theory that when employees are given more power to determine outcomes they should have a financial stake in enterprise success.

A second policy area is training. The implementation of flexible work systems seems to require higher levels of skills than are typically afforded employees in traditional mass-production systems. One would therefore expect investments in training to be higher in transformed work systems.

As already noted, there are strong reasons to believe that companies engaged in work reform must be prepared to provide enhanced levels of job security. On the other hand, there have been widespread recent layoffs, even in such companies as IBM and DEC, which are thought to exemplify flexible work organization.

The National Survey of Establishments asked a series of questions regarding these human resources practices, and the relationships with work reform are displayed in Table 3.7. The fact that establishments engaged in work reform are more likely to provide training is consistent with earlier arguments, but the fact that there is no relationship between work reform and job security is a surprise. Overall, however, the patterns do support the idea that sustainable work reforms need to be underwritten by broader shifts in HR systems. Enhanced training and innovative compensation policies are linked to sustained workplace reform.

What Explains Variation in Work Innovation?

The goal of this section is to help us understand why some companies engage in work reorganization and others do not. This is a question of more than just academic interest. We cannot predict the rate or extent of diffusion of high-performance work systems without first understanding what considerations underwrite its adoption. In this section we review some of the key findings from the National Survey of Establishments. The patterns described here have been analyzed in greater statistical detail in Osterman (1994).

Before beginning with the survey, however, it is important to

Table 3.7. Supporting Human Resources Practices

	All	Establishment has at least one flexible work practice with 50% penetration	Establishment has no flexible work practice with 50% penetration	t-Statistic
Gain sharing	.137	.144	.126	.946
Pay for skill	.304	.364	.197	4.676**
Profit sharing/bonus	.447	.478	.393	2.008*
Percent in off-the-job training	.320	.375	.219	4.838**
Percent in cross-training	.451	.529	.314	7.456**
Employment security policy	.398	.394	.404	.179

Note: The t-statistics are based on equations that include core occupation and industry controls.

** = significant difference at 1% level
 * = significant difference at 5% level

103

understand that broad contextual considerations, which cannot be captured in a survey, can influence adoption of work systems. One such set of factors includes laws and regulations affecting the workplace. For example, in Germany most employers are required to establish works councils that provide a formal mechanism through which employees can voice their concerns and ideas. These institutions are likely in turn to lead to a variety of work practices that we would consider to fall under the high-performance label (Streeck, 1988). In a similar vein, the reluctance of Japanese companies to poach labor from each other leads to low turnover, which in turn permits considerable investment in the human capital of the incumbent workforce and work systems designed to take advantage of that investment.

Another contextual factor is the nature of the product and the production process. Some of the most powerful explanations of work reform come from the auto industry, where the evidence suggests that "lean production" systems of manufacturing require innovative systems of work organization and, in turn, training to make those systems function (MacDuffie and Kochan, 1995). Presumably the gains from high-performance work systems are weaker, if not nonexistent, when the work is relatively simple and can be standardized. That this is true is suggested by Milkman's study of Japanese transplants in California's electronics assembly industry. The Japanese managers of these companies were certainly knowledgeable about high-performance work practices and were under no constraints from their home offices in establishing them. Yet Milkman found in her survey of fifty Japanese-owned electronic assembly plants that

> the Japanese-owned plants in California bear little resemblance to the Japanese management model. Relatively few have quality circles or the equivalent; flexible teams are even more exceptional; and most of the managers we interviewed laughed outright when asked about just-in-time delivery or the like. One "Japanese practice" is more typical of these plants, however; most are committed, in principle, to avoiding layoffs. However, even this is tempered by the fact that these plants typically have high turnover rates. (Milkman, 1991)

This general point about context is supported by the National Survey of Establishments, which found that the skill level of the production process was an important determinant of whether transformed work systems were adopted (Osterman, 1994). Putting the matter most starkly, even the most enthusiastic advocate of high-performance work systems should agree that they are not appropriate under all circumstances.

Turning now to other findings from the survey, an important

Table 3.8. Competitive Strategies of Businesses

	All	Manufacturing
Quality	168*	177*
Variety	88*	88*
Service	227*	182*

*Points to quality, variety, and service relative to 100 points given to cost-based competition.

Source: National Survey of Establishments (Osterman, 1994).

place to start is with companies' competitive strategies. The National Survey of Establishments assigned 100 points to the strategy of competing on cost and then asked respondents to indicate how many points their establishment would assign, relative to this, to competing on the basis of quality, variety, and service. Many commentators believe that enterprises that emphasize these last three strategies are following what might be termed the "high road," and it is important to see, first, how widespread such strategies are and, second, whether they are related to adoption of new work practices.

Table 3.8 shows the average score of the respondents with respect to each of the strategies. Evidently, product variety is not central to the strategy of most establishments but, relative to cost, quality and service rank quite high. It is worth noting in passing that the weak support given to product variety somewhat undercuts the emphasis in the literature on what has been termed "flexible specialization" (Piore and Sabel, 1984).

Table 3.9 shows the relationship between each of the strategic elements and the establishment's use of innovative work systems. It is apparent that businesses that place a high value on quality as a

Table 3.9. Product Market Strategy and Flexible Work Organization

	Variety		Quality		Service	
	Above	Below	Above	Below	Above	Below
Teams	39%	39%	45%	35%	54%	36%
QC	29	26	40	28	19	29
TQM	24	26	44	21	22	26
Rotation	28	25	42	23	36	24

Note: Percent of "core" employees involved in each practice by whether score on product market strategy is above or below average.

Source: National Survey of Establishments.

competitive strategy make much greater use of all four new work systems than do other enterprises. By contrast, there is essentially no relationship between stress on variety and work organization, and the relationship between work organization and service is inconclusive. The conclusion, then, is that a key determinant of whether companies engage in work reform is whether their competitive strategy emphasizes quality.

An additional aspect of an establishment's competitive position that proves to be important is whether the establishment was among the 32 percent in the sample that competes in international markets. The average penetration (percent of core employees involved) in TQM was 38 percent for establishments that competed internationally and 19 percent for those that did not. This is a not unexpected finding, since these establishments are more likely to face competition from other businesses that employ various forms of high-performance work systems and since international exposure provides learning opportunities.

Among the most interesting findings is the strong role that employer values play in influencing the adoption of flexible work systems. It is well known from anecdotal evidence that businesses that appear to observers to be similar with respect to markets, technology, and other structural characteristics nonetheless may differ considerably in their human resources practices. One possibility is that the value of each company—for example, the extent to which the employees of the enterprise are seen as a community or a "family"—might be important. This consideration is given weight by the observation that Japanese employers have more of a community or stakeholder view of their enterprises than do Americans and that this difference helps explain various work practices (Dore, 1973; Lincoln and Kalleberg, 1990).

It is difficult to measure directly the entire range of possibly relevant values. However, the National Survey of Establishments did seek to measure one particular set of values, attitudes toward helping employee families, and this can be seen as a proxy for more general employee-friendly values.

About 50 percent of the survey instrument was composed of a long series of questions about benefits, particularly work-family benefits, and about enterprise values regarding these benefits. This portion of the questionnaire was administered earlier than the portion on work organization that is the subject of this chapter, so the respondents' replies on values were unrelated to any suggestion that might have been implanted by the work organization section. Respondents were asked, "In general, what is your establishment's philosophy about how appropriate it is to help increase the well-

Table 3.10. Relationship of Establishment Values and Work Practices

	It is "very" or "extremely" appropriate	Other reply
Percent teams	47%	29%
Percent QC	36	16
Percent TQM	29	19
Percent rotation	31	20

Source: National Survey of Establishments (Osterman, 1994).

being of employees with respect to their personal or family situations?" On a five-point scale, 1.7 percent said, "not appropriate," 9.4 percent said, "a little appropriate," 33.0 percent answered, "moderately appropriate," 42.8 percent said, "very appropriate," and 12.8 percent responded, "extremely appropriate."

Table 3.10 shows the penetration of the less traditional work practices in relation to whether the establishment replied that it was "very" or "extremely" appropriate to help with the personal family situation of employees. It is apparent that the relationship is very strong.

There are several commonly discussed factors that prove *not* to be important in influencing whether establishments adopt flexible work systems. Notable among these are establishment size and union status. Many observers would have predicted that small companies are less likely to implement high-performance work systems because they lack resources for training and implementation as well as, often, knowledge concerning the best way to proceed. However, it is also important to recall that the sample is limited to establishments with fifty or more employees, so the smallest companies are not included. The failure of the union status variable to prove important probably reflects the fact that we lack a measure of the nature of the bargaining relationship. It is clear from many of the examples presented here (Saturn, Xerox, and Corning) that when the relationship is healthy, unions can play an important role in supporting and sustaining the transition to high-performance work organizations.

Perhaps the most fundamental lesson to be taken from this section is the close relationship between a company's business strategy and its approach to work organization. Both international competition and a "high-road" competitive strategy drive the adoption of new forms of work organization. This clearly places human resources at the core of a company's competitive strategy, but it also means that it is difficult to conceive of altering work organization without first addressing the issue of product market strategy.

Work Organization and Performance

As we have already noted, the current wave of work reorganization is driven by performance considerations rather than by the "softer" concerns with work humanization that motivated the earlier (and failed) wave of innovations. However, the fact that hope for better performance lies behind recent reforms is a double-edged sword, because these reforms will ultimately take root only if they succeed in these terms. What evidence do we have that work reform brings with it tangible benefits?

As a preliminary point, it is important to recognize that in the discussion that follows, the research is held to a very high standard, so many of the remarks will be cautionary. This should be put in context: Virtually all research can be criticized on some grounds, and very little research on managerial practices is even as good as the research reviewed here. On balance, as we will see, the evidence does support the conclusion that high-performance work organizations can deliver higher levels of performance.

One of the problems is that the metric for benefits is not clear. In some circumstances, work reform might increase physical output per employee (labor productivity), yet be so difficult and costly to implement that the net effect on the business's bottom line is negative. Most research has focused on physical output (often for a small work group, not even an entire production line or office) and misses this complication. The foregoing problem suggests that gains from work reform may be overstated in the evaluation literature. A problem that biases research in the opposite direction is the reasonable possibility that gains from work reform take a number of years to develop, yet most evaluations look at the short term. Beyond these two issues, there are a number of other difficulties inherent in measuring the gains from work reform, and we will discuss these at the end of the chapter. First, however, it is important to review what the literature does tell us.

The literature on performance falls into two broad categories: anecdotal and social science-based. The anecdotal research typically consists of success stories from companies that have implemented new systems. These success stories are often striking and compelling. There are, however, important questions about how seriously we should take them. First, we generally hear about success, not failure, since no one wants to publicize a failure. Yet the appropriate research question is not whether introduction of new work systems ever succeeds but rather how often it succeeds. To answer this, we need to know the incidence of failure as well as of success. Another problem concerns measurement. The anecdotal cases typically use a wide range of different outcome measures, making comparisons difficult. Furthermore, it is hard to know just what is being measured (e.g., how are defects calculated?) and what is being controlled for (was new technology introduced at the same time as the new work organization, and, if so, what was its contribution relative to the work organization?).

These caveats aside, we have to take the anecdotal evidence seriously both because the accounts are so compelling and also because, as we will see shortly, the social science evidence also leaves much to be desired. A flavor of the kinds of gains that are reported can be gained by Applebaum and Batt's (1994) review of experience of some Baldridge Award winners:

> Milliken reported a significant increase in on-time delivery and a 50 percent reduction in defects in goods over 10 years; Motorola developed methods for measuring quality in white-collar settings, and improved quality ten-fold between 1981 and 1986; at Xerox, defects in component parts dropped from 10,000 per million in 1980 to 360 per million in 1989; at IBM's Rochester plant write offs for scrap and excess inventory dropped 55 percent between 1984 and 1990.

Turning to the social science literature, the huge research in the behavioral sciences on workplace reform typically examines performance effects at the level of the individual worker or, sometimes, the group. The results suggest that interventions like employee participation, job redesign, and quality circles, have at best modest effects on improving performance (Cotton, 1993).

Levine and Tyson (1990) reviewed both case studies and surveys that focus on relationships with organizational performance and productivity. They reached the following conclusions:

1. If participation is limited to quality circles, the impact is not likely to be great. Quality circles and other forms of purely advisory shop-floor arrangements do not lead to lasting productivity increases without broader changes in work organization.

2. The consensus of studies is that in organizations with substantive participation (e.g., work teams), productivity does rise, and the improvement is maintained. Again, however, these forms of participation seem to have their most positive effect when they are linked to other transformations in work organization.

3. Representative participation (e.g., labor-management com-

mittees or works councils) can improve performance if it is one element in a larger set of workplace reforms. Taken alone, it does not seem to have a substantial impact.

Modest conclusions about the impact of participation schemes are also reached by other literature reviews (e.g., Miller and Monge, 1986). In general, the effects are seen as positive but not overwhelmingly so. More important, what seems to determine whether there are positive productivity effects is how deeply the work reforms penetrate into other aspects of the organization. An example that illustrates the importance of this consideration is the careful evaluation of autonomous work teams that was conducted by Wall et al. (1986). They did not find any productivity benefit, despite the fact that the teams were introduced into a greenfield (i.e., brand new) site and were done so in a very careful way under the supervision of experts. Presumably, an important source of the failure was the fact that other aspects of the company's internal labor market did not change; in particular, there was no shift in compensation toward more contingent arrangements, nor was there an increase in training expenditures.

There are, however, more optimistic stories. In a recent study of Xerox, a company that sought to implement a transformed internal labor market, Cutcher-Gershenfeld (1991) collected productivity data on work areas (i.e., particular stations on the shop floor). He measured labor hours per unit of product, as well as additional output indicators such as scrap. He then measured whether a work area was "transformed," using an index that included use of informal conflict resolution, worker autonomy in planning production, and the use of problem solving groups such as quality of work life. He found clear evidence that those work areas that had moved the farthest in the direction of transformed work systems were the most productive. What distinguished Xerox from other organizations that had instituted similar procedures but not gained productivity seems to be that at Xerox the work reorganization efforts were part of a larger agreement between the management and the union to reform collective bargaining, provide job security, and reform the compensation scheme (Cutcher-Gershenfeld, 1988).

These studies lead to a paradox. We believe that transformed work organization leads to high levels of productivity. Our basis for believing this is observation of the successes of many Japanese companies and some European ones and of U.S. companies that have reorganized their internal labor markets. Yet at the same time, the careful studies of aspects of work reorganization, such as work teams and QWL, which we reviewed earlier, lead to much more modest conclusions. Why is this so? The best conclusion is that work reorganization alone does not lead to impressive gains. It pays off only when it is part of a reorganization of the entire production system that includes substantial shifts in other aspects of internal labor markets. When these prerequisites are met, there can be considerable gains.

This conclusion is reinforced by two careful studies, one of the automobile industry and the other of the steel industry.

The automobile research is that of MacDuffie (1995) in his international study of automobile assembly plants. MacDuffie examined ninety assembly plants and measured their output on the basis of labor productivity and quality. There were very substantial variations across the plants and also variation by region.[4] He also collected data on human resources systems, technology, product complexity, size of the plants, age of the plant, and other relevant variables. Table 3.11 presents the findings by examining the differences across plans that perform very well and those that do not perform as well. More sophisticated statistical techniques, which MacDuffie reports in his dissertation, confirm these findings.

It is apparent that there is a relationship between technology and performance, but the relationship is not extremely dramatic. What is dramatic is the relationship between human resources systems and performance. Most strikingly, the best-performing plants are those that combine technological sophistication with transformed internal labor markets.

There is additional evidence, also drawn from the automobile industry, that work organization systems that entail high levels of

Table 3.11. Productivity, Technology, and Human Resources in Automobile Assembly

Performance Zone	*n*	Total automation	Work system	HRM policies
Low productivity/low quality	18	15.7%	25.0	27.4
High productivity/low quality	6	31.6	34.1	26.7
High productivity/high quality	15	29.3	42.6	58.2
World class productivity/high quality	6	36.4	82.6	75.6

Source: McDuffie (1995).

Definitions:

Productivity = hours per vehicle assembled

Quality = results from the J.D. Powers Survey

Automation index = the share of all steps in painting, welding, and assembly

The Work System = the extent to which teams, problem solving groups, job rotation, and decentralization of quality tasks are employed

Human Resource Management Policy index = the extent to which broad skills are sought in recruitment and hiring, the use of contingent compensation, the extent of training, and the extent to which status differentials are minimized unresolved grievances reduce productivity; typically, grievance levels are lower in transformed organizations). In separate studies based on plants in one of the Big Three automobile companies, researchers found a significant inverse relationship between productivity and increases in grievance filings (Katz, Kochan, and Gobeille, 1983; Katz, Kochan, and Weber, 1985). This finding was confirmed by Ichniowski (1986) in his study of paper mills. It is not entirely clear through what channels this effect works (some authors argue that the simple act of dealing with grievances uses up time; others argue that high levels of grievances signal morale problems that reduce output), but it does appear certain that the effect is real and substantial.

A recent study of the steel industry by Ichniowski, Shaw, and Prennushi (1994) supports conclusions derived from the auto study. The authors collected monthly productivity data in thirty steel-finishing lines. Their measure of productivity was the amount of unscheduled downtime in each line. They also collected data on the range of practices associated with high-performance work systems (teams, employment security, communication, training, and incentive compensation). They entered these practices into an equation for productivity in two ways. First, they studied the impact of each practice separately and found small effects. Second, they examined the impact of introducing clusters of practices (i.e., human resource management or internal labor market systems). This had a substantial effect. The authors then identified four levels of systems, from the least to the most innovative, and found that going from the former to the latter increased uptime from 88 percent to 98 percent, a very substantial gain. The lesson, therefore, is twofold: Innovative work systems improve productivity but only do so when introduced in clusters.

As noted earlier, the relatively low-technology apparel industry has experimented in recent years with innovative work organization. The survey conducted by Bailey (1994) shows that these innovations are fairly widespread. In a recent study, Berg et al. (1994) studied a matched set of plants using alternative production and human resources systems. They found that the factories that used so-called modular systems, which entail relatively high levels of employee involvement, were more physically productive and produced higher-quality products. In addition, unit costs were lower with the innovative modular system.

As noted earlier, physical productivity gains or quality gains from high-performance work systems may be offset by the costs of implementing those systems (e.g., the costs of extensive training or employment continuity provisions). The best way to check this possibility is to examine the relationship between corporate profitability and work systems, but there is very little research that takes this approach. One problem is the difficulty that large, diversified organizations face in collecting accurate financial data on the particular unit (i.e., the establishment or the business unit) where the work reform occurs.

In a recent study, Huselid (1994) sought to overcome this problem by limiting his sample to companies with one business line. He surveyed human resources managers at 3,400 businesses with more than 100 employees. The companies were U.S.-owned, not part of a holding company, and not a business unit of a larger corporation. The questionnaire collected data on a variety of human resources practices and had a response rate of 29 percent. Financial performance measures of several types were collected from public sources.

Huselid created an index of human resources practices in which higher scores represented increased use of state-of-the-art techniques. For the purposes of this chapter this index is too limited, because it includes items such as use of performance assessments, employee surveys, formal job analysis, and preemployment testing, which, while of interest, are not directly related to work reform. Nonetheless, the results are interesting because they seem to support the general importance of HRM in influencing financial performance. Huselid found that a one-standard-deviation increase in his index was associated with an increase in profits of about $33,000 per employee.

The research we have discussed was based on organization- or establishment-level data, that is, averages collected for worksites regarding work organization and performance. Cappelli and Rogovsky (1993) make the point that data on individuals that relate individual performance to work organization would be an important supplement to the more aggregate approach. In their study, they collected data on 553 employees in eight public utility companies and for each employee gathered performance data from supervisors as well as descriptions of working conditions from the employees. The researchers found that employees who worked in jobs providing high levels of autonomy and information sharing had higher levels of performance than did other employees. This is clearly supportive of the idea that high-performance work systems elicit greater effort and improve organizational performance.

Although the foregoing literature review focused on the performance gains associated with new forms of work organization, there is also a literature on the impact of personnel policy innovations that are typically part of the overall shift. Perhaps the most important of these involves adoption of innovative compensation schemes aimed at both increasing the incentives offered to employees and encouraging employees to feel that they are part of the larger enterprise. Under a typical gain-sharing plan, a base level of output and wages is determined, as well as a method for valuing additional (or reduced) output. All members of the group receive pay increases (or decreases) depending on whether output increases or decreases relative to the base. Profit sharing is similar to gain sharing in that it links pay to company performance, although in this case the outcome variable is profits rather than a more direct measure of productivity gain.

Much of the evaluation evidence on gain-sharing plans tends to resemble case studies more than carefully controlled research. A few high-quality statistical studies are available, however, and these, along with the case studies, tend to paint a positive picture. For example, the U.S. General Accounting Office in its survey found that those companies with gain-sharing plans in place for more than five years averaged an annual 29 percent reduction in labor costs (Mitchell, Lewin, and Lawler, 1990). The seeming precision of this result is undermined by the poor quality of the company-based data that underlie it (Ehrenberg and Milkovich, 1990). A more careful analysis by Schuster (1984), however, also found positive results, although they tended to plateau after a period of time. Additional evidence comes from a review by Weitzman and Kruse (1990) of attitude surveys. They uncovered six surveys of employees who participated in gain-sharing or profit-sharing plans and fifteen attitude surveys of employers. A typical survey of employees was that conducted by Bell and Hanson of 2,703 workers who were in twelve different profit-sharing plans. Ninety-one percent of the workers were positive about the plan in general, 51 percent said that it made people work more effectively, and 86 percent said it was good for the company and the employees. The fact that people were more positive about the plan on dimensions other than work effort suggests that the plan improves the atmosphere or the working conditions of the company. The surveys of employers also yielded positive responses, with between 73 and 100 percent reporting that the plans were successful.

In an important econometric effort, Kruse (1988) examined a sample of 2,976 companies, of which 1,198 had some form of profit sharing. He found positive and significant effects on sales per employee, effects that persisted even after he attempted to control for the fact that the companies most likely to introduce profit sharing are the ones that would benefit from it. Weitzman and Kruse (1990) summarized the results of fifteen other econometric studies that also found positive impacts of either profit or gain sharing upon productivity. In a recent study of one variant of gainsharing (the Improshare system), Kaufman found that participating companies increased their productivity by 8 percent the first year after the plan was implemented and that cumulative productivity gains rose to more than 17 percent. A substantial portion of the gains was due to a reduction in defects and downtime (Kaufman, 1990).

Returning to the evaluations of work organization, it is important to note the limitations of most of the research on this topic. We have already noted three difficult issues: the measure of performance that is used, the need to consider long-run as well as short-run payoffs, and the need to consider the full range of organizational changes (or the lack of them) as well as more narrow shifts in work organization. Beyond these concerns are even more difficult issues that center on the problem of causality. Let us assume that we discover a positive relationship in a cross-section of businesses between profitability and work reform (i.e., businesses that have engaged in work reform are more profitable). Does it follow from this that work reform caused profitability? Although such causality is certainly one possibility, another and perhaps equally plausible theory would be that more profitable companies engage in work reform for a variety of reasons: They may simply have more time and managerial resources to alter work arrangements, and they may choose to take the opportunity because it seems like a better way to treat people (recall the importance of managerial values). In this case, the positive relationship would be from profitability to work organization, and not the reverse.

One solution to this kind of problem is to work with longitudinal data. With these kind of data the researcher can study changes in profitability that follow from changes in work organization; the causality problem can be addressed by taking advantage of the timing in the data. Good longitudinal data on work reform and performance are hard to find but in principle are available. In fact, the steel industry study described earlier used this technique, although most other studies do not.

Unfortunately, even such longitudinal data are not adequate to resolve all issues. First, there may be something about companies that determines whether or not they engage in work reform that is not controlled via the longitudinal data technique. In the steel study, for example, field work suggests that it is the Japanese-associated businesses (either directly owned or in joint ventures) that engage in the most substantial work reform. The technique of examining the impact of changes in HRM systems on changes in performance does not control for a consideration such as this, which determines which companies choose to change their HRM systems. We cannot be sure whether something distinctive about these companies both leads to better performance and leads them to achieve it via improved HRM systems.

Another way of seeing this point is to consider the following: What if companies that engage in work reorganization do so because the managers have reason to believe on the basis of information available to them but not to researchers (i.e., the special knowledge that all managers have about their companies) that work reorganization will pay off given the internal and the external circumstances of the business? By the same token, companies that do not engage in reform may fail to do so because the managers have reason to believe that reform would not pay off. In this circumstance one would again find a positive relationship between work reform and performance, but it would not follow that if work reform were instituted in a randomly selected organization, it would pay off.

The truly valid solution would be to launch an experiment in which work reform took place in a randomly selected set of companies and did not in a randomly selected control group. Such an experiment would solve the research problem but, of course, as a practical matter is impossible. Where, then, does this leave us?

In the end, our assessment of the return to work reform will have to rest on informed judgment based on the results, taken as a whole, of as many studies as possible. For the reasons stated earlier, none of these studies will be the "right" one, and none will be definitive. Instead, the analysis will have to weigh the balance of a set of flawed studies and reach an informed but inevitably uncertain conclusion.

Such a conclusion, based on available evidence, would seem to be positive one: that work reform does improve productivity. Such gains, however, depend upon the introduction of a cluster of changes, not simple, small, incremental programs. Several caveats, however, are important. First, very little research is available that weighs the benefits of reform against its costs. We are therefore even more uncertain about the net effect on profitability than we are regarding the impact on productivity. Second, the research is very context-dependent. The best studies have been in the heavy-capital goods industries such as automobiles and steel. We have much less evidence regarding the impact of work reform on services, finance, trade, and less capital-intensive manufacturing. Third, very little of the existing research controls for the amount of work intensity or employee effort that is generated by the new systems. One criticism of these "transformed" systems is that they are simply a "speed-up" and that the greater productivity is due to increased effort that in turn is generated by fear of job loss rather than by any beneficial effects of new approaches to management. This is a criticism that must be taken seriously and that the current research literature does a poor job of addressing.

The discussion so far has focused on the consequences of transformed work organizations for the employer. But there are other consequences as well. With respect to unions, for example, alternative work systems that allow direct employee participation were often seen as a threat to unions because they represented a different avenue for addressing individual problems outside the grievance and collective bargaining system. And, in some cases, employee participation plans have been part of union avoidance programs.

In unionized settings, on the other hand, labor is increasingly embracing employee participation programs and pressing for their expansion (AFL-CIO, 1994). Work reform efforts that are jointly initiated and administered by labor and management are less likely to threaten either side and are more likely to be successful (Kochan and Osterman, 1994).

These new methods for organizing work also have important effects on employees that are discussed in more detail in chapter 5. Briefly, they seem to demand more of workers: more of their talent and ideas, more responsibility (both of which employees appear to value), and new skills, especially in communication and problem solving. At the same time, these reforms typically reduce the number of employees—especially the number of supervisors—and create significantly more work per employee.

Prospects for Diffusion

What are the prospects for the survival of innovative work practices in those companies that have them and for the further diffusion of these practices to additional employers? There is certainly reason to be concerned about these questions. Arguments for expanding employee involvement in the workplace along the outlines noted above have a fifty-year history in the United States, and each set of arguments was associated with experiments that did not survive. The QWL plans established in the 1970s, for example, were perhaps the most significant of these experiments and yet had a very low survival rate. According to Goodman (1980), 75 percent of the plans five or more years old were no longer functioning. This poor record may reflect the fact that these efforts were not tightly linked to the broader competitive strategies of the organizations, whereas the current reforms are very much driven by product market considerations.

Evidence from the National Survey of Establishments suggests that plans that survive do so because they are embedded in a larger system of changes. Table 3.12 shows the fraction of establishments having zero through five practices (at the 50 percent level of adoption) that have been in place for five or more years, which we will take as our standard for sustained innovation.

Table 3.12.   Distribution of Sustained Practices

Number of practices	Percentage of businesses with sustained practices*
0	63.0%
1	23.8
2	9.9
3	2.1
4	1.0
5	0.0

*A practice is "sustained" if it involves 50 percent or more of core employees and has been in place for five years or more.

Source: National Survey of Establishments (Osterman, 1994).

It is apparent that the percentage of establishments that meet the sustainability criterion of five or more years falls well below the percentage that have innovative practices in place regardless of length of time (described earlier in Table 3.1). Sixty-three percent of the sample have no innovative practices that are "sustained," 24 percent have one, and only 10 percent have two practices that cover at least 50 percent of their core workers and that have been in place for at least five years. This divergence does not necessarily imply that most innovations fail to last. Some of the difference is simply due to the fact that the spread of these policies is fairly new, and some have not had the chance to meet the five-year test (recall that the survey is cross-sectional, so it is difficult to draw inferences about behavior over time). Nonetheless, it is striking that the distribution of long-lasting innovations is so limited.

Can these practices be diffused more broadly in U.S. businesses than they have been to date? In order to answer this question we need to consider the obstacles to diffusion. Among the most important of these are the following:

- Small and mid-size companies may lack the resources, knowledge, and available managerial time to implement substantial changes. In addition to these resource constraints, smaller enterprises operate on the margin and cannot afford to take the risks associated with broad transformations in how they do business.
- Financial markets limit the willingness of many enterprises to invest substantially in human resources development because

these investments are harder to measure than those for more tangible items such as plant, equipment, and research and development. They are therefore undervalued by financial analysts even though, as we have seen, their payoff may be substantial.

- Related to the foregoing point is the legal structure for corporate governance of American businesses that gives more weight to the interests of stockholders (the financial markets) compared to the interests of other stakeholders (e.g., employees). This is in contrast to the governance systems in other nations such as Germany and Japan that provide mechanisms for valuing employee and other stakeholder interests. However, responsible corporate leaders constantly strive to balance these competing interests.

- Even companies whose leadership wishes to undertake substantial work reform may face internal obstacles. These may include middle and lower-level managers, who may be threatened by shifts that empower employees, as well as unions that are unwilling to move away from traditional adversarial relationships.

Some of the obstacles may be overcome by imaginative private-sector leadership and creative public policy. The problems facing small companies, for example, can be addressed by assistance programs that provide training grants and technical assistance. Examples of effective programs along these lines are the Prairie State 2000 program in Illinois and some of the small manufacturing assistance centers (National Institute of Standards and Technology or NIST centers) supported by the U.S. Department of Commerce. Typically these programs help assess the business plans of small enterprises and assist them in introducing new production processes or technology and in establishing programs to meet quality standards. These efforts often involve retraining employees.

The internal political problems facing companies are not insurmountable, particularly if the perceived gains are large enough. This is a lesson that can be learned from examples such as Xerox and even Saturn. However, broader changes in the governance structure are more problematic. The prospects for substantial labor law reform are uncertain, and the chances of establishing stakeholder governance structures are even murkier.

An assessment of work reform over the past few years does suggest that considerable progress has been made. We have no true longitudinal data, but the two waves of Government Accounting Office surveys, those for 1987 and 1990, show substantial growth in activity. In addition, the National Survey of Establishments finds that there is much more activity than was previously thought, and this conclusion is generally supported by the other surveys reviewed here.

Set against this optimistic assessment is the fact that many businesses are engaged in widespread layoffs, no doubt in part made possible by the productivity gains inherent in high-performance work systems. It is reasonable to assume that these layoffs will make further progress difficult, since logic suggests that new work systems depend on a committed and cooperative workforce. Even this, however, is not entirely clear. Some of the results presented earlier suggest that employment security is not central to the adoption of transformed work systems. Furthermore, we have very little research on the impact of layoffs on employers' ability to undertake work reform.

The conclusion is that we are in a period of flux and uncertainty. Shifts in work organization are under way in many settings, but we cannot be sure about the extent of diffusion. Certainly, however, the impulse to reorganize employment is more deeply embedded and more likely to have a long-term impact than at any other time since World War II.

Appendix A

Following are the definitions the interviewers used when the respondent requested clarification.

Self-directed work teams: Employees supervise their own work and make their own decisions about pace, flow, and, occasionally, the best way to get work done.

Job rotation: Self-explanatory example: In some banking firms employees spend six months in the real estate division, six months in pension plans, and so on.

Problem-solving groups/quality circles: Quality programs in which employees are involved in problem solving.

Total quality management: Quality control approach that emphasizes the importance of communications, feedback, and teamwork.

Notes

1. The material on Corning is taken from interviews conducted in the company. Similar information has been widely reported in the business press.

2. The survey did not directly observe the actual work practices. There may be a tendency of respondents to exaggerate, in the direction of socially acceptable responses, their actual practices. However, considerable care

was taken to work with the most knowledgeable available respondent. Furthermore, as the statistical results demonstrate, the responses are not simply noise; they are correlated in sensible ways with explanatory variables. Nonetheless, as is true in all surveys of this kind, the point estimates of the practices should be treated with caution.

3. Jan Klein suggests that this may be because self-managed work teams place strains on the inventory management system in manufacturing. See Klein (1991).

4. Although regional differences are not the focus of this discussion, they are of interest. The productivity measure was hours per assembled vehicle. Japanese plants located in Japan needed 16.8 hours; Japanese plants in the United States, 21.8; U.S. plants in North America, 24.9; European plants, 36.9; and newly industrialized countries, 41.1. On the quality index the respective numbers of defects per 100 vehicles were 60, 65, 82, 105, and 88.

4

Job Training Programs
and Practices

Job training programs loom increasingly large in U.S. companies' struggle for competitive advantage within the turbulent world economy. Many analysts find that worker and employer investments in job training produce substantial earnings gains, productivity increases, and greater job security. Despite their diminished presence in the labor force, unions are stimulating innovative joint training programs with progressive companies. Restructured workplaces demand new configurations of both technical and social skills by front-line employees and their managers. Providing these skills in a timely and cost-effective fashion will tax the ingenuity and the imaginations of the reorganized companies. Of particular concern is whether emergent new employment systems, which are shifting substantial economic risk from companies to the labor force, will jeopardize significant sources of economic prosperity for both employers and workers.

Under the old employment system, businesses created complex internal labor markets that buffered workers from external market forces while assuring employers of predictable supplies of higher-quality labor. Companies could hire entry-level employees who lacked basic opportunities because the companies provided sufficient training and development opportunities for the newly hired workers to acquire necessary job skills. In addition to informal on-the-job learning activities, a variety of formal skill-upgrading programs was offered at all occupational levels, ranging from apprenticeships for craft workers to college curricula for aspiring managers. Larger companies could maintain comprehensive job training centers run by their human resources and personnel departments to assess, teach, and evaluate trainees. The erection of elaborate job ladders further solidified the position of company-provided training as a key part of the internal labor market, along with seniority and performance criteria. As developed within the traditionally largest companies of basic industries such as automobiles, steel, chemical, electronics, and banking, the internal labor market hired young workers without skills at entry-level jobs, provided them with experiences and improved skills through formal and informal on-the-job training, and then promoted them to next-level positions that carried heavier responsibilities and higher compensation (Osterman, 1984).

Evidence from a national survey of diverse organizations reveals that workplaces maintaining elaborate internal labor markets for the hiring and promotion of their employees sustain much broader arrays of formal job training activities (Knoke and Kalleberg, 1994; Knoke and Ishio, 1994). But recent shifts toward high-performance work designs in many organizations—toward the use of more teams, job rotations, quality circles, and total quality management practices—pose numerous challenges to the traditional internal labor market model of employment. Indeed, Osterman's (1995) more recent establishment survey finds no relationship between internal labor markets and the extent of employer training. Company-provided job training is likely to be transformed along with the reorganization of the workplace.

In their relentless quest to lower costs, improve quality, and boost productivity, businesses seem compelled to reconfigure and relocate their internal training programs and practices. Ironically, as company internal labor markets unravel, the erosion of training efforts threatens not only to worsen employee well-being and morale but also to imperil the very supply of workforce skills on which companies depend for improving their productivity, quality, and profitability. An understanding of the diverse sources and trends in company training programs and practices is crucial to determining whether ongoing changes in the employment contract will create a more or less competitive U.S. economy.

The continual restructuring of corporate operations carries contradictory implications for company job training efforts. As businesses increase their use of temporary and contingent workers, many employees do not remain long enough for companies to recover their full training investments through upgraded productivity. As downsizing organizations reshuffle their remaining personnel into redesigned positions, however, those displaced workers need retraining to perform their new assignments, sell new products, serve new customers, interact with new coworkers, and renew their commitments to the organization. Unionized employees can effectively pressure their companies to develop jointly governed training opportunities, including basic education, apprenticeships, and retraining programs. The continually expanding applications of scientific and technical knowledge demand an increasingly "technized" labor force, the burden of whose education and skill acquisition falls on both employees and employers at a time when the public education system is producing graduates with serious deficiencies:

> As the technical infrastructure becomes increasingly computational, even blue-collar workers will be asked to process abstract, symbolic information and to engage in procedural and mathematical reasoning in order to accomplish their work. Computer-integrated technologies demand that workers understand the larger production system of which they are a part and make decisions formerly reserved for occupations with higher status. (Barley, 1992, p. 9)

Despite their financial straits, many organizations have little alternative to revamping their training programs if they hope to restore their competitive edge.

Company efforts to procure competent employees may follow external or internal strategies; an organization's decision whether to "make or buy" training depends on its relative assessment of efficiency and institutional criteria that constrain its capacity for rationalizing the workplace during turbulent times. In a cost-cutting mode, a hard-pressed company may conclude that trying to maintain its own training staff is an inefficient use of scarce resources; a more skilled company workforce can be sought through externalizing the training function by: (1) more careful searching and screening of job applicants to cream only the most talented candidates who have acquired the necessary human capital through their personal investments; (2) "poaching" workers already trained by other employers, further eroding those companies' incentives to train their workforces; and (3) purchasing more ready-made, "off-the-shelf" training packages from commercial and public-sector vendors, such as community colleges, who thus assume the costs of producing and marketing such services. Osterman's (1995) analysis finds exactly this trade-off: Establishments that give a greater priority to skills when hiring (as opposed to potential, attitudes, or other characteristics) are significantly less likely to provide training themselves.

Resisting the thrust toward moving training activities outside the organization's boundaries are several institutional impediments, including: (1) the difficulties that external agents encounter in acquiring competence in company-specific training requirements, not only in "technized" production processes but especially in understanding the unique corporate cultures readily accessible only to insiders; (2) effective demands by important organizational stakeholders, particularly labor unions and human resources professionals, who seek to retain some control over the administration and benefits from training activities linked to corporate internal labor markets; and (3) the pressures from interorganizational environments—competitors, customers, suppliers, government regulators, professional and industry associations—to conform to normative expectations about appropriate organizational forms and functions, in which company job training efforts signal allegiance to contemporary conceptions of responsible corporate citizenship.

Answering the question of how employers deal with the contradictions between efficiency and institutional standards in their actual company job training programs and practices requires a detailed empirical examination of training activities among diverse work organizations. Although direct evidence is limited about company training trends over an extended period, some recent employer surveys reveal that worker training is a highly complex, multifaceted process that defies simple summarization.

Theories About Company Training

This section examines the principal attempts to answer to the question, "When do businesses provide their employees with job training?" Answers have been offered by four major theoretical perspectives on the prevalence, causes, and consequences of employer job training: human capital, credential-screening, social structural, and institutional.

Human Capital Theories

Human capital explanations of employers' efforts to train their workers emphasize the employer's rational decision to invest in upgrading employees' skills with expectations of generating productivity, quality, and competitiveness gains for the organization (Becker, 1964). An economically rational company can be expected to provide job training only when it anticipates capturing sufficient increased worker productivity to offset its training costs. *General training,* for example in such easily portable skills as reading and arithmetic, does not allow an employer to reap the benefits of improved employee productivity because a trained worker's wage will rise in a competitive labor market by exactly the amount of the increased marginal product. In contrast, *specific training* increases the productivity of workers only within the company that provides it (Becker, 1964). Because company-specific skills and knowledge (for example, operating a unique machine or serving a special clientele) are useless elsewhere, companies are willing to pay for such training. Larger profits will result from the specially trained workers' increased productivity. Unfortunately, measuring general and company-specific skills has proven elusive, making impossible an empirical test of the human capital hypothesis that company training tends predominantly to be company-specific.

Credential and Screening Theories

Credential and screening explanations suggest that an employer selects new employees partly on the basis of the likelihood that they will remain with the company long enough to repay any company investments in informal work experience and formal job training (Berg, 1970; Spence, 1974). Thurow's (1975) job-competition model, for example, consists of a labor queue in which job applicants are lined up according to their perceived trainability potential. Formal schooling credentials serve as indirect evidence of "absorptive capacity," even if no relevant cognitive skills were learned in school. The further that students persisted with formal schooling, the more likely they are to be compliant at order taking, punctuality, and test taking and to exhibit stick-to-itivity. A company places such candidates higher in its hiring queue as preferred low-training cost applicants. Evidence that workers with higher education credentials receive more company training than those with less education supports this hypothesis. Supervisors make post-hire appraisals about new recruits' technical and social skills and learning capacity, evaluating their potential for enhanced productivity through various employer training programs. Only those workers who are judged to possess higher capabilities will be retained in the employer's workforce beyond the probationary period.

Social Structural Theories

The structure of work settings may facilitate or constrain individual job training opportunities. In this perspective, the primary factors determining which individuals will receive company-provided training lie not so much in personal resources as in workers' access to bureaucratic employment systems, to specialized internal labor markets, and to social networks linking organizations, industries, and occupational communities (Baron and Bielby, 1984; Granovetter, 1985). The particular job-training structures and processes that employers create for matching workers to jobs extend well beyond the initial screening/hiring phase during which formal credentials loom largest. During the post-hiring period, the organization's demands for company-specific skilled labor grow increasingly important. The company must decide whether the new recruits are sufficiently reliable in the entry job to warrant retention and whether additional training (general and/or specific) would enhance their future performances. The recruits must decide whether their career prospects seem sufficiently rewarding to stay with the company or whether a search for alternatives (including leaving the labor force) would be more advantageous. Thus, probation involves mutual sorting processes that increase the over-time complementarity between jobs and workers. Company training policies serve an important function in this matching process: They are both an outcome and a determinant of the matching process.

Institutional Theories

Training decisions are driven in part by prevailing institutional conventions, in the society at large and among peer organizations, regarding appropriate behaviors. Institutional theories emphasize that organizational forms and actions emerge and persist, not only through conscious rational-choice designs but also through cognitive and cultural conventions that come to assume a rule-like status in social thought and action (Scott, 1992). Cultural environments induce substantial uniformity among organizational practices, including job training programs and policies, by conferring greater legitimacy on organizations that adopt more conventional structures. Since World War II, personnel practices in the largest corporations have encouraged strong organizational ties to employees, inducing their commitment by offering education and training, job security, comprehensive benefits, and career opportunities (Baron, Dobbin, and Jennings, 1986). Employers' job training practices inevitably came to reflect a pervasive elaboration of employee job rights, as educational opportunities became legitimated and diffused across many employment contexts (Scott and Meyer, 1991; Monahan, Meyer, and Scott, 1994). Where such institutionalization was most strongly entrenched, company conformity to external training norms was strongest.

In summary, the four theoretical perspectives we have sketched each offer distinct answers to the question of which companies provide job training to their employees. The human capital approach asserts that rational organizations invest only in company-specific training skills whose costs can be recaptured through improved worker productivity; employees must pay for their own general skills training. The credential-screening principle emphasizes that training is one component in an elaborate recruitment, hiring, and promotion process. Employers use formal school certifications as proxies for other worker characteristics to select and slot workers perceived as most receptive to skill enhancement. Organizational structuralists point to the constraints and opportunities that formal work settings impose on training, particularly the impact of organizational size, unionization, and internal labor markets. And the institutionalist perspective underscores the normative and cultural influences in the external environment that shape an organization's decisions about appropriate training activities. To the extent that each theoretical approach encompasses crucial factors in the organizations' training decisions, we must anticipate that as these factors undergo major transformation, organizational training programs will change accordingly. These themes recur later in this chapter as we turn next to the empirical examination of work organization training programs and practices.

Measuring Training

This section seeks answers to the question, "How much job training occurs in U.S. companies?" Estimating the volume and trend in employer training is complicated by conceptual and measurement problems, resulting in inconsistent estimates across studies of how many employees receive training and from which sources. The contexts within which questions appear in survey interviews affect the responses as well. Informal on-the-job training, which involves workers learning through watching others at work and through feedback from immediate supervisors, is exceedingly difficult to quantify in terms of hours and dollars, even when based on self-reports. More surprising, reliable information on formal training programs, which presumably have identifiable participants and well-defined starting and ending points, is also difficult to obtain. The two primary sources of evidence on the extent of training activity are surveys of employees and employers.

Employee Surveys

Estimates of worker training based on employee surveys often lack details on the types of training and their providers. Despite measurement inconsistencies across surveys, Lynch's (1991) review succinctly summarizes the major findings from studies of young workers: Managers, professional, and technical employees are most likely to receive company training, while union members are more likely to be trained on the job or be apprentices. Nonwhites receive less training than whites, and men are more likely than women to be trained on the job. Company training drops when the local labor market has high unemployment but increases in industries experiencing rapid technological change. High school and college dropouts receive less employer training than those workers who have graduated. Bishop's (1994a) survey adds that the jobs that are more likely to offer training are those with higher value added, where more expensive technology is used, and where the skills are not useful elsewhere in the community, that is, where employees are less likely to leave. One conclusion from these surveys is that more advantaged workers in better jobs also seem to get more training.

Brown (1990) concluded that most employee surveys reveal that 85 to 90 percent of workers never receive formal training from their employer. During the 1986–1991 half decade, about 38 percent of the National Longitudinal Survey of Youth (NLSY) cohort experienced some formal training, with company training the leading source (24 percent), followed by seminars outside work (11 percent) and vocational-technical institutes (5 percent) (Veum, 1993). Other evidence on changing training trends points to modest increases during the 1980s (U.S. Bureau of Labor Statistics, 1985, 1992). The 1983 Current Population Survey reported that 55 percent of all employed workers needed some education or training to qualify for their current jobs. By 1991 that figure had increased only slightly to 57 percent, with the largest change among those receiving school training (from 29 percent to 33 percent). Formal company training to qualify for the current job crept up from 10 percent to 12 percent of all workers. However, the number of employees whose qualifying training in schools was sponsored by their companies "more than doubled since 1983, from 2.1 million to 5.4 million in 1991" (U.S. Bureau of Labor Statistics, 1992). Upon obtaining their current jobs, 41 percent of workers in 1991 received some form of skill improvement training, an increase from 35 percent in 1983. A "rapid expansion in the use of formal company programs was the driving force behind the 6-percentage-point increase" (U.S. Bureau of Labor Statistics, 1992), with 16 percent of 1991 workers obtaining formal skill improvement training in their companies, compared to just 11 percent in 1985. Hence, while employers appeared reluctant to provide basic training necessary for unqualified new workers to acquire their jobs, they significantly enlarged their investments in upgrading the jobs skills of those workers once they were hired.

The NLSY panel contains further evidence from individuals about training trends. Figure 4.1 displays the cumulative company-training experiences for four birth cohorts born between 1957 and 1964. Because many of these youths were still completing their educations in the early 1980s, annual company training enrollments

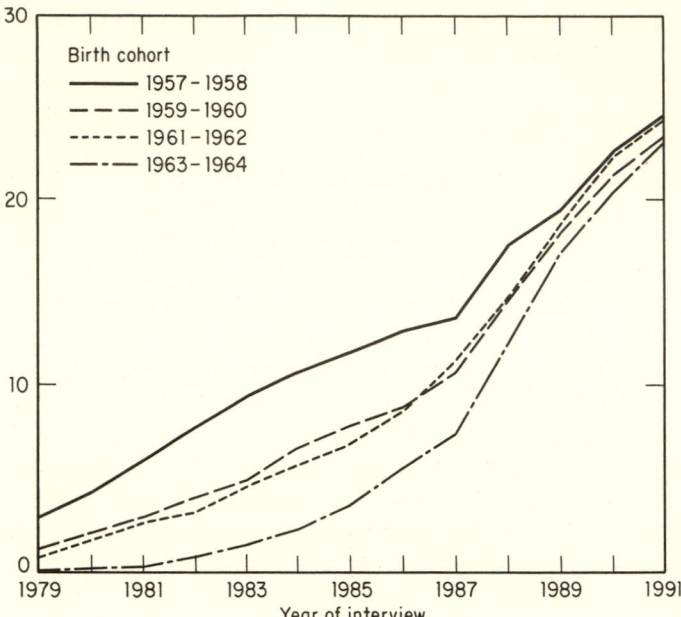

Figure 4.1. Cumulative Company Training. *Source:* National Longitudinal Survey of Youth 1979–1991.

were only slightly above 1 percent during the initial NLSY survey period (1979–1986). As these respondents entered the labor force in increasing numbers in the following five years, however, annual company training rates nearly tripled. Hence, the cumulative training experience grew rapidly, reaching about one fourth of each birth cohort by 1991, with no indication that a plateau had been reached.

Constantine and Neumark (1994) examined changes in reported levels of training between 1983 and 1991 using the Current Population Survey. They looked at the proportion of workers reporting that training was needed to qualify for their current job and, in particular, formal training paid for and provided by the employer. The incidence of such training was essentially unchanged for the workforce as a whole, but the length of training, a proxy for the amount of training provided, declined substantially, especially for high school dropouts. For workers with fewer than ten years' seniority, the incidence was unchanged but the decline in the length of such training was especially great.

The incidence of employer-provided training intended to improve workers' skills on their current jobs, on the other hand, rose over this period. On average, the length of such training was unchanged except for high school dropouts, for whom there was a substantial increase in training time.

Employer Surveys

Direct evidence on company formal training programs comes from a handful of employer surveys, few of which are comparable over time. As with the employee studies we have cited, inconsistencies in question wording and differing definitions of the organizational population generate divergent estimates of the volume and trend of company training across surveys. The 1982 Employment Opportunity Pilot Project (EOPP) asked informants how many hours the most recently hired employee spent during the first three months of employment in formal training by specially trained personnel, informal individualized training by line supervisors, informal training by coworkers away from other tasks, watching others at work, and job orientation by company personnel (Barron, Black, and Lowenstein, 1989). The typical worker received a total of 133 hours in some form of training, but only 10.7 hours were spent in formal training programs (Bishop, 1991). This survey underestimated training activity in the labor force because it focused on the most recently hired worker and thus over sampled low-wage jobs having rapid turnover and including many workers with prior job experience, who are less likely to receive training. A 1992 national replication that asked similar questions about training during the first three months found a total of 152 hours, of which only 18.6 hours were for formal training (Black, Berger, and Barron, 1993). Instead, "new hires spend most of their time either watching others do the job or being shown the job by supervisors and coworkers" (Bishop, 1994a). The 1991 National Organizations Survey (NOS) of establishments of all sizes asked informants, "Apart from on-the-job training, in the past *two years* did [organization name] provide *any* employees with formal job training, either on or off the premises?" The responses reveal widespread training activity. Formal training programs were reported at workplaces that, collectively, employed more than 90 percent of the U.S. labor force. Organizations with training programs reported training an average 56 percent of their employees during the two years, at a median estimated cost of $365 per trainee (Knoke and Kalleberg, 1994).

The 1992 Organization of Work in American Business (OWAB) survey of establishments with fifty or more employees identified "core workers" as the largest group of nonsupervisory and nonmanagerial employees directly involved in producing goods and services (Osterman, 1995). Informants were then asked, "[O]ver the course of a typical year, what percentage of (core employees) attend off-the-job training programs paid for by the company? (Including classroom instruction, vestibule training, training provided by a vendor, or at a formal educational institution)." About 38 percent of these establishments' core employees received formal training in a "typical year," averaging more than eight days per year. A 1991 national survey of 406 large businesses revealed that, on average, they retrained 58 percent of their core production workers from 1986 to 1991, with the most active employers retraining every one to three years (25 percent) or every year (34 percent) (Useem, 1993). A survey of 1,226 manufacturing and nonmanufacturing companies reported that 8 percent and 6 percent, respectively, offered a workplace education program, defined as training in basic reading, math, problem solving, or interpersonal skills (Bassi, 1993). A 1993 survey of 1,062 chief executive officers of manufacturing, service, and trade companies found that more than 70 percent characterized workforce training as very important, and 58 percent of the companies offered some type of formally structured program (American Society for Training and Development, 1994).

The 1993 Bureau of Labor Statistics survey of 11,991 private nonagricultural establishments found that 71 percent provided some type of formal training, covering 90 percent of the labor force. Nearly half of all establishments offered job-skills training, one third provided orientation, safety and health, and workplace-related training, but fewer than 3 percent gave remedial instruction in basic reading, writing, arithmetic, and English as a second language (U.S. Bureau of Labor Statistics, 1994).

Finally, the National Employer Survey (National Center on the Educational Quality of the Workforce, 1995), a national probability survey of establishments with more than twenty-five employees, found that 81 percent of establishments provided some kind of formal training, including that offered through vendors or outside schools, and 97 percent provided informal instruction. Fifty-seven percent reported that training had increased over the past three years, with only 2 percent reporting a decrease.

Training, a magazine for professional trainers published by Lakewood Publications, conducts an annual survey of company training practices based on samples from its subscriber list and other databases. Because the survey targets organizations with 100 or more employees, it ignores about a third of the U.S. labor force. A further caveat is that the survey response rates have been abysmal (typically around 15 to 20 percent of mailed questionnaires). Nevertheless, the *Training* industry reports offer the only available longitudinal glimpse of formal company programs. The general impression from these surveys is that formal company training activities expanded steadily along several dimensions from the late 1980s to the early 1990s. Table 4.1 shows that total spending on company training and the numbers of employees trained increased markedly from 1988 to 1994 (by 28 percent and 26 percent, respectively), with notable dips following the 1990 recession. Most of this budgetary increase was consumed inside the organizations, with "outside purchases" of services, materials, and hardware making up less than 10 percent of the $11 billion rise in training expenditures between 1988 and 1994. The percentage of companies reporting some type of remedial training nearly doubled from 11 percent to 22 percent (and reached 40 percent among businesses employing ten thousand or more people). The number of companies with formal programs targeted toward specific occupational groups showed smaller increases across the seven-year interval. Comparing averages for the first four years to averages for the last three years, training programs for professionals and customer service employees both increased by 7 percent, programs for executives and production workers rose 6 percent, while sales personnel training barely budged. Middle manager training fell by 2 percent, perhaps because these positions were most often eliminated in downsizing companies. Programs to train higher-level employees (executives, managers, administrators, and professionals) were still more prevalent in 1994 than were programs aimed at front-line workers (first-line supervisors, customer service, sales, and production employees). In 1994, the higher-level occupations accounted for 40 percent of all persons trained, more than twice their proportion in the labor force.

In sum, the evidence from worker surveys suggests less job training activity than do data from diverse employer samples. These

Table 4.1. Company Training Activities (1988–1994)

	1988	1989	1990	1991	1992	1993	1994
Total budgeted expenditures ($ billion)	39.6	44.4	45.5	43.2	45.0	48.2	50.6
Outside budgeted expenditures ($ billion)	9.0	9.4	9.2	8.7	8.8	9.4	9.9
Number trained (million)	37.5	35.6	39.5	36.8	41.0	47.2	47.3
Remedial training (%)	11	11	15	23	19	21	22
Executive training (%)	65	65	67	65	70	74	70
Middle managers (%)	78	72	76	77	73	76	72
Professionals (%)	60	56	60	61	65	70	66
Customer service (%)	45	43	45	50	57	52	50
Salespeople (%)	43	37	40	42	44	41	42
Production workers (%)	35	27	33	35	38	37	40

Source: Annual issues of *Training* Magazine's "Industry Report." Adopted with permission from *Training*, Lakewood Publications, Minneapolis, Minn.

discrepancies may arise in part from different understandings of "training," but a more likely reason is underreporting by workers and overreporting by employers. These participants have different incentives for drawing more or less inclusive boundaries around the various activities likely to be labeled formal company training. Because employee samples almost never include information about their employers or program details, the remainder of this chapter concentrates on analyses of the 1991 National Organizations Survey, which represents all U.S. employers and which provides detailed characteristics about them (Kalleberg, Knoke, Marsden and Spaeth, 1996).

Dimensions of Company Training

This section seeks answers to the question, "Does it matter who trains which workers for what purposes?" Our ability to reach any clear conclusions on this point is hampered by uncertainty about how changes in the employment contract might affect company training programs; the erosion of internal labor markets, the restructuring of workplace relations, and employer demands for improved employee skills each imply substantial transformations of training practices. One strategy for studying the question is to examine current variation in employer programs along basic dimensions such as industry, establishment size, unionization, and employment contingency. The subsections that follow investigate what types of companies train which kinds of workers for what purposes, using various instructional methods at diverse locations, under alternative administrative controls and program evaluations. The detailed portrait that emerges from this mosaic permits a well-informed speculation about the future of company training in the United States.

Extent of Formal Training

How does formal company training vary by industry, establishment size, employment contingency (combinations of full-time, part-time, and subcontracted workers), and core employee unionization? As shown in Table 4.2, some kind of formal training program is available in 72 percent of all establishments. Formal programs are especially prevalent within the manufacturing-transportation and professional–public administration sectors (both more than 80 percent), but relatively rare in the agriculture-mining-construction sector (43 percent). The very smallest establishments (with fewer than five employees) seldom provide any formal training program (15 percent), while the very largest workplaces (with a thousand or

Table 4.2. Extent of Formal Training by Organizational Characteristics

	Percentage of establishments offering any formal training	Percentage of employees trained in past year	
		All orgs.	With training programs
Mean	71.7	7.0	21.5
Industry			
Agriculture, mining, construction	42.9***	2.8***	27.4***
Manufacturing, transportation	80.8	8.0	16.4
Wholesale, retail trade	57.3	4.3	21.8
Finance, services	61.5	4.3	19.3
Professional, public administration	82.3	12.3	26.3
Establishment size			
Fewer than 5 employees	15.4***	1.0***	37.0**
5–9 employees	56.8	5.0	30.0
10–99 employees	73.3	8.0	23.1
100–999 employees	91.3	12.7	17.6
1,000 or more employees	95.7	18.5	22.4
Employment contingency			
All full-time	64.4***	5.3***	22.0
Subcontractees, no part-time	65.8	6.4	26.6
Part-time < 50 percent, no subcontractees	80.1	9.6	21.3
Part-time < 50 percent, subcontractees	89.9	13.7	20.3
Part-time > 50 percent	52.3	3.3	19.5
Union status			
No core worker union	64.8***	5.6***	23.1*
Core worker union	90.7	12.9	18.5
(*N* of establishments)	(688)	(650)	(455)

*p < .05
**p < .01
***p < .001

Source: 1991 National Organizations Survey.

more workers) almost always have some program (96 percent). The distribution of any training by employment contingency shows that formal training is provided by 90 percent of establishments with both subcontractees and a minority of part-time employees but by barely half the establishments with a majority of part-time employees.

Establishments with union representation of their core production workers are much more likely to have a training program (91 percent) than are employers without a unionized staff (65 percent). Further analyses of these data by Knoke and Ishio (1994) found that union impact on training varies inversely with the presence of company internal labor markets; that is, where organizations' internal labor markets were poorly developed, unionized workplaces trained their core production workers more often than did nonunionized establishments. Among organizations with highly developed internal labor markets, however, unionized and nonunionized establishments were equally likely to provide worker training programs. One implication is that, in the face of weakening company internal labor market structures, unions effectively fight to preserve company training opportunities for core production workers.

Osterman's (1995) analysis revealed that establishments that provided more training were more likely to pay wage premiums as well. These premiums helped bind employees to the employer so that the investments in training could be recouped and may have served as substitutes for internal labor markets.

Informants in the NOS were asked to estimate the number of employees who received formal company training during the preceding two years. Their estimates were divided by the total number of employees, then halved to obtain the average annual percentage of employees trained. The mean proportion of employees trained by all establishments was 22 percent per year (with a 99 percent confidence interval of 19 percent to 25 percent), but the median value was only 14 percent, indicating a substantial positive skew: About 5 percent of employers trained half or more of their workforces every year. Column two of Table 4.2 shows the percentage of employees trained for all establishments, while column three displays the corresponding values only for those organizations that had formal training programs. Both training measures covaried significantly with the four basic characteristics, with the exception of contingent worker status for programs only. Looking at column 2, it is evident that the professional–public administration sector trained the highest percentage of its employees, while agriculture-mining-construction trains the least. When employers without formal training programs were eliminated, however, agriculture-mining-construction rivaled professional–public administration for the highest training rate, while the manufacturing-transportation sector had the lowest percentage of workers trained. The percentage trained increased strongly with the establishment-size variable among all organizations, but, if only companies with formal programs were considered, the smallest organizations trained the largest percentages of their workers. A similar reversal occurs for the unionization variable: The percentage of core workers trained by all establishments was higher where they were unionized, but nonunionized establishments with programs actually trained a larger percentage than did the unionized programs. Finally, among all establishments, training was lowest where a majority of employees were part-time, highest for companies employing subcontracted workers and a minority of part-time workers. Among organizations with formal programs, however, temporary work status was unrelated to the extent of worker training.

The recent organizational restructuring trends discussed earlier carry contradictory implications for company training. On the one hand, a weakened employment contract thrusts many previously internal training functions outside the organizational boundaries. As companies contract by peeling away layers of highly trained middle managers, fewer promotion opportunities remain that require managerial training programs for advancing up the corporate ladder. Expanding companies can hire managers made redundant at other companies, thereby saving substantially on the costs of growing their own. Similarly, the increased turnover of production workers through mass layoffs and plant closings means that many companies become reluctant to maintain their own training programs, given the increased risk of losing their investments before employees can pay back the training costs through increased productivity. Employers who hire temporary, part-time, and subcontracted workers find little incentive to train people with no long-term attachments to the company. And the continual shrinkage of union membership in many sectors bodes ill for this collective voice on behalf of job enrichment and skill upgrading efforts.

Some evidence suggests that many employees already pursue the strategy of not training to get the skills they needed. In the 1993 U.S. Bureau of Labor Statistics survey, for example, the majority of the establishments surveyed did not provide training to upgrade workers skills or prepare them for new jobs in the organization; of these, 28 percent reported that they did not offer training because they hired only workers who already had the skills needed for the jobs. For the larger establishments with more than fifty employees, the ones more likely to have internal labor markets and who employ the majority of the workforce, the figure was actually higher—35 percent reported that they hired only workers who already had the skills that would be needed for new jobs (Frazis, Herz, and Horrigan, 1995). On the other hand, competition and technological change generate heavy demands for improved skills that companies must meet either with current employees or with new hires. Downsizing organizations reassign the remaining employees to new positions involving new job responsibilities, which places a premium on workers who have the most general skills. Redesigned workplaces that rely on teamwork and other interdependency concepts put heavy demands on employees to acquire sophisticated social skills and combinations of formal training and experience (MacDuffie and Kochan, 1995). Because many restructurings increase the need for company-specific skills, companies cannot rely solely on the external market to satisfy their demands for skilled labor. Ironically, the same worldwide economic turbulence that is busily destroying many rationales for company-provided training also generates new ones. Which of these contradictory trends will dominate the training effort depends very much on the particular configurations of industry, size, employment contingency, and unionization that individual organizations confront.

Purposes of Training

Employers seem to offer training for almost as many reasons as they have employees, but at least five broad categories appear to constitute a minimal typology that captures the general diversity among formal training programs:

1. Basic skills training. Given the woeful state of U.S. public education, lamented for over a decade in official publications such as *A Nation at Risk* (U.S. National Commission on Excellence in Education, 1983), some employers experience difficulty in recruiting qualified entry-level job candidates (Useem, 1993). Consequently, they attempt to rectify their new hires' basic literacy and numeracy deficits by providing remedial training programs, although the ready transferability of these general skills to other employers would appear to violate rational investment strategies (Becker, 1964).

2. Skills upgrading. Many industries face rapidly changing high technologies, substantial workplace health and safety concerns, and fierce sales and service competition from their domestic and foreign rivals. The installation of new machinery and software programs is a typical occasion for elaborate instructional endeavors because they change the skills required to fill jobs. Current employees need to improve their job skills if the company is to adapt successfully to changing production and service requirements. An employer will invest in retraining efforts aimed at enhancing workers' company-specific human capital in the expectation that it will reap the rewards of the employees' augmented productivity. Employers may also provide training to their suppliers' employees to improve their service capabilities, for example, by teaching them just-in-time inventory delivery procedures.

3. Social skills training. Relevant work skills are not restricted to basic or highly technical activities. Service-sector industries in particular depend heavily on employees' developing strong interpersonal proficiencies, communication skills, and social aptitudes, especially in professional, sales, and managerial jobs. Companies operating in international markets need managers familiar with foreign languages and local cultural norms. Hence, many corporations continually provide seminars in effective communication, affirmative action, peer counseling, and similar sensitivity training. Employees' promotions within career ladders leading to higher administrative posts may require their successful completion of extensive courses on interpersonal skills; even at lower levels, new hires and contingent workers are often required to participate in formal orientation programs to help them fit into the corporate culture.

4. Teamwork training. As organizations restructure their production and service systems around teamwork concepts, they require special attention to training in group dynamics. Collective decision making, team leadership, interpersonal communication, and related cooperation skills are vital to success in work units ranging from hospital operating theaters to nuclear power plants to air and sea transport businesses where human errors can trigger catastrophic consequences. Programs that teach coworkers how to interact more effectively with one another, often by simulating or role-playing critical situations, are in vogue among cutting-edge companies.

5. Displaced worker retraining. During the recent decade of enormous corporate downsizing and reorganization, a few companies concluded that they should not leave the fates of their laid-off and reallocated employees to chance. They created formal units within their human resources departments to offer career counseling, outplacement, and reassignment services to employees at all skill levels. Unions became particularly sensitized to retraining and relocation issues involved in "flexibility" about employment security. Most companies, however, view displaced worker retraining and placement as outside their purview (see Congressional Quarterly [1994] for a comprehensive overview of federal programs).

Several studies reveal a prevailing diversity of training purposes. The 1993 Current Population Survey examined five types of training obtained by individuals and concluded that "occupation-specific technical training was the most often cited form of skill improvement training," with computer-related and managerial-supervisory training of secondary importance, while basic reading, writing, and math training was a distant fourth (U.S. Bureau of Labor Statistics, 1992). A 1990 survey of 276 large unionized companies found that the largest amounts of training provided to "unskilled" blue-collar workers dealt with safety and health, quality improvement, and technical skills upgrading and refreshers, but very little time was devoted to remedial English literacy and basic math (Katz and Keefe, 1993). The National Employer Survey conducted by the National Center on the Educational Quality of the Workforce (EQW) found a similar pattern. The amount of training time varied considerably by topic. Safety training was the most important topic, and very little time was spent on basic academic skills. Such employer disregard for basic skills training was consistent with a 1991 survey of 360 National Association of Manufacturers members showing that, despite acknowledged shortages in the availability of skilled job applicants, "employers believe that the most important problem with applicants for entry-level jobs is behavioral, the perception that candidates would not fit into the work environment. Academic skills were of substantially less concern" (Cappelli and O'Shaughnessy, 1993). Less than one company in eight mandated that employees who needed remedial education obtain it.

Although the 1991 NOS did not ask about the training of workers displaced by corporate reorganization or downsizing, some indirect evidence can be gleaned by comparing the training activities by organizations that changed their employee sizes over the preceding three years. Both growing and declining organizations seemed more likely to offer employee training programs than were stable organizations, but for different reasons: Growing organizations need to train their newly hired employees, while shrinking organizations must retrain their remaining workers for new assignments. Table 4.3 shows how workplace growth, decline, and stability affect training activities. The first column shows the percentage of establishments with any formal training program. Both declining and growing businesses were significantly more likely to offer training (81 percent and 84 percent, respectively) than were unchanged organizations (56 percent). But the effect occurs almost entirely among the smallest establishments (those with fewer than 100 employees); of these, declining and growing organizations were respectively 65 percent and 75 percent more likely to provide worker training than were stable employers (41 percent). Among the largest establishments (those with 100 or more workers), no significant variation in availability of training was evident (more than 90 percent offered formal training, regardless of their growth experiences).

The last five columns of Table 4.3 display, for establishments that had formal training programs, cross-tabulations between size changes and changes in the amount of resources devoted to training during the preceding two years. Organizations experiencing changing employment should be more likely than stable employers to increase their training effort. Declining organizations may, however, find that effort more difficult to achieve than growing organizations, given the disparities in the resources available for coping with change. A much larger percentage of growing establishments boosted their training resources than did either stable or declining firms (71 percent versus 49 percent and 53 percent for all orga-

Table 4.3. Changes in Training Resources by Changes in Number of
Employees

	Any training	Change in training resources in past 2 years? (%)				
		Increase	Same	Decrease	Total	(N)
All establishments						
Declining	80.7*	53.0*	28.2	18.8	100.0	(117)
Same	55.9	48.6	45.8	5.6	100.0	(142)
Growing	83.5	70.7	24.7	4.5	100.0	(198)
Total	71.9	59.3	32.2	8.5	100.0	(457)
(N of establishments)	(636)					
Small establishments (1–99)						
Declining	64.7*	50.0*	34.1	15.9	100.0	(44)
Same	41.3	42.1	53.9	3.9	100.0	(76)
Growing	75.2	73.4	24.1	2.5	100.0	(79)
Total	55.7	56.3	37.7	6.0	100.0	(199)
(N of establishments)	(357)					
Large establishments (100+)						
Declining	94.8	54.8*	24.7	20.5	100.0	(73)
Same	93.3	56.1	36.4	7.6	100.0	(66)
Growing	90.2	68.9	25.2	5.9	100.0	(119)
Total	92.5	61.6	27.9	10.5	100.0	(258)
(N of establishments)	(279)					

*p < .001

Source: 1991 National Organizations Survey.

nizations). Although the percentage of declining organizations increasing their training efforts nearly equaled that of stable organizations, more of these contracting employers were forced to devote fewer resources to training (19 percent versus 6 percent), presumably because those assets were more urgently needed for organizational survival. These patterns were essentially identical among both small and large employers.

These relationships once again foreshadow future diminutions in company training, given the contemporary metamorphosis in the U.S. workplace. Downsizing organizations can less afford to divert scarce resources from the struggle to stay afloat. As company payrolls shrink, their simplified internal labor markets and nonunionized workforces require fewer specialized training programs. The shifts of employment away from the manufacturing and public-professional sectors into the service and trade sectors similarly reduce the requirement that employers provide training in technical skills for their workers. As more part-time and subcontracted employees are taken on board, companies are unwilling to underwrite both remedial and technical skills training, on the presumably accurate perception that such workers will not remain with the company long enough to pay back their investments. As other studies have found (Bishop, 1994a; Osterman, 1995), employers reduce training when they are more involved in the outside labor market for skills. Consequently, substantial diversity among organizational job training programs may be lost.

Occupational Training

Mainly on the basis of employee surveys, several researchers have reported that the chance of receiving company-provided training varies by the worker's occupation. Training programs heavily favor managers and professionals over other white-collar and blue-collar employees (Boston, 1990; Rumberger, 1984). Brown (1990, p. 103) concluded that "the largest difference is between different occupational groups, with estimates for professional, technical, and managerial workers roughly twice as high as those for service workers, with other white- and blue-collar workers falling in between." The OWAB survey of large establishments revealed that 51 percent of their professional and technical workers but only 27 percent of their core blue-collar workers received formal training away from their work stations, a difference that remained significant after controlling for a variety of organizational characteristics (Osterman, 1993). However, the NOS found few differences among all establishments by type of core occupations, since "formal training programs for core workers and their managers have apparently diffused widely across the entire occupational spectrum" (Knoke and Ishio, 1994).

The NOS asked informants whether any of the establishment's core production workers had received formal training in the previous two years. About 90 percent of the organizations that offered formal programs also provided some training specific to their core employees. Unions exerted a clear impact on core worker training: Establishments with union representation were 15 to 21 percent more likely to offer training at every occupational level, with the greatest difference—an enormous 50 percent gap—occurring in upper blue-collar workplaces. (Four categories were compared: upper white-collar (professional and managerial occupations); lower white-collar (sales and clerical); upper blue-collar (craftsmen, foremen, and transportation); and lower blue-collar (operatives, laborers, service, and farm workers).) A slight bias towards high-status occupational training was evident in the significantly greater training provided to upper white-collar workers (72 percent of establishments with these core workers), but the next highest group was lower blue-collar workers (66 percent), and at least half the organizations with lower white- or upper blue-collar core workers offered them formal training. No significant differences occur in remedial skills training, although both blue-collar categories had slightly higher levels than the white-collar organizations. Training in the safe use of equipment was very clearly concentrated among the blue-collar groups, with rates some 25 to 35 percent higher than in white-collar establishments. Training in computer usage was highest in establishments employing upper white- and upper blue-collar core workers and lowest among lower blue-collar core employees. Management skills training was most often provided by establishments with upper white- and upper blue-collar core workers. Such management instruction was probably directed at non-core employees, that is, the establishment's administrators and supervisors, rather than at the core employees themselves.

If the distribution of occupational training programs across organizations remains fairly stable, changes in the employment relationship carry contradictory implications. For companies that are expanding their upper-level white- and blue-collar workforces, the amount of training devoted to computer and management instruction is likely to increase. At companies following a deskilling strategy of hiring more lower-level employees, in contrast, company occupational training is likely to contract, particularly programs in equipment safety instruction. Although occupational training seems unaffected by the shift from a full-time to a more contingent workforce, reductions in organizational size and unionization rates would strike a major blow against occupation-specific training programs. With the exception of lower white-collar training, the trend of employment from the manufacturing and the public sectors into service and trade industries also would seriously constrict the availability of occupational training offered by employers.

Joint Training Programs

The vast majority of company training activities are wholly instigated and administered by the company, even those programs involving external providers. However, small but important segments involve genuine collaborations with other organizations, particularly governments and unions. The federal Job Training Partnership Act of 1982 (JTPA), which replaced the much larger Comprehensive Employment and Training Act, emphasized training of disadvantaged youths, minorities, and dislocated workers with the goal of eventual job placement. It gave program funding and oversight to states and private industry councils composed mainly of business leaders, prohibited public service employment, and severely limited work experience, allowances, and support services to trainees (Pines and Carnevale, 1991). In the NOS data, fewer than 10 percent of establishments with training programs report receiving any JTPA funds, with little variation across organizational characteristics. However, a general question—"Is any of the formal training paid for by federal, state, or local government agencies"— was answered affirmatively by one third of establishments with formal programs. Governmental support varied significantly across all four organizational characteristics, with the well-off employers generally benefiting the most. Forty-six percent of unionized establishments but only 26 percent with nonunionized core workers obtained public training dollars; 55 percent of training programs in the professional–public administrative sector but only 5 percent in the wholesale-retail trade were underwritten by public monies; governments supported training programs in 46 percent of the largest organizations (1,000 or more employees) but paid for just 6.3 percent of the smallest units' programs; and government training funds were dispensed to 40 percent of places hiring a minority of part-time employees and no core subcontractees but to just 13 percent of workplaces with a majority of part-time workers.

Labor unions constitute perhaps the most important organizational participant in company training programs (Knoke and Ishio, 1994). Unions press for more company training for their members, encouraging employers to invest more resources in skill upgrading. Although only 15 percent of the NOS establishments' training programs were offered because of stipulations in union contracts, these programs encompassed 36 percent of the sites where core production workers were unionized. Furthermore, 44 percent of the unionized manufacturing and transportation establishments had training programs created under union contracts (the next most prevalent sector was professional–public administration, where 32 percent of training programs in unionized organizations were due to union contracts). Unfortunately, the NOS provides no further details about how these union-company training programs are governed, particularly whether they involve shared administrative efforts.

Training programs that are jointly conceived, implemented, monitored, and evaluated by unions and management are a recent innovation in industrial relations, often growing out of apprenticeship and employee-involvement programs (Ferman et al., 1991). Genuine joint training involves codetermination of decision making, a degree of shared resources, and local control of program content (Ferman et al., 1990). The condition favoring its emergence is prevailing strong unionization in the context of declining or changing industrial performance, which gives both management and labor an incentive to seek mutual benefits from cooperative rather than adversarial arrangements. Because unions represent less than 17 percent of the U.S. labor force, the impact of joint programs is relatively limited and may decline with further deunionization. In contrast to employer-initiated training, joint programs "democratize access to training (within the union membership)" by imposing fewer eligibility requirements on enrollment (Ferman et al., 1990). Participants generally self-select into training on the basis of their expressed needs and aspirations, resulting in joint programs more oriented toward personal development than toward the narrow vocational training needs of the organization. These programs are more likely to emphasize employment security in the form of lifelong job holding by combining personal and technical skills than to concentrate on the company's immediate internal labor market needs. Further, joint training programs are more likely to be sensitive to the real needs of participants and less likely to be subject to short-term changes, such as revised priorities, that often plague other training programs (Roberts and Wozniak, 1994).

To date, most of the evidence about joint training comes from case studies of specific unions and employers, such as the United Automobile Workers' efforts with Ford and General Motors (Tomasko and Dickinson, 1991; Schurman et al., 1991). Several state government programs have sought to assist unions and management in retraining workers dislocated by plant closings (Baker, 1991). The first employer survey to focus on joint training efforts was conducted in 1988 on a sampling frame of 204 union-employer pairs created in 1978 by the U.S. Department of Labor (Hoyman and Ferman, 1991). Of the 107 pairs responding, 42 percent had conducted some form of joint training, with larger companies more likely to start such programs. Half the joint programs originated in a desire to extend cooperative industrial relations, while nearly a third cited competition as a driving force. External pressures were evident, with a majority of joint programs in industries experiencing decline or undergoing a great deal of change. Multiple objectives were sought by these programs; about half had "traditional purposes" such as safety and health training or upgrading job skills, and half emphasized "nontraditional" goals such as developing communication skills and assisting displaced workers. Despite the implication that joint training reflects common concerns of labor and management, a number of divisive issues may undermine their aims, such as control over financing, staffing, and evaluation (Ferman et al., 1990). More research is needed on joint efforts, particularly on their effectiveness relative to alternative arrangements.

Training Program Administration

Employee training may be provided under a variety of administrative arrangements. The employer's primary choice is a make-or-buy decision: Should the organization create its own permanent staff to train its workers, or should it use outside training vendors? Company training activities are likely to remain inside whenever they involve company-specific expertise or proprietary knowledge and when there is adequate time to create an internal training staff. The decision to purchase training from outsiders is more likely when companies have important needs that cannot be met within the time and funding available to produce proprietary programs. Smaller organizations, operating at the margin of profitability, usually cannot afford the luxury of maintaining their own internal training operations.

A variety of external training vendors offer both highly specialized and generic training packages on as-needed bases. This thriving industry encompasses nonprofit vendors, such as local community colleges, voc-tech schools, and community-based (low-income) organizations, as well as commercial training consultants who package and sell short courses (Carnevale, Gainer, and Villet, 1990). External vendors also include the larger organization (parent) of which an establishment is a branch or subsidiary unit. Many large companies, for example, operate centralized training institutions that seek to standardize employee instruction, ranging from the General Motors Research Institute for engineers and designers to "Hamburger University" for new McDonald's franchise managers.

Table 4.4 shows the training arrangements of NOS establishments that had formal programs. Four basic provider types are distinguished, organizations that (1) maintain no training staffs of their own but rely entirely on nonparental external vendors, such as "outside agencies, consultants, or schools" (23 percent of all establishments); (2) use only their own training staffs or only trainers provided by a parent organization (5 percent); (3) use *both* their own training staffs plus external vendors (35 percent); and (4) use their own training staffs, plus parent organization trainers, plus outside vendors (37 percent). Virtually no establishments (fewer then 3 percent) relied exclusively on their own training staffs. Even when organizations maintained training staffs, they almost always collaborated with other vendors of training services. These results suggest how far the training function has been pushed onto the outside market.

These generic methods for delivering training vary significantly across the four organizational characteristics. The manufacturing-transportation and professional–public administration sectors were most likely to use all three provider arrangements (40 percent and 43 percent respectively), while the three other industry sectors were more likely to use outside training vendors exclusively (29 percent or more). The wholesale and retail trades were also the most likely to

Table 4.4. Types of Training Providers by Organizational Characteristics

	Only outside vendors	Only own staff, or parent organization	Own staff & outside vendor	Own staff, parent organization & outside vendor	Total	(N)
Mean	23.2	5.1	34.9	36.8	100.0	(487)
Industry**						
Agriculture, mining, construction	30.0	5.0	30.0	35.0	100.0	(20)
Manufacturing, transportation	21.7	3.5	35.0	39.9	100.0	(143)
Wholesale, retail trade	28.8	13.6	30.5	27.1	100.0	(59)
Finance, services	30.6	11.1	34.7	23.6	100.0	(72)
Professional, public	19.2	1.6	36.8	42.5	100.0	(193)
Establishment size**						
Less than 5 employees	76.9	7.7	7.7	7.7	100.0	(13)
5–9 employees	45.8	12.5	33.3	8.2	100.0	(24)
10–99 employees	32.3	6.6	27.9	33.3	100.0	(183)
100–999 employees	15.2	4.5	38.8	41.6	100.0	(178)
1,000 or more employees	6.7	1.1	46.1	46.1	100.0	(89)
Employment contingency*						
All full-time	35.8	6.0	27.6	30.6	100.0	(134)
Subcontractees, no part-time	26.9	3.8	26.9	42.3	100.0	(26)
Part-time < 50%, no subcontractors	18.1	4.2	36.3	41.4	100.0	(215)
Part-time < 50%, subcontractors	12.9	3.2	50.0	33.9	100.0	(62)
Part-time > 50%	22.0	10.0	34.0	34.0	100.0	(50)
Union status**						
No core worker union	26.6	5.9	38.1	29.4	100.0	(323)
Core worker union	16.5	3.7	28.7	51.2	100.0	(164)

*p < .01
**p < .001

Source: 1991 National Organizations Survey.

use only their own trainers plus those from the parent organization (14 percent). Not surprisingly, the complexity of training programs varied strongly by establishment size. More than 75 percent of the very smallest establishments, generally lacking their own training staffs, purchased training exclusively from external sources, while better than 90 percent of the very largest organizations combined their own training staffs with those from parental and/or external providers. Companies that hired only full-time employees were the most likely to rely exclusively on outside vendors (36 percent). Organizations that employed a minority of part-time workers were most likely to provide training by combining their own staffs with outside trainers and/or parental organization training staffs (84 percent and 78 percent, respectively, of establishments with and without subcontractees). Finally, a majority of organizations with unionized core employees obtained training from all three types of providers (51 percent), while nonunionized establishments more frequently used only external vendors (27 percent) or external vendors plus their own staffs (38 percent).

The changing employment contract has obvious implications for training program administration. Downsizing organizations will rely less on their own training staffs and more on outside vendors to provide training. The shift away from manufacturing and public sector employment to service and trade industries likewise will reduce in-house provision of training. A countertrend is that a growing contingent workforce may retard the exclusive dependence on outside training vendors. Companies with a minority of part-time workers may combine outside training vendors with their own staffs more often than those with entirely full-time workforces, which are more likely to rely completely on outside vendors. But, when a majority of the workforce becomes part-time, organizations may turn to outsiders to meet all their training needs.

Program Financing

Data on the costs and methods of financing company training are scarce. Estimation is complicated by uncertainty about whether to count only the direct costs of instructors and materials or also to include worker productivity lost by being taken off-task. During the 1980s, annual U.S. employer investment in workplace training was about $210 billion, counting all forms of instruction from apprenticeships to informal demonstration and coaching (Carnevale, Gainer, and Villet, 1990). Only $30 billion of that amount, however, was spent directly on formal training programs, amounting to just 1.4 percent of the national payroll (Carnevale and Gainer, 1989). Even the largest employers usually committed less than 5 percent of their budgets to formal training. Smaller employers (those with fewer than 100 workers) paid for only 23 percent of the training taken by their workers outside the workplace, while larger companies covered 40 percent of these external training costs. The *Training* magazine surveys of the late 1980s and early 1990s estimate about a 3.5 percent annual increase in direct-cost expenditures, roughly the rate of inflation (see Table 4.1).

The NOS informants were asked how much money, "including staff time and all other costs," their establishments had spent on training in the past two years. More than one in five informants could not give a dollar estimate, suggesting some uncertainty about how to calculate such expenditures. For organizations providing these data, the mean biennial formal training expenditure was $590 per employee and $1,206 per person trained (medians were $153 and $365, respectively). These amounts did not vary significantly across the four organizational characteristics, with the sole exception of the industry sector. Mean expenditures per person trained were $2,853 in the finance, insurance, and real estate (FIRE)–services sector, $1,498 in manufacturing-transportation, $670 in professional-public administration, $581 in wholesale-retail trade, but just $282 in the agriculture-mining-construction sector. Formal training costs, a tiny percentage of establishments' total operating budgets, varied significantly only across industry: the wholesale-retail trade spent 0.8 percent, FIRE-services 0.6 percent, manufacturing 0.5 percent, professional–public administration 0.3 percent, with agriculture-mining-construction again last at only 0.1 percent of operating costs.

The overwhelming majority of organizations with formal training programs also paid their employees' tuition for training courses taken off the premises (91 percent), as well as provided release time from work to participate in such activities (82 percent). Again, such financial support did not vary significantly across the four organizational characteristics. This apparent willingness of companies to pick up the tab for their employees' training investments indicates that formal programs have become a widely institutionalized employer function (Knoke, 1994). Most notably, smaller establishments with programs appear to spend about as much per capita in training their workforces as the very largest companies, and even companies employing substantial numbers of part-time workers seem as committed to training them as do companies employing full-time labor.

The available evidence on actual company training costs does not reveal whether these expenditures are optimal for fulfilling employers' human capital needs. Indeed, programs may be underfunded relative to the demand for skilled labor if companies are unwilling to pay for skill upgrading that might not be recaptured in future worker productivity. As the restructuring of the employment contract proceeds, organizations are likely to spend less on training because their simplified internal labor markets now have fewer opportunities for promotion that require training. And, as worker tenures grow shorter and more contingent, a companies' commitment to continuing investments in its human capital steadily erodes. If the organizational training function persists, it is more likely to be transferred to external vendors while the internal training staff is first reduced, then disbanded.

Program Benefits and Evaluation Methods

Bishop's (1994b) careful assessment of the impact of previous job training on newly hired employees acknowledged that nonrandom selection processes render definitive conclusions difficult. Nevertheless, he found a tendency for employees having relevant work experience, vocational education, and prior employer-sponsored training "to require less training, to be more productive, and to be paid higher wages both initially and after one year." Further, Bowers and Swaim (1992) found that the overall returns to training rose from 1983 to 1991. Such apparent benefits to both workers and employers from company-sponsored training underscore the need for research on the long-term consequences of training at both the individual and the organizational level.

For several decades the applied psychology and personnel management disciplines have generated enormous literatures on training procedures (see periodic reviews by M. L. Goldstein [1980] and Wexley [1984]). This research emphasizes such microlevel issues as "what tasks are performed, what needs to be learned to perform these tasks, what ways these tasks should be performed, what should be taught in training, and what should be learned on the job" (Wexley, 1984). Training program designers draw heavily from social learning theories about how individuals acquire cognitive skills (e.g., Patrick, 1992). Hence, their instructional techniques heavily rely on principles from the full panoply of psychological processes —behavior modeling and modification, role playing and simulation, feedback and reinforcement, positive transfer—to change trainees' knowledge and job skills. Not surprisingly, most evaluations of training program effectiveness emphasize pre- versus post-training learning measures (A. P. Goldstein, 1981). Self-reports predominate over behavioral observations (Phillips, 1990), while studies of training program impacts on organizational performance, such as increased productivity and financial gain, are rare.

The NOS establishments are no exception to this microlevel

approach to training program evaluation. Presented with four procedures, informants reported that 73 percent of the organizations with formal training relied on the trainees' opinions; 73 percent employed supervisors' evaluations of employee performance; 67 percent used the program director's assessment; and 53 percent formally tested the trainees. The establishments used a mean of 2.6 training assessment methods. Establishments with unionized core workers applied 0.31 more assessment techniques than the non-unionized companies; the FIRE-services sector used the fewest evaluation techniques and the wholesale-retail sector the most; and larger companies employed more than twice as many methods as the smallest places.

Although current trends in workplace restructuring imply that leaner times may lie ahead for company training programs and practices, the quality of training evaluations paradoxically may improve. A resource-scarce environment should turn employers into more cautious consumers of training services, more resistant to razzle-dazzle technologies lacking demonstrable results. As employers increasingly seek a better accounting of their training dollars, they will pressure trainers to produce solid evidence that their programs actually change workers' skills and that they subsequently contribute in measurable ways to enhanced company performance. Thus, one side benefit of the changing workplace is likely to be more accurate assessments of the value and limitations of company-provided job training.

Toward a New National Training Policy

Training plays a central role in the success of individual workers in the labor market and contributes to important labor market outcomes such as wages and promotion prospects. Changes in the distribution of earnings and of opportunities in the labor market that capture the attention of policy makers focus attention on training as a mechanism for addressing those issues. The 1994 School-to-Work Opportunities Act, for example, which mandates the creation of state-level programs for integrating school and work, was driven in part by the perception that those entering the labor force from secondary school had a difficult time securing the skills needed for a successful worklife.

As these arguments suggest, training is also becoming a central issue for employers. The changes in the nature of employment and of work organization that we have noted are generating a series of challenges for employer-provided training. Organizational restructuring and new systems of work, for example, demand new skills that somehow have to be learned. Yet downsizing and other efforts that reduce the attachment of employees to employers make it more difficult for employers to recoup investments in training and, in turn, to undertake them at all.

With the election of Bill Clinton as president, job training seemed poised finally to move onto the national policy agenda. As the governor of Arkansas, Clinton enacted a youth apprenticeship program, and during the presidential campaign he embraced a "play-or-pay" scheme similar to those of other advanced industrial nations such as Germany and France, where companies either train their own workers or contribute to a pool of training funds administered by the government (Loveman, Piore, and Sengenberger, 1990). Clinton's appointment of Robert Reich as secretary of labor was widely viewed as a signal of his commitment to the play-or-pay proposal. Other issues, however, crowded onto the agenda. Even Reich, sensing the sea change, began advocating a consolidation of overlapping federal training programs and the channeling of the savings into vouchers for individual workers to use to purchase their own training (Wartzman, 1995). Regardless of whatever specific proposals ultimately emerge, a national debate over job training policy must grapple with many issues, including these:

- Employers face a "make-or-buy" decision with respect to securing the skills they need. While it may make perfect sense for individual employers to "buy" skills by hiring them from the outside labor market, typically away from other employers, this strategy may not be optimal from the perspective of the society as a whole.

  How employers can be encouraged to make investments in training and skill, raising the quality of the entire workforce, is a central question. A related issue is how to accommodate the special problem of small businesses whose smaller scale makes it more difficult for them to mount formal training programs.

- Training seems closely related to high-performance work organizations and other desirable forms of investment and restructuring. Whether training could—or should—be used as a lever to facilitate these other changes is an important issue.

- Among the most successful training programs are joint labor-management-sponsored training programs and unionized apprenticeship programs. These operate with minimal government assistance. How can these programs be expanded to cover more workers, and are there any equivalent arrangements that might work in the nonunion sector?

- Any government effort to intervene directly in employer-provided training raises a series of issues. Perhaps the first issue is to define what counts as training and what the minimum standards should be. What auditing and oversight mechanisms would prevent companies from operating frivolous executive boondoggles, for example, and ensure that front-line production and service workers get their fair share of company training expenditures?

Second, how should the training programs be administered? Are there alternatives to the federal or state and local bureaucracies, such as consortia of private vendors that could be subsidized to implement these programs? Should the government create assistance programs to provide companies with research, information, and advice on best practices, or should it simply stick to financial support and monitoring?

- Is it possible to concentrate incentives on employees as a means of increasing employer-provided training? Allowing employees to claim a portion of their companies' remitted funds for their individual training, low-interest loans and tax-deductible training accounts (similar to IRAs) for personalized training programs, training vouchers, and other, similar arrangements might increase work-based training and skills by creating a market for training. The problems of monitoring quality still remain, however.

- Federal training programs for displaced, disadvantaged, and unemployed workers exist independent of any efforts to encourage employer training. Whether these programs could be integrated with other employer training efforts—or, indeed, with welfare reform—is an important question.

The success or failure of national training policies that extensively involve private-sector companies, workers, and unions will depend on a solid understanding of current needs and practices and of the impediments to change. We hope that the analyses reported in this chapter contribute in some useful ways toward developing that knowledge.

5

Implications for Policy:
A "Skills Gap"?

The previous chapters in this volume have considered the forces that have driven the restructuring of employment relations and the characteristics of the new system as it is evolving. One of the more important questions raised so far is whether restructuring has changed what jobs require in ways that the workforce will find hard to meet. Is there a mismatch between what jobs will require and the skills available in the labor market?

The notion that such an imbalance may lie ahead for the U.S. economy has been an important part of recent public policy debates. Assessing the likelihood of a skills gap begins with understanding what we know about how jobs are changing and how the skills of the workforce are developing.

Jobs and Skills in the Future

What effect will the restructuring have on the kind of jobs available in the future? The effect on skill requirements is perhaps central, because skill levels are associated with important outcomes such as pay and worker control. Perceptions of changing skill levels help drive public attitudes toward education policy. The literature analyzing changes in skill requirements goes back at least to Adam Smith and takes two forms. Studies of individual jobs and occupations tend to show how technological change and management practices (scientific management in particular) "deskill" jobs through automation or other techniques; studies of the labor force as a whole show how the least skilled jobs tend to be eliminated as the distribution of employees shifts toward higher-skilled functions.

The *Workforce 2000* report (Hudson Institute, 1986) helped fuel contemporary interest in changing skill requirements in the United States by arguing that this shift toward higher-skilled jobs might outstrip the rise in educational levels, thus creating a "skills gap." Reanalyses of the data used in that original study suggest that the case for rising skill requirements may have been overstated and that a large proportion of the new jobs were predominately lower-skilled (Mishel and Teixera, 1991). An historical look at changes in the distribution of employment by Howell and Wolfe (1991) found that while there was a shift toward higher-skilled jobs in the 1980s, the rate at which employment was shifting away from lower-skilled positions was actually declining compared to previous generations.

Studies of the manufacturing sector find results consistent with the changes in work organization described in chapter 4 that push responsibility—and skills—down to lower levels of the organization. Cappelli (1993) found that skill requirements are rising for production jobs in manufacturing for two reasons: The skill levels needed for individual job titles, such as assembly work, are rising and the distribution of employment has shifted away from the simplest jobs and toward more complex ones. Berman et al. (1993) also found that employment in U.S. manufacturing has shifted toward higher-skill jobs.

Another look at the Hay data on organizational structure presented in chapter 2 suggests how restructuring is influencing skill requirements inside organizations (Cappelli and O'Shaughnessey, 1995). Figure 5.1 uses measures of the skill requirements for each job to assess how skills have changed by management level from 1986 to 1992. While skill requirements are rising marginally for jobs within each management level, the sharp reduction in middle management jobs and the expansion of lower-level positions, associated in part with the kind of employee empowerment described in chapter 4, has shifted the distribution of employment across jobs in such a way that the overall skill level in these companies has fallen sharply. This result suggests the important distinction between the trend of rising skill requirements for particular jobs and changes in the occupational structure, both of which result from the redesign of work organization.

Projections by the U.S. Bureau of Labor Statistics suggest that the number of jobs requiring a college degree will rise 39 percent between 1990 and 2005, compared to an increase of 20 percent in the overall number of jobs (General Accounting Office, 1990). But the rate of growth in these college jobs is declining sharply compared to that for the 1980s, and it is important to note that a good

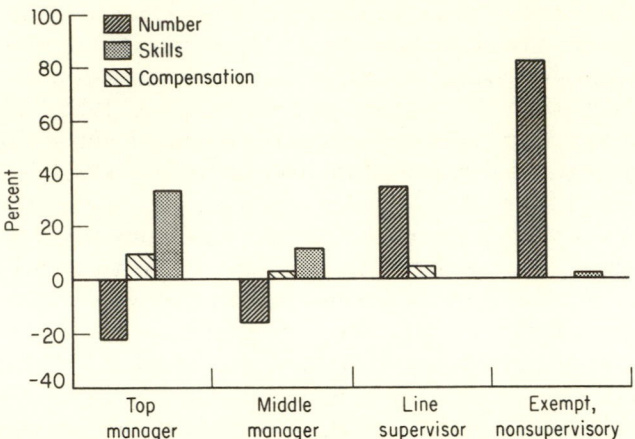

Figure 5.1. Percentage Change in Number, Skill, and Compensation. *Source:* Cappelli and O'Shaughnessey (1995).

deal of the "upgrading" of job requirements may have occurred simply because the excess supply of college graduates makes it cost-less to do: At present, only about 70 percent of college grads will find jobs that require a college degree. The rest will find positions for which they are overqualified (Shelley, 1992).

In chapter 3, it was suggested that changes in work organization may create substantial upgrading of skill requirements for front-line workers performing tasks such as production work, upgrading that sharply reduces the demand for poorly trained, unskilled employees. But the demand for highly skilled managerial jobs may well be falling because of reengineering and related changes in work organization. Whether these changes in demand will be associated with shortages at current wage levels—a "skills gap" effect—will depend on changes in the supply of skill.

One general area where demand seems to be outpacing supply is in technician jobs. Several developments appear to be behind this trend. First, the importance of applied scientific work to organizations is rising rapidly, as are the skill requirements for these jobs. Second, no coherent system exists for acquiring the skills to become a technician; even if a worker has an adequate background in the relevant scientific material, most of the truly important skills for technical jobs are work-based and can be learned only on-the-job. As traditional career paths and related aspects of internal labor markets break down, it becomes more difficult to develop informally the skills needed for technical work. Third, technicians increasingly communicate and learn from each other through networks that cut across companies. This development has contributed to a craft-like occupational structure where the outside labor market is dominant and technicians increasingly hop from company to company.[1]

The rising demand for technician skills and the lack of infrastructure for producing them is creating problems that might be seen as more extreme versions of the general changes described throughout this volume. In this case, the breakdown of the internal system for training at a time when demand is growing is creating a relative skills shortage. Whether this will happen in other work areas as well is an important question.

Employers' Needs

Another and more direct way to learn about the demand for workers' skills is to ask employers directly about the skills they need. A variety of surveys examine the skills that are needed by workers and the skills that employers report as being most difficult to find. The consensus is that employers are experiencing limited difficulty in hiring entry-level workers and somewhat greater difficulty in filling positions for more senior positions that require specific skills.[2] In general, companies report that only about 50 percent of recent high school graduate applicants are qualified for entry-level positions, although the pool of applicants is large enough to allow employers to find some good candidates. Employers are also likely to report that deficiencies in computational and problem-solving skills are among the most serious deficiencies that workers have, although inadequate writing and verbal skills are also reported to be a problem. But deficiencies in interpersonal skills and poor attitudes toward work and/or an "inability to fit in" are reported as the most important deficits among entry-level applicants.

Whether skills are deficient is a relative question; the answer depends on how the job is defined and what one expects from applicants. A job may "require" higher-order computer skills, for example, but it would seem unreasonable to expect applicants to have such skills if the job paid only minimum wage. Without knowing what employers expect from applicants, it is difficult to interpret their assessment of deficiencies among applicants. It is also difficult to know whether current complaints are more—or possibly less—significant than those at other times in U.S. history. Nevertheless, some insights can be gleaned from these surveys. For example, the employers in the National Association of Manufacturers survey that report the most serious skill deficiencies among their workers are also engaged in the most fundamental restructuring of the way their organizations operate (Cappelli and O'Shaughnessey, 1994). Analysis of data from the National Center on the Educational Quality of the Workforce (EQW) (1995) suggests that employers who see their own workforces as less proficient are the ones engaged in more

Table 5.1. **Relative Ranking of Factors in Making Hiring Decisions**

Applicant characteristics	Rank*
Applicant's attitude	4.6
Applicant's communication skills	4.2
Previous work experience	4.0
Recommendations from current employees	3.4
Previous employer recommendation	3.4
Industry-based credentials (certifying applicant's skills)	3.2
Years of completed schooling	2.9
Score on tests administered as part of the interview	2.5
Academic performance (grades)	2.5
Experience or reputation of applicant's school	2.4
Teacher recommendations	2.1

*1 = not important or considered; 5 = very important

Source: Derived from Question 57 of the National Employer Survey by the National Center on the Educational Quality of the Workforce (1995): When you consider hiring a new nonsupervisory or production worker (front-line worker), how important are the following in your decision to hire?

fundamental restructuring of work organization and technological change.[3] It may simply be the case that skill deficiencies emerge as a fundamental problem only when a company is in the midst of major change. Put another way, companies that are undergoing major restructuring of their work may require a more skilled workforce.

Why is it that businesses restructure their work if this causes skill deficiencies? The consensus from the surveys is that work restructuring is driven by imperatives that overwhelm any short-term concern about skills. A fundamental threat to survival, from increased domestic or foreign competition, seems to be what causes companies to engage in fundamental restructuring of work. The techniques for addressing these competitive challenges, such as new production technologies or systems of work organization, demand higher skills from employees.

The fact that work attitudes and behavioral skills feature so prominently in concerns about skill shortages, especially for entry-level jobs, seems to reflect two different forces. First, many entry-level jobs demand relatively few occupational skills (e.g., retail sales), making interpersonal skills and work attitudes more important. Second, team-based and other new forms of work organization increasingly make demands on workers' behavioral skills.

The Supply of Skills

Changes of the magnitude described throughout this volume do not happen without substantial disruption and turmoil. The impact has rippled through society, touching other important aspects of life in the United States, including education.

It is not coincidental that as these changes at work were unfolding, the nation's school system came under intense attack; the perception that schools had "failed" in their job of providing skills, especially skills for the workforce, became increasingly commonplace.

The 1984 report by the National Commission on Excellence in Education, *A Nation at Risk,* arguably one of the most influential reports ever published by the U.S. government, riveted the nation's attention on the skill levels of the nation's young people. Its dramatic language and the claim that "a rising tide of mediocrity threatens our very future as a nation and a people" resonated with an unspoken, and by and large unarticulated, concern that had been felt by much of the nation for more than a few years. More than a decade later, the report's findings and recommendations continue to influence debate and action across the nation's thousands of school districts.

The central premise of *A Nation at Risk* was that the U.S. school system had failed. It had failed to produce graduates who were capable of performing the simple computational, reading, and communication tasks that are required of almost every worker in every workplace in the economy. It had failed to produce even minimal levels of literacy in more than 13 percent of all seventeen-year-olds. It had failed to produce students who could measure up to their counterparts in other nations; on nineteen academic tests, U.S. students never ranked first or second and, in comparison to students in other industrialized nations, scored at the bottom on seven. The comparisons of mathematical competence and knowledge of basic scientific material are particularly striking. The one measure by which U.S. students are ranked above those of any other nation is the number of hours watching television. Students in the United States report watching an average of twenty-four hours of television per week, while students in Canada and Switzerland, for example, watch thirteen and ten hours per week, respectively (Bishop, 1990).

These comparisons do, indeed, paint a very grim picture, and even the most cursory review of them leads almost inevitably to the conclusion that the school system has failed miserably in its job of educating the nation's youth. *A Nation at Risk's* conclusions, however, are based on comparisons of achievement levels from the 1970s with levels from the 1960s. The important issue is whether the trends in poor achievement have accelerated or improved.

The high rate at which students drop out of high school has, for example, been used as evidence of the failure of the schools. And while the current dropout rates, which in some inner cities approach 50 percent, are indeed alarming, the situation has not deteriorated. In fact, dropout rates have declined. Table 5.2, which shows

Table 5.2. Percentage of High School Dropouts among Persons 16 to 24 Years Old, by Sex and Race/Ethnicity (October 1967–October 1994)

	Total				Men				Women			
Year 1	All races 2	White, non-Hispanic 3	Black, non-Hispanic 4	Hispanic origin 5	All races 6	White, non-Hispanic 7	Black, non-Hispanic 8	Hispanic origin 9	All races 10	White, non-Hispanic 11	Black, non-Hispanic 12	Hispanic origin 13
1967[2]	17.0	15.4	28.6	—	16.5	14.7	30.6	—	17.3	16.1	26.9	—
1968[2]	16.2	14.7	27.4	—	15.8	14.4	27.1	—	16.5	15.0	27.6	—
1969[2]	15.2	13.6	26.7	—	14.3	12.6	26.9	—	16.0	14.6	28.7	—
1970[2]	15.0	13.2	27.9	—	14.2	12.2	29.4	—	15.7	14.1	26.6	—
1971[2]	14.7	13.4	23.7	—	14.2	12.6	25.5	—	15.2	14.2	22.1	—
1972	14.6	12.3	21.3	34.3	14.1	11.7	22.3	33.7	15.1	12.8	20.5	34.9
1973	14.1	11.6	22.2	33.5	13.7	11.5	21.5	30.4	14.5	11.8	22.8	36.4
1974	14.3	11.9	21.2	33.0	14.2	12.0	20.1	33.8	14.4	11.8	22.1	32.2
1975	13.9	11.4	22.9	29.2	13.3	11.0	23.0	26.7	14.5	11.8	22.9	31.8
1976	14.1	12.0	20.5	31.4	14.1	12.1	21.2	30.3	14.2	11.8	19.9	32.3
1977	14.1	11.9	19.8	33.0	14.5	12.6	19.5	31.6	13.8	11.2	20.0	34.3
1978	14.2	11.9	20.2	33.3	14.6	12.2	22.5	33.6	13.9	11.6	18.3	33.1
1979	14.6	12.0	21.1	33.8	15.0	12.6	22.4	33.0	14.2	11.5	20.0	34.5
1980	14.1	11.4	19.1	35.2	15.1	12.3	20.8	37.2	13.1	10.5	17.7	33.2

1981	13.9	11.4	18.4	33.2	15.1	12.5	19.9	36.0	12.8	10.2	17.1	30.4
1982	13.9	11.4	18.4	31.7	14.5	12.1	21.2	30.5	13.3	10.9	15.9	32.8
1983	13.7	11.2	18.0	31.6	14.9	12.2	19.9	34.3	12.5	10.1	16.2	29.1
1984	13.1	11.0	15.6	29.8	14.0	12.0	16.8	30.6	12.3	10.1	14.3	29.0
1985	12.6	10.4	15.2	27.6	13.4	11.1	16.1	29.9	11.8	9.8	14.3	25.2
1986	12.2	9.7	14.2	30.1	13.1	10.3	15.0	32.8	11.4	9.1	13.5	27.2
1987	12.7	10.4	14.1	28.6	13.2	10.8	15.0	29.1	12.1	10.0	13.3	28.1
1988	12.9	9.6	14.5	35.8	13.5	10.4	15.0	36.0	12.2	8.9	14.1	35.4
1989	12.6	9.4	13.9	33.0	13.6	10.3	14.9	34.4	11.7	8.5	13.0	31.6
1990	12.1	9.0	13.2	32.4	12.3	9.3	11.9	34.3	11.8	8.7	14.4	30.3
1991	12.5	8.9	13.6	35.3	13.0	8.9	13.5	39.2	11.9	8.9	13.7	31.1
1992[3]	11.0	7.7	13.7	29.4	11.3	8.0	12.5	32.1	10.7	7.5	14.8	26.6
1993[3]	11.0	7.9	13.6	27.5	11.2	8.2	12.6	26.1	10.9	7.7	14.4	26.9
1994[3]	10.5	7.7	12.6	30.0	12.3	8.0	14.1	31.6	8.1	7.5	11.3	28.1

[1]"Status" dropouts.

[2]White and black include persons of Hispanic origin.

[3]Because of changes in data collection procedures, data may not be comparable with figures for earlier years.

—Data not available.

Note: "Status" dropouts are persons who are not enrolled in school and who are not high school graduates. People who have received GED credentials are counted as graduates. Data are based on sample surveys of the civilian noninstitutional population.

Source: National Center for Education Statistics (1995).

how high school dropout rates among those between sixteen and twenty-four years of age have varied over time, indicates steady improvement over the course of many decades. While there has been only modest improvement in school completion rates over the past two decades, there has certainly been no decline in those rates. Furthermore, among minorities, the situation has improved quite dramatically. For example, in 1973 only 71 percent of African Americans between eighteen and twenty-five years of age had completed high school; by 1990 this figure had increased to 82 percent (Bishop, 1990). At the same time, the content of high school course work has become more rigorous. From 1982 to 1992, for example, the percentage of high school graduates whose course work included the number of "core" academic subjects recommended by the U.S. Department of Education rose from 13 to 47 percent (*Condition of Education*, 1994).

Evidence from the Iowa Test of Basic Skills finds improvements in achievement among minorities as well. While white students have experienced only a very modest gain in their test scores on basic skills, minority students' test scores have demonstrated a fairly steady improvement over the past two decades. And the National Assessment of Educational Progress, an essay-based achievement test, shows improved scores for all age groups from 1982 to 1992 (*Condition of Education*, 1994).

Nor does the evidence on the achievements of those who have completed high school reveal any deterioration in the skill levels of young people in the United States. The Scholastic Aptitude Test (SAT) offers one of the only measures of student achievement that has been consistently collected over time. Table 5.3, which shows how SAT scores have varied over time for a variety of racial and ethnic groups, indicates that with the exception of whites, every racial group's performance on the SAT improved between 1975 and 1994.

The much discussed decline in the average SAT score during the early 1970s appears to have been caused in large part by a change in the composition of the student group taking the test, rather than an absolute deterioration in students' abilities. Since a greater percentage of all high school seniors (and, therefore, a less educationally elite group) have chosen to take the SAT exam with each passing year, the average SAT scores would have increased more than they actually did during the 1980s had the percentage of all students taking the exam remained constant (Bracey, 1992). In other words, the performance of students with average ability on the SAT exam has probably risen.

Tables 5.2 and 5.3 taken together indicate that the school system has not failed. In fact, these data indicate just the opposite—the

Table 5.3. Scholastic Aptitude Test Score Averages by Race/Ethnicity: 1975–1976 to 1993–1994

Racial/ethnic background	1975–76	1977–78	1978–79	1979–80	1980–81	1981–82	1982–83	1983–84	1984–85	1986–87	1987–88	1988–89	1989–90	1990–91	1991–92	1992–93	1993–94
1	2	3	4	5	6	7	8	9	10	11	12	13	14	15	16	17	18
SAT-Verbal																	
All students	431	429	427	424	424	426	425	426	431	430	428	427	424	422	423	424	423
White	451	448	444	442	442	444	443	445	449	447	445	446	442	441	442	444	443
Black	332	332	330	330	332	341	339	342	346	351	353	351	352	351	352	353	352
Mexican-American	371	370	370	372	373	377	375	376	382	379	382	381	380	377	372	374	372
Puerto Rican	364	349	345	350	353	360	358	358	368	360	355	360	359	381	388	387	367
Asian-American	414	401	396	396	397	398	395	396	404	405	408	409	410	411	413	415	416
American Indian	388	387	388	390	391	388	386	390	392	393	393	384	388	393	395	400	396
Other	410	399	393	394	388	392	386	386	391	405	410	414	410	411	417	422	425
SAT-Mathematical																	
All students	472	468	487	485	486	487	486	471	475	476	476	476	476	474	476	478	479
White	493	485	483	482	483	483	484	487	490	489	490	491	491	489	491	494	495
Black	354	354	358	360	362	386	389	373	376	377	384	386	385	385	385	388	388
Mexican-American	410	402	410	413	415	416	417	420	426	424	428	430	429	427	425	428	427
Puerto-Rican	401	388	388	394	398	403	403	405	409	400	402	406	405	406	406	409	411
Asian-American	518	510	511	509	513	513	514	519	518	521	522	525	528	530	532	535	535
American Indian	420	419	421	426	425	424	425	427	428	432	435	428	437	437	442	447	441
Other	458	450	447	449	447	449	448	450	448	455	460	467	467	468	473	477	480

Note: Possible scores on each part of the SAT range from 200 to 800. No racial/ethnic group data are available prior to 1975–76. No data are available for 1985–86 due to changes in the Student Description Questionnaire completed when students registered for the test.

Source: National Center for Education Statistics (1995).

system seems to be doing at least marginally better than it was twenty years ago. And the percentage of high school graduates who go on to some form of higher education has also risen, from about 47 percent in 1972 to about 62 percent in 1992, suggesting an even greater expansion of the education-based skills and knowledge of the workforce (National Center for Educational Statistics, 1993).

What this assessment of the school system's performance does not reveal, however, is the variation in the experiences of the young people within it. While hard evidence is difficult to come by, many analysts believe that the real "failing" of the U.S. education system can be found in the difference in achievement between those who are bound for universities and those who complete high school but do not go on to any form of postsecondary education.

In every nation, it is certainly the case that those students who pursue advanced education have typically done better in schools than those students who do not. These differences in achievement, however, are believed to be especially pronounced in the United States. Consider, for example, a mathematics test that was administered to students at the beginning and the end of the school year. Among Japanese students, the difference in test scores between those scoring well below average and those scoring well above average at the beginning of the school year was reduced by the end of the school year. For U.S. students, however, the difference between students at the bottom and those at the top at the beginning of the school year was much larger by the end of the school year (Bracey, 1992). In other words, the U.S. system seems to increase the inequality in student performance.

Most telling perhaps on the issue of inequality is that the United States spends a small percentage of its educational resources on those who do not go on to college, and this percentage is much smaller than that spent in other nations. While the United States spends .03 percent of its gross domestic product on programs designed to help youth in the labor market, for example, West Germany spends twice that amount in relative terms (Organisation for Economic Co-operation and Development, 1988). Even in primary and secondary school, U.S. students have fewer resources devoted to them: the United States spends 14 percent less than Germany, 30 percent less than Japan, and 51 percent less than Switzerland (Berliner, 1993).

These statistics are particularly troubling, given that completing a college education in the United States remains the exception, rather than the rule. Eighty-six percent of young people complete high school or have earned a general equivalence degree (GED) by the time they are in their late twenties; 62 percent of those who have completed high school go on to postsecondary schooling; but only

45 percent of those students complete four years of college by the time they are 30 (National Center for Education Statistics, 1991). If these percentages remain constant over the next decade, only 23 percent of the current crop of high school freshmen will earn a four-year college degree by their late twenties.

Many analysts of the education system believe that it is unrealistic to expect that the percentage of young people completing college can be increased substantially beyond its current level. Among other issues, expanding participation in higher education is an expensive way to raise average education in the labor force, and real improvement in the education system can be achieved only by improving outcomes for the vast majority of young people who do not graduate from college.

U.S. schools have not, in fact, "failed." Rather, the changes at work have resulted in a growing need for workers who can adapt well to a rapidly changing work environment, learn and implement new technologies, and even change occupations when necessary. It is the increase in the demand for these types of traits—traits that are more common among highly educated individuals than among those with low education levels—that has led to the growing dissatisfaction with the nation's secondary school system.

Although the need for flexible and adaptable workers has grown, the supply of them has not, despite modest improvements in school performance. Consequently, the highly educated have, in general, fared relatively well in the labor market, while the less well educated have suffered.

From School to Work

Perhaps the most obvious evidence of a serious mismatch between the demand for and the supply of skills operates at the intersection between school and work where school leavers enter the labor market. This mismatch appears as higher jobless rates for school leavers and long periods of dead-end jobs. The unemployment rate for youth ages 16 to 19 is as much as three times higher than that for the population as a whole, and there is some evidence that this ratio may be increasing. In 1986, for example, when the overall unemployment rate was 7 percent, the rate for those ages 16 to 19 was 18.3 percent; in 1993, when the overall rate was somewhat lower—6.8 percent—the youth rate was higher—19 percent—despite a relative decline in the number of people in the 16–19 age group associated with the passing of the baby boom (*Monthly Labor Review*, 1986, 1994).

The United States has a very weak—some might argue nonexistent—system for facilitating students' transition from school to work.

While society's post–high school investment in college students is substantial, virtually nothing is invested in those individuals who do not attend college (General Accounting Office, 1990). Most of the post-school investment that is made in the noncollege-bound is remedial in nature, such as Job Corps or some other form of government-provided "second-chance" education or training program. Evaluations of these programs, however, have been unable to find any evidence that the programs really help students acquire labor market skills or make the transition from school to work (see, e.g., Long, Mallar, and Thorton, 1981). As a result, the process of making this transition is a difficult and awkward one for the majority of the nation's noncollege graduates.[4]

The process seems to be less problematic in other nations. In Japan, for example, approximately half of all of those leaving the school system find jobs with employers that have traditionally made a lifetime guarantee of employment.[5] In Germany, the vast majority of those young people who do not attend a university are enrolled in an extensive apprenticeship program that spans the course of several years and makes the transition from school to work much less disruptive than it is in the United States.

This is not to say that these nations have not also had difficulties with their labor markets. In recent years, German unemployment rates have been high relative to those in the United States. But even when the German labor market is slack, the transition from school to work is not as problematic there as it is in the United States.

For school leavers in the United States, finding a job at all is hard enough, but the real problems concern the type of jobs that they find. The best way to describe the labor market experience for these workers is as a kind of "churning," where they move from one low-wage, low-training job to another. By the time they reach age 30, only about 55 percent of high school graduates are in jobs that they have held for more than two years; only 28 percent of high school dropouts have jobs with that level of tenure (Osterman, 1993), and half have held their current jobs for less than a year (Burtless, 1993).

The lack of career opportunities and employer investment in these young workers contributes to their high turnover rates, and the high turnover rates then discourage employers from investing in these workers, creating a vicious cycle. Minimal investment in young workers by employers may be both the cause and the consequence of high turnover. These young workers, with their high turnover rates and skill levels that appear to be increasingly deficient, eventually turn into mature workers and become the nation's workforce.

Another aspect of the school-to-work problem is the lack of a relationship between performance in school and success in the labor market. Except for students who are bound for a university education, "success" in school does not seem to help one get a good job (Bishop, 1990). Recent research suggests that superior academic skills have essentially no payoff when students enter the labor market, presumably because the kind of "dead-end" jobs available to them make no use of those skills. These skills begin to earn higher wages for workers after the workers have spent about six years in the labor force, presumably when they have finally found jobs that make greater demands on them (Murnane, Willett, and Levy, 1993; Bishop, 1992). Evidence suggesting that skill deficits are greater for workers who have been with their employers longer—when skill demands have increased—supports this point (Cappelli and Rogovsky, 1994).

Getting the credential of a high school diploma does have an important effect on a student's labor market success. But while getting good grades, taking difficult classes, and attending school on a regular basis are all very important for those students who are headed toward college, research indicates that exemplary behavior and achievement in school make very little difference—at least initially—in the earnings and the employment prospects of those who go directly to work.

It appears that at least part of the explanation for the lack of relationship between school performance and initial success in the labor market is attributable to the fact that most entry-level jobs have traditionally demanded so little from workers in terms of skill. Another explanation for the relatively small relationship over the long run turns on the absence of any universally agreed-upon skill standards or nationalized tests to measure performance. Those who do well in school but do not go on to college have no reliable method for communicating the relevant accomplishments of their school years to prospective employers. Wages rise years later when workplace situations finally make evidence of their skills obvious to employers. As a result, the labor market does not reward those accomplishments. If this explanation is correct, then the "failure" of the schools is that they are irrelevant to the majority of the students in them, providing them with no payoff for hard work and learning.

Some observers claim that it has long been the case that success in secondary school was largely unrelated to success in the labor market. In the bygone era when growth in manufacturing based on a mass-production technology fueled an ever-rising standard of living in the United States, basic literacy was all that was required of the majority of workers. Under these circumstances, the schools were "successful" as long as they managed to instill minimal skills and discipline in the majority of students.

The appearance of "failure" among schools coincides with the decline of the mass production era and its low demand for skills. While schools continue to do what they have always done, that may no longer be enough to ensure that students have a secure future in the labor market. The changes in work organization and employment relations have together created a slow but steadily growing need for those leaving school to possess more than minimum basic skills. At the same time, the mechanisms inside companies for developing unskilled workers into trained employees appear to have declined, shifting the burden of providing skills increasingly onto schools. Whether they can—or even should—be asked to cope with the need for higher skills in the entering workforce, especially work-based skills that are best learned on the job, is an open question.

Employer Choices

If the "skills gap" issues discussed in this chapter are in large measure the result of restructuring efforts that have raised skill requirements, then employer choices as to how they restructure work may be able to influence some of these issues, such as how best to help school leavers gain access to the labor market. The growing supply of potential workers whose education and skills are relatively inadequate, which manifests itself in declining real wages and increasing unemployment, may even provide employers with options on how they organize work. At least some employers may find it more advantageous to choose systems of work organization that make greater use of such workers. Almost everyone has seen the cash registers that have pictures on them, rather than numbers, allowing the registers to be used effectively by cashiers with limited numerical skills. While it takes time and money to create such technologies, there can be a payoff since they enable companies to hire minimum-wage workers.

Employers who invest in technology that allows less skilled workers to perform jobs with greater value added might generally be applauded for helping to put such workers into jobs and for raising productivity.[6] The more troubling issue arises when employers fail to adopt new technologies or innovate because they are concerned about whether their workers have adequate skills to use them. If companies have responded to "skill shortages" by failing to adopt new technologies that would require greater basic skills of workers, then the result could well be a decline in overall economic performance and in the real wage levels of many workers.

A number of recent surveys have asked employers directly whether or not they have changed the content of jobs in order to accommodate workers with inadequate basic skills (which would amount to dumbing down jobs). Very few companies say that they are investing in techniques that would enable them to use less-skilled labor. But there is evidence that employers do adapt aspects of work organization to the characteristics of their labor forces; employers who employ more working mothers, for example, have more flexible hours in order to tap that supply of workers (Sherer, 1992). There is ample historical evidence that employers have introduced technology and work systems to reduce the level of skill required of workers and thus their wages. But there is also evidence that upskilling is greater where workers are overall in shorter supply and average wages are rising (Cappelli, 1993), perhaps because skilled workers are a means of economizing on total labor.

Cheapening the cost of skill might reduce the incentives to introduce these deskilling techniques. But it is difficult to make the case that cheapening skill per se could lead to production choices that require higher skills. Employers do not choose production systems from a clear continuum of choices. Often a technology is so dominant that the price of skill is essentially irrelevant. Secretaries, for example, would have to work virtually for free to make typing positions economically competitive with word-processing technology. New technologies tend to revolutionize functions so thoroughly that old jobs simply become obsolete.

The current move toward high-performance work systems, perhaps the work system most associated with higher skills, is based on the notion of tapping knowledge that the workforce already has— skills that are basically free. It is difficult to see how any further cheapening of workforce skill will matter much to that transformation. On the other hand, the skills needed to tap worker knowledge, such as general communications and interpersonal skills, may be in short supply, as are the management skills associated with operating under these new arrangements. There is some evidence that higher skills may make it easier to adopt new technology and otherwise innovate (Bartel and Sicherman, 1993).

The policy consequences that come from increasing the supply of skills are complex. They include, for example, lowering the relative wages for skilled workers. Paradoxically, they may also include a reduction in some of the incentives for employers to introduce participative management; one of the reasons for pushing tasks down onto front-line workers is to reduce the need for high-priced supervisors, a need that declines if supervision becomes cheaper. These arguments suggest that more powerful forces for change are likely to come from the demand side. Changes in skill demands driven by the decision to introduce new management techniques or workplace organization can raise skill requirements dramatically and create a demand for skills and training. Helping employers to adopt new work systems seems therefore to be a point of considerable leverage for intervention. Some programs to facilitate the adoption of new work systems, such as the technical assistance programs run by the U.S. Department of Commerce for manufacturers, have the potential to exert considerable leverage.

The choices concerning work organization often come down not so much to changing tasks as to determining who will perform them. When numerically controlled machines were introduced in manufacturing, for example, the important issue was whether the programming of these machines would be handled by the machinists themselves or by the industrial engineers. In practice, the determination seems to have been based on issues of bargaining power between the two groups associated with trade union influence (Kelley, 1989). Changing the supply of skill here would simply change the relative price of engineers and machinists, shifting the programming task back and forth between them.

While few employers appear to be deliberately dumbing down their work, many more, as described in chapter 3, indicate that they are restructuring work to use more fully the capacity that their workforces possess. In other words, an option besides introducing technology that allows employers to substitute low-paid, low-education workers for highly paid, high-education workers is to change what it is that the highly paid workers do.

Once companies make these changes and increase what jobs require of workers, they can be expected to change their hiring practices in an attempt to screen out more effectively those individuals who do not have the prerequisite skills or abilities. Recent survey results indicate, for example, that many businesses report that they intend to change their hiring strategies because of their increasing awareness of the relationship between the basic skills of their workers and the company's ability to compete (Cappelli and O'Shaughnessey, 1995).

One of the implications of a strategy of shifting to more skilled workers is that if it is pursued by enough companies, the wage premiums for highly educated, skilled workers will become even more pronounced as employers more aggressively pursue these workers. Another implication, suggested elsewhere in this volume, is that employers who increasingly rely on hiring to meet their skill needs will also have to rely more on firing to make room for the new workers when they come in.

The alternative strategy is obviously to develop skills inside the organization, to invest in training and related programs that raise skills and retrain workers as skill needs change. The difficulty with this strategy is that developments in the labor market outside the company are pulling in the opposite direction: If other employers increasingly hire from the outside, and if employees who see their careers as spanning many different companies increasingly hop from job to job, then the ability of any employer to hold onto a worker it has trained declines. And when employee retention falls, so does the ability to recoup training investments. The new work systems that get rid of traditional job and promotion ladders also make it more difficult to develop skills from within (see chapter 7).

Employers who want to pursue the alternative strategy of investing in employees therefore need to address the problem of recouping training costs. A typical solution to this problem is to find ways for employees to share in the costs of training. Particularly for general skills where all the benefits eventually accrue to workers, it seems both efficient and fair that workers should help pay for that training. As noted in chapter 7, however, the current wage and hour laws in the United States prohibit employees from paying for training that is required for their current jobs. An alternative is to pay lower wages to workers who receive general skills training, an approach associated with apprenticeship programs. Whether it is efficient for companies to provide general skills training, even at reduced wages, depends on how well their systems of work organization can combine productive work and learning. In other words, can they secure something productive from those employees who are receiving training?

There are many occupations where work and learning are effectively combined. Medical students serving internships and residencies are classic examples that benefit from licensing rules that prohibit practicing without having completed these training periods. But there are also examples from occupations that are far less regulated. Management consulting and accounting firms, for example, get great value from new entrants at relatively low wages, first, because they organize tasks so that work and learning go easily together (i.e., team projects with close supervision) and, second, because the junior workers know that the experience they gain will have a big payoff in the labor market.

The survey evidence indicates that those companies that have embarked on a path of considerable work restructuring are precisely the companies that are most likely to be simultaneously implementing a workplace education program that is sponsored and paid for by the company. While there is preliminary evidence that this strategy can be a profitable one, that evidence is based on a self-selected group of innovative businesses that have led the way (see, e.g., Mavrinac, Jones, and Meyer, 1994). Diffusion of this strategy among large numbers of more typical employers might produce

results very different from those it has generated among the selected few.

Notes

1. These arguments are developed in Barley (1992).

2. Although all of the surveys summarized here have been done within
the past few years, it is likely that some variation in the responses is due to
the timing of the surveys. A survey that was conducted in mid-1990 (prior to
the onset of the recession), for example, is likely to conclude that employers
were reporting more difficulty in finding the skilled workers that they
needed than would a comparable survey conducted during mid-1991 (in the
midst of the recession). Furthermore, the surveys differed in focus and
scope. One of the surveys, for example, focused exclusively on large, unionized companies, while another focused primarily on small employers. Each
of the surveys was designed with a somewhat different emphasis. One was
intended to produce information on human resource policies, another focused on labor-management relations, and still another on education policy
within companies.

3. These are preliminary results from the National Employer Survey
(NES) analysis reported in National Center on the Educational Quality of
the Workforce (1995).

4. While this statement certainly applies to many graduates of the nation's university system as well, individuals in this fortunate group at least
find themselves at the top of the hiring queue.

5. This system has had serious drawbacks, perhaps the most substantial being the almost total exclusion of women from it. Furthermore, many
analysts point to pressures that are likely to reduce the guarantees that large
Japanese corporations are able to offer to their employees (Komiyo, 1991).
This prospect does not, however, diminish the significance of these practices in the past.

6. Such employers have also been criticized, however, for having a less
altruistic motive. The de-skilling of manufacturing work during the early
part of the twentieth century did make it possible to employ waves of often
unskilled immigrants. But it forced down wages in the process and helped
break down the control that skilled workers had over their jobs. How much
of the deskilling was designed to increase control over workers by making
them expendable is an open question.

6

The Effect of Restructuring
on Employees

The focus of this chapter is the important question of how the restructuring of employer-employee relations that has been occurring throughout the U.S. labor market is affecting employees. At least in the short run, it seems that employees are bearing many of the adjustment costs associated with restructuring.

The problem facing those who wish to examine the consequences of restructuring for employees is the great difficulty of securing information specifically about employees in organizations that have undergone restructuring or related changes. As a result, we must often rely on data drawn from the labor force as a whole.

The difficulty with generic labor force data is that they may understate the consequences of changing employment practices on employees because only a part of the labor force is in companies that have made these changes. The kind of organizational restructuring, downsizings, work reform, and training programs described in the earlier chapters of this book are mainly features of larger organizations. Smith (1988) calculates, for example, that the kind of job evaluation systems that were integral to internal labor markets are not cost effective in organizations with fewer than about 500 employees. Yet the majority of the U.S. labor force works in establishments of fewer than fifty employees, often with very informal structures and arrangements that could not be restructured in the manner described in earlier chapters. So the kind of changes associated with large companies would have to be very dramatic in order to change labor market data on the labor force as a whole.

But there are other reasons for paying attention to labor market data. Labor is arguably the most important of all markets in the economy, generating nearly three quarters of all income (*Economic Report of the President*, 1990). Because of the centrality of the labor market to the nation's economic well-being, its outcomes shape Americans' individual and collective understanding of whether the country is on the "right track." Changes in the labor market shape not only the average experience on outcomes like wages and unemployment but also the distribution of those outcomes in the society as a whole.

Trends in Unemployment

Perhaps the change in employee outcomes most identified with the new employment relationship is the apparent difficulty in finding jobs and the lack of job security once one has a job. Figure 6.1 indicates that overall, the unemployment rate has been trending slightly upward for many years for both white-collar and blue-collar jobs. In 1967, at the peak of a business cycle, the unemployment rate was 3.8 percent; in 1989, also a peak year in the business cycle, unemployment was 5.3 percent.

While the rate of unemployment clearly cycles up and down with changes in the macroeconomy, there has been an unmistakable upward trend also in the duration of unemployment spells. Taken together with the higher average level of unemployment, this indicates an increase in the degree of dislocation in the labor market— an increase in the difficulty that workers experience matching the skills they possess with the skills that are demanded of them.

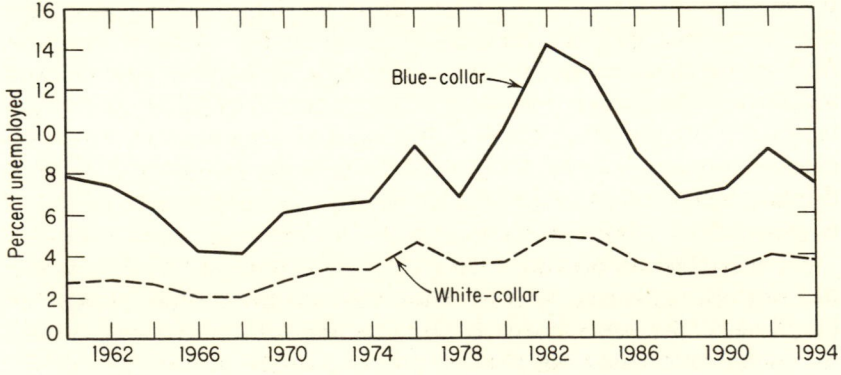

Figure 6.1.   White- and Blue-Collar Unemployment Rates, 1960–1994.

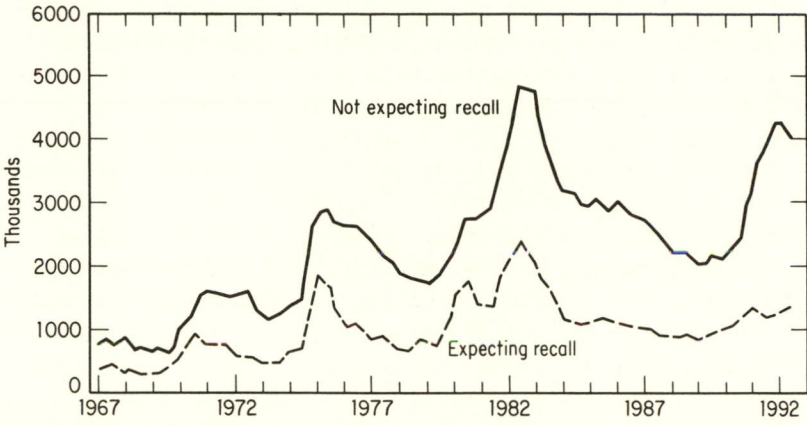

Figure 6.2. Unemployed Job Losers by Recall Status, 1967–1992. *Source:* Nardone et al. (1993).

These problems are most pronounced for those with the lowest levels of education and labor market experience. The probability of experiencing a long spell of unemployment after being laid off from one's job is greatest for those who are newest to the labor market and those who have the least formal education (Advisory Council on Unemployment Compensation, 1994). While education and skills are not synonymous, there is a very important link between an individual's education and what ultimately happens to that individual in the labor market.

An aspect of unemployment that helps illustrate the changing prospects for job security is the increase in the percentage of layoffs from which workers cannot expect to be recalled. In previous decades, layoffs were typically associated with business cycles and recessions; production workers in particular were laid off until business improved and then recalled, generally in the order of seniority. As Figure 6.2 indicates, however, beginning in the early 1980s, more and more layoffs were permanent, creating displaced workers. And in the 1990s, the proportion of layoffs that are permanent has increased further. Ninety percent of the increase in unemployment during the recession of the late 1980s and early 1990s was the result of permanent job losses (Nardone et al., 1993).

This figure compares to estimates as low as 40 percent for previous recessions, when more workers could expect to be recalled from layoffs (Mishel and Bernstein, 1992). The U.S. Bureau of Labor Statistics estimates suggest that only 15 percent of those laid off in the 1992–1993 recession could expect to be recalled, compared to about 44 percent in the previous four recessions. And half of those who eventually found new jobs in the most recent recession had to change industries to do so (Gardner, 1993). Farber (1993) found that those who have been permanently displaced are more likely to end up in part-time jobs, if they are employed.

Layoffs and Job Security

Job security might best be measured as one's risk of being laid off, and the evidence suggests that this risk is high and has increased. A quick review of the kind of downsizing described in detail in chapter 2 helps set the stage for this discussion. A survey by Louis Harris and Associates (1991) found that roughly 50 percent of the companies surveyed had laid off "substantial" numbers of employees during the previous five years; a survey of employers in 1993 found that 72 percent had implemented layoffs in the previous three years (Wyatt Company, 1993). The Family and Work Survey, a national probability survey of individuals who were employed full-time, found that 42 percent of all employees reported that their companies had a downsizing in 1993. Twenty-eight percent of the companies had a specific cutback in management, and 18 percent were involved in a merger or acquisition. All of these restructurings were more prevalent among larger businesses; 40 percent of those with more than 500 employees had management cutbacks, for example, and 28 percent had a merger or acquisition (Galinsky et al., 1993).

Forty-seven percent of the 8,000 companies included in the American Management Association's (AMA) annual survey of employers concerning personnel practices reported that in 1992–1993 they had had a reduction in force, about the same percentage as in 1991–1992, but the cuts were even deeper, representing 10.4 percent of the workforces compared to 9.3 percent in 1991–1992. The percentage of companies planning to downsize actually rose between 1993 and 1994. The surveys also found that workforce reductions are increasingly "strategic or structural in nature," rather than a response to short-term economic conditions (AMA, 1994) and that layoffs are increasingly targeted at white-collar and managerial jobs. While salaried employees held roughly 40 percent of all jobs in 1993–1994, they accounted for 62 percent of all the jobs cut. The number of supervisory positions eliminated as a percentage of all jobs that were cut doubled between 1990–1991 and 1993–1994 to 26 percent (AMA, 1994).

Nor are these layoffs limited to low-seniority workers. The Health and Retirement Survey, a national probability survey of individuals over age 55 conducted by the Institute of Social Research, reports that 15 percent of those polled had been laid off from jobs where they had at least ten years' seniority. Forty-seven percent of those who left employment took advantage of an "early-out" offer;

only about half of the 30 percent of men who reported having no current job were retired (Gustman et al., 1995).

It is difficult to know how these figures compare to earlier periods because there appear to have been no systematic efforts to survey companies about downsizing (as opposed to cyclical layoffs) before the 1980s. The displaced worker surveys conducted by the U.S. Bureau of Labor Statistics (BLS) suggest something about trends in layoffs during the 1980s, however. BLS defines displacement as permanent job loss for workers who have had at least three years' experience with their employer. A comparison of the surveys conducted so far reveals that the rate of displacement was highest in the 1979–1983 period—8.5 percent of employees lost a job permanently during that period—then declined somewhat to 6.4 percent in 1985–1989 but rose again between 1987 and 1991 to reach 7.9 percent. Displacement in the 1980s does not appear to be a short-term phenomenon.

In the early 1980s, durable manufacturing accounted for the largest share of all displacements—49 percent—but this figure had fallen to 34.5 percent by the end of the decade (Gardner, 1993). The abolition of one's shift—associated with reengineering and "thinning" the organization—has increased the most as a cause of displacement since the 1990 survey (Farber, 1995). Partly because the distribution of employment has been shifting toward white-collar work (1989–1991), this was the first recession in which more white-collar workers were laid off than blue-collar. And the category of jobs containing executive, administrative, and managerial positions experienced the largest increase in displacements among white-collar jobs.

Other studies of individuals have reported a sharp increase in layoffs compared to earlier periods. Medoff (1993) found that the proportion of prime-age male workers (ages 35–54) who were permanently displaced from their jobs almost doubled between the 1970s and the early 1990s. Displacement among college graduates, for example, was 18 percent higher in 1990–1991 than in 1982–1983.[1] Using data from the Panel Study of Income Dynamics (PSID), Boisjoly, Duncan, and Smeeding (1994) found that job losses were higher between 1980 and 1992 than between 1968 and 1979, even for older and more educated workers. Job losses were also somewhat higher over the period for white-collar workers. Overall, they found that the percentage of people laid off rose by one third during this period, while the percentage fired doubled.

Job Tenure

How long an employee and employer stay together is another measure of job security. If there is an overall decline in job security in the United States, we might expect to see a reduction in the average length of time that an employee spends with an employer, other things equal.

There are problems in using job tenure to proxy job security, however. Job tenure is a consequence of employee turnover, which, in turn, is driven both by employer separations (layoffs and firings) and by employee quits. The quit rate has generally been roughly twice the employee separation rate and varies mainly with the availability of jobs in the labor market. We think of job security typically as referring to the ability of an employee to remain if he or she wants to and therefore to the probability of layoffs and firings, not quits. Tracking changes in job tenure rolls quits and separations together and, as a result, may not be the best measure of changes in job security. Furthermore, because layoffs and quits are inversely related, they build stability into turnover over time and, as a result, into average tenure: When layoffs are up, quits are down, and total turnover remains more or less the same.

Changes in employee tenure nevertheless indicate something about whether the attachment between employer and employee is changing. Among the recent empirical work, Swinnerton and Wial (1995) observed a substantial overall reduction in job tenure in the United States since the mid-1970s. Using similar data from the Current Population Survey (CPS) and arguably better techniques, both Diebold, Neumark, and Polsky (1995) and Farber (1995) reported that overall rates of job tenure were remarkably constant over the same period. Using longitudinal data from the Panel Study on Income Dynamics (PSID) and a question that is less susceptible to error (explicit job change as opposed to months of tenure in current job),[2] Gottschalk and Moffitt (1994), Marcotte (1995), and Rose (1995) all found a substantial increase in the frequency of job changes for men in the 1980s compared to the 1970s. The data from the PSID indicate that both employer separations and quits increased over this period.

A simple overall picture of job stability seems hard to capture, but even the CPS results showing overall job stability indicate important changes for some subgroups. Because women are now less likely to quit their jobs when they get married or have children (Wellington, 1993), for example, their job tenure is increasing for reasons that reflect—in part—changes in their behavior. Changes in the tenure of men would seem to be more indicative of a change in the nature of employers' relationship with employees—and average tenure for men in all of the studies except Diebold, Neumark, and Polsky (1995) showed some overall decline over time. In addition, demographic changes that have occurred since the 1970s have been operating to raise tenure in the workforce,[3] so the fact that overall tenure for men seems to be falling suggests that some other, very powerful development has been operating in the other direction, such as declining employer attachment.

Even the studies that show aggregate stability find that the decline in tenure for less educated men has been substantial. For those with less than a high school education, average tenure has fallen by a full year as compared to twenty years ago, and the probability of remaining in a job less than one year rose 6 percent (Farber, 1995). Older white men, the group historically most protected by internal labor markets, have seen their job stability decline (Marcotte, 1994), and there has also been a fairly sizable decline in retention rates for those with less than six years in their current jobs, for blue-collar workers and for those in goods-producing industries (Diebold, Neumark, and Polsky, 1995).[4] These results seem consistent with earlier arguments that entry-level jobs are less secure, especially for young, less-educated workers in whom employers are less likely to invest.

Rose's (1995) study, which follows the same cohort over time and focuses on prime-age men, showed a particularly dramatic, overall decline in job stability. The percentage of men with "weak" employer attachment (with the same employer less than five out of the past ten years) doubled from the 1970s to the 1980s to 24 percent. When workers were asked about staying in the same occupation as opposed to remaining with the same employer, however, the results suggested remarkable stability in the two periods; 4 percent of these men had "weak" attachment to an occupation in the 1970s, a figure that rose only one percentage point to 5 percent for the 1990s. Not only was the attachment to an occupation stronger, but the gap between workers' attachment to their employers and to their occupations grew sharply. While workers were much more likely to change employers in the 1980s, they were likely to keep their occupations. Bishop (1994) reported a similar finding using CPS data.

This change in apparent career prospects is not lost on employees, who manifest relatively low levels of commitment to their current employer. Despite the fact that middle management jobs seem to be taking the biggest cuts and although the prospects for job security as a middle manager certainly seem poor, this group of employees exhibits with the highest commitment to current employers, as indicated in Figure 6.3. The reason appears to be that they have no place to go; no one is hiring middle managers.

A Yankelovich survey of individuals (*Time*, 1993) found that 66 percent of respondents believed that job security was worse than it had been two years earlier; 53 percent believed that the decline in job security was permanent (with 10 percent unsure). The Family and Work survey reported that 17 percent of employees believed

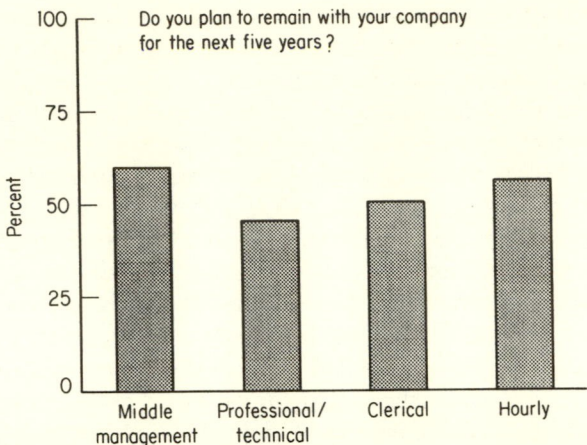

Figure 6.3. Employee Commitment. *Source:* Hay Research for Management.

that they would be permanently laid off within the next year (Galinsky et al., 1993).

Temporary Jobs

As noted in chapter 2, the rise of contingent work has been an important component of the restructuring of employment. While contingent workers may give an employer added flexibility, from the perspective of the employee contingent work creates real insecurity for those forced to accept part-time jobs despite a desire to work full-time. Involuntary part-time work is the category that distinguishes those who would like to work full-time but cannot find a position from those who have chosen part-time work. Another way to think about involuntary part-time workers is that they are partially unemployed.

Some estimates suggest that the number of involuntary part-time workers averages almost two thirds again the number of unemployed (Mishel and Bernstein, 1992). Approximately 4 percent of U.S. workers are in this involuntary part-time category. Of the twenty industrialized countries that form the Organization of Economic Cooperation and Development (OECD), only the Netherlands reports a higher figure despite overall levels of unemployment that are considerably higher (*Employment Outlook,* 1993). Three quarters of the part-time workforce would rather have full-time jobs (Mishel and Bernstein, 1993). Leete and Schor (1994) calculated that the total of all those who would like to work more hours but are unable to do so (involuntary part-timers and the unemployed) as a group rose from 7.2 percent of the labor force in 1969 to 14.5 percent in 1989. Other estimates suggest that modest increases have occurred since then (Nardone et al., 1993).

Temporary help represents an important component of part-time work. In a Yankelovich poll (*Daily Labor Report,* 1993) of employers, a majority reported that they had never considered replacing permanent jobs with temporary workers, but another 34 percent had already begun to hire temps without paying them employee benefits. The Wyatt Company survey found that 21 percent of employers were using temps in place of permanent workers (Wyatt Company, 1993). For workers, temporary help may now represent an important port of entry to a permanent job. In a 1994 survey conducted by the National Association of Temporary Services (NATS) (1994a), 76 percent of temporary workers believed that temporary help is "a way to get a full-time job," and this belief was an important factor in their decision to become temps. Thirty-eight percent had been offered full-time jobs at the organizations to which they were assigned. As noted in chapter 5, now that the level of initial training has declined for young workers, temporary help agencies may be one of the most important avenues for new entrants to learn skills. About 30 percent of temporary workers received twenty or more hours of formal training from their agency (NATS, 1994b).

Wages

Many of the changes associated with restructured employment would be better tolerated if jobs delivered high standards of living for employees. Many employees are willing to work longer hours or trade off other aspects of their jobs for higher pay. Perhaps the main factor attracting attention to the employment picture is the fact that real wages have been declining since the early 1970s (see Figure 6.4). The factors associated with that decline clearly predate the current restructuring of employment and lagging productivity as well as the entry of the baby boom cohort and the increasing participation of women in the labor force, both of which depressed wages by raising the supply of labor. The decline of real wages continues to affect the generation of workers who entered the labor force after 1970 (Levy, 1988) even as they enter middle age.

While the slowdown in the growth of compensation has occurred in all major industrialized countries, the relative decline has been sharpest in the United States, as indicated in Figure 6.5, which includes benefits and wages in its measure of compensation per person.

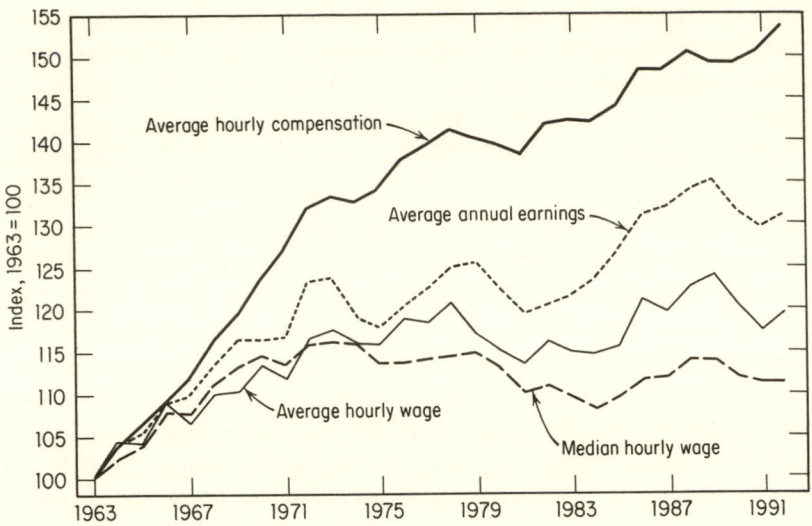

Figure 6.4. Growth in Various Measures of Real Pay. *Note:* CPI-U-X1 is used as the deflator. *Source: Economic Report of the President* (1995).

Women's experience with earnings growth has been somewhat different from that of men. As the social barriers to employment have eroded for women, employment opportunities have increased, especially for those with substantial work experience or a college education. In 1973, for example, women's median hourly wages in real terms averaged about 65 percent of men's. By 1993, that ratio had climbed to 78.2 percent. While the real median hourly wage for men declined by more than 10 percent in the 1980s, it rose by almost 5 percent for women (Mishel and Bernstein, 1994).

The biggest factor contributing to poverty in the United States appears to be low wage rates, not unemployment or involuntary part-time employment. The difficulty is that these labor market problems come bundled together. When we look at them separately, we find that only 13.9 percent of those in poverty in the early 1990s were unemployed (i.e., without a job and actively seeking work). Those with low wages and working full-time accounted for 32 percent of those in poverty. The remainder experienced more than one problem, such as involuntary part-time employment (see Gardner and Herz, 1992).

The restructuring of organizations and jobs appears to be directly responsible for at least some of the changes in the wage structure. Recent job displacement, for example, has shifted more people to the lower end of the income distribution. As shown in Figure 6.6, those who do not find a job obviously suffer income losses, but many of those who get new jobs apparently do so as well. A majority

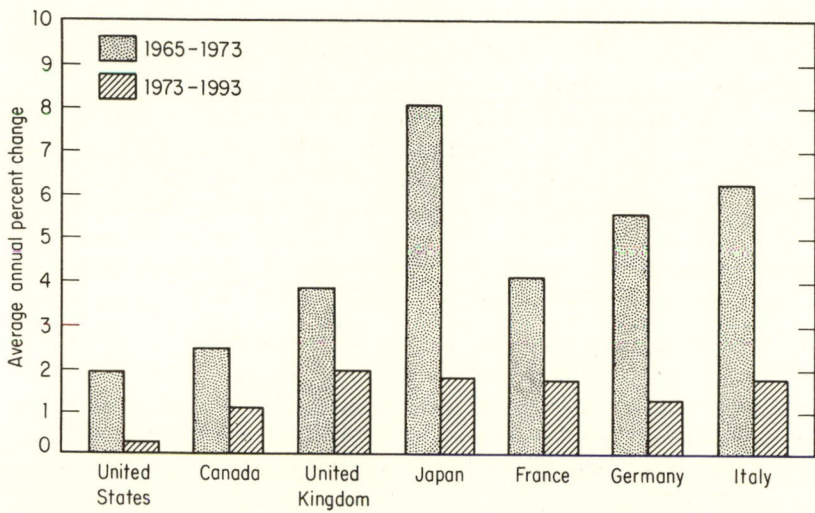

Figure 6.5. Growth in Real Compensation per Person Employed. *Note:* Data for Canada begin with 1966. *Source:* Organization for Economic Cooperation and Development.

of the displaced workers surveyed by the BLS in 1992 who found jobs took pay cuts, an increase in that category over previous years. The number of workers with much lower earnings—20 percent lower than in their previous jobs—rose substantially over previous periods (Gardner, 1993).

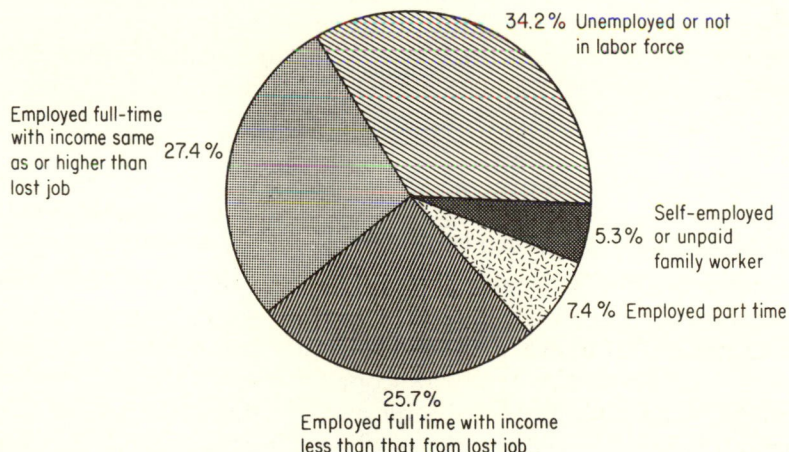

Figure 6.6. Outcomes for Workers Who Are Laid Off. *Source:* U.S. Department of Labor, Bureau of Labor Statistics.

Rose (1995) calculated that the proportion of men who had lower earnings at the end of the decade than at the beginning increased from 24 percent in the 1970s to 36 percent in the 1980s and that half of this increase resulted from the decline in job stability (Rose, 1995). The increase in part-time work also contributed to an overall increase in earnings inequality, offsetting modest reductions in the wage rate inequality for some jobs (Grubb and Wilson, 1992).

Dominance of the Outside Labor Market

The rising importance of the outside labor market in setting pay, and the corresponding decline in the role of factors internal to companies, is clearly one of the most important developments in the restructuring of employment. Katz and Krueger (1991) concluded that wages were more sensitive to the influence of local labor markets in the 1980s than they were in the 1970s, which is another way of saying that they were less protected from local market conditions. Changes in occupational differentials within organizations also seem more clearly related to the strength of the outside labor market for particular occupations.

Among the most compelling evidence of the increased role of the outside market is the effect of job changes on earnings. Management jobs are more clearly tied to companies' internal labor markets than are professional jobs. Rose (1995) calculates that managers with medium attachment to their employer (those who had been with the same employers between five and eight of the past ten years) earned $30,000 less than those with strong attachments to their employers (those who had been with the same employer eight of the last ten years); professionals with medium attachments earned only $18,000 less than those with strong attachment (on average, professionals earned more overall than managers). Rose (1995) also reported that while workers who stayed with one employer tended to earn more, the earnings penalty for changing employers seemed to decline in the 1980s compared to the 1970s.

The apparent decline in the return to tenure with the same employer is powerful evidence of a change in the traditional employment relationship. As Medoff and Abraham (1980) showed, pay systems traditionally have rewarded seniority; whether that is an explicit reward to ensure long service and loyalty or simply the fact that workers who have been with a company for a long time have clearly made a good match is an open question. Using CPS data, Chauvin (1994) found that the returns to seniority with the same employer have collapsed since the 1980s. Using data from the PSID, Marcotte (1994) also observed a sharp decline in returns to seniority, about a $3,000 annual decline between the 1970s and 1980s for workers with ten years of seniority. He noted that during the late 1980s, the costs of job changing dropped dramatically; workers who changed jobs every other year saw almost the same earnings rise during that period as those who had kept the same job for ten years.

These results suggest that the relationship between employer and employee is becoming less important in determining an employee's long-term success. By default, what must be becoming more important are factors outside the relationship with an individual employer—factors in the outside labor market.

Earnings and Education

One of the most striking trends in the labor force during the 1980s was a marked increase in the dispersion of earnings of individuals according to their level of education. As a group, individuals with a college education have always earned more than those without one. But during the past decade, the premium on higher levels of education increased sharply. As Mishel and Bernstein (1994) noted, real hourly wages for high school dropouts fell by 17.4 percent between 1979 and 1989 and by 12.3 percent for high school graduates. During the same period, they rose by 0.3 percent for college graduates and by 9.8 percent for those with two or more years of graduate school. By the mid-1980s, the ratio of earnings for college graduates to high school graduates was the highest since records have been kept (Goldin and Margo, 1992).

As one might expect, these changes in earnings by education were most pronounced for the youngest workers, new hires just entering the labor force whose pay was more sensitive to the outside labor market. The drop in real wages for high school graduates in entry-level jobs in the 1980s was far greater than that for high school graduates already in employment. Similarly, the rise in real wages for college graduates in entry-level jobs was far greater than that for college graduates already holding jobs (Mishel and Bernstein, 1994). For those without college educations, this wage pattern suggests that the school-to-work transition has become more problematic.

One way to think about these changes is to consider the possibility that the labor market is reducing the rewards to brawn and increasing the rewards to brains. One reason why the transition from school to work has become more problematic, then, particularly for those without a college degree, might be that it is much more difficult for workers to signal what they know than what they can lift.

Little is known about what components of education are most important in generating these favorable labor market outcomes.

One potentially important clue, however, has begun to emerge from a number of research studies—an individual's level of achievement in mathematics (in terms of either number of courses taken or test scores) is a powerful indicator of later earnings capacity (Murnane, Willett, and Levy, 1993). It is not yet clear whether mathematics education per se causes labor market success or whether mathematics is merely a proxy for some underlying trait that is important in the labor market. Whichever (or both) of these explanations is ultimately found to be significant, it is likely that mathematics education either teaches—or serves as a proxy for—an individual's capacity to solve problems. The evidence summarized earlier indicates that problem solving is precisely the ability that employers report as being increasingly important for their workers to possess.

In general, additional years of formal education continue to be associated with better performance in the labor market. But even the returns to a college degree have begun to erode in recent years; median hourly wages for men with bachelor's degrees dropped about 3 percent in real terms between 1989 and 1993 and rose only modestly, by 0.4 percent, for women. Changes for entry-level jobs reveal sharper declines—a drop in real wages of 6.1 percent for both men and women college graduates between 1989 and 1993 (Mishel and Bernstein, 1994) and may predict future declines in overall wage levels.

Earnings Inequality

The distribution of earnings has shifted in part because of changes in the returns to education but also for other reasons. After decades of relative stability, earnings inequality began to increase in the 1970s and then accelerated during the 1980s. Inequality also rose during the 1980s in all major industrialized countries except Germany, suggesting that at least part of the explanation may be changes common to all industrialized economies (Organization for Economic Cooperation and Development, 1993b). The greatest increases were in the United States and in the United Kingdom. The fact that trade union wage-setting power was weakened the most in these countries and that their arrangements for training the least-educated workers are particularly poor may explain their disproportionately larger increases (Freeman and Katz, 1995). Declining real wages in the United States, especially for the lowest paid, seemed to be the factor that contributed most to the growth of inequality in the United States (see Figure 6.7). At least half of the growth in the inequality of wealth, which rose sharply in the 1980s, can be attributed to rising income inequality (Wolfe, 1992).

Changes in inequality are usually measured first for white men

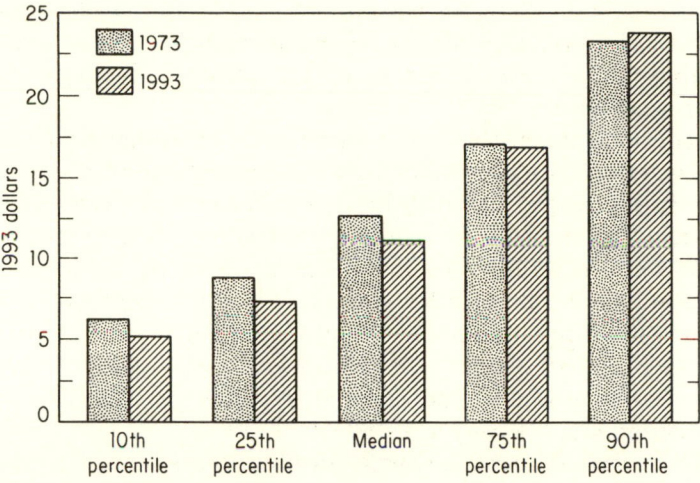

Figure 6.7.   Real Hourly Wages for Men by Wage Percentile. *Source:* Economic Report of the President (1995).

because their employment experience has been more stable, less influenced by public policy developments such as equal pay legislation, and more indicative of underlying economic trends. During the 1980s, the distribution of earnings for white men widened; real earnings fell for those below the median and rose substantially for those in the top 10 percent (see Levy and Murnane [1992] for a summary). There is evidence that for men (although not for women), the number of middle-class jobs—that is, those providing earnings in the middle of the income distribution—seems to have diminished. And the increase in inequality seems driven by changes in wage rates rather than in hours of work (Burtless, 1993).

Changes in inequality can be thought of as resulting in part from labor market adjustments based on changes in supply and demand as well as from changes in labor market institutions that set wages. Research during the 1970s suggested that changes in supply, in demography, were having perhaps the most important effects on inequality as the entry of the highly educated baby-boom generation drove down wages for that age cohort relative to others (Easterlin, 1980) and returns to education in particular (Freeman, 1976).

Part of the growth in wage inequality within cohorts is driven by changes in the supply of skilled workers; increases in the immigration of relatively low-educated workers and the decline in the rate of growth of college graduates over the 1980s may have depressed wages for lower-paid jobs. But inequality in earnings rose even within demographic groups of otherwise identical workers—those of the same gender, with the same level of education, and in the same age cohort. Some estimates suggest that the majority of the growth in inequality in the 1980s occurred within age and education cohorts (Grubb and Wilson, 1992).

Arguments during the 1980s suggested that demand-side factors not associated with particular cohorts were accounting for the increase in inequality. Specifically, some researchers suggested that the restructuring of the economy—the decline of high-wage industries or "deindustrialization," in particular—was driving an increase in inequality (Bluestone and Harrison, 1982), as were new technologies, including organizational systems, that increased the demand for more educated workers. Individuals who used computers on the job, for example, were found to earn sizable wage premiums, other things being equal (Krueger, 1993).

The decline of union power is another important component of the changing wage structure and is related to some of the restructuring pressures described in chapter 1. Blackburn, Bloom, and Freeman (1990) concluded, for example, that about 6 percent of the decline in real wages for high school dropouts could be attributed to the decline in union coverage; the effect on other education groups was nil, contributing to some of the growth in inequality with respect to education described earlier. Groshen (1993) found that the wages of nonunion employers showed the greatest departure from average levels in their labor markets in recent years.

The rise in inequality is not simply the result of shifts in jobs across industries or in union status. Davis and Haltiwanger (1991) found, for example, that most of the increase in wage inequality for nonproduction workers was within the same facility; some part of the increase in within-facility inequality was attributable to disproportionate increases for the best-paid employees. Surveys of white-collar pay suggest that the jobs with the largest increases in pay are those that already have the highest pay and responsibility (Ryscavage and Henle, 1990). A survey conducted by *Business Week* reported that the compensation for chief executive officers rose by 300 percent between 1980 and 1989, while pay for production workers rose by only 54 percent. And Bok (1993) reported evidence of growing inequality of earnings within management ranks (top executive earnings outstripping other managers). In 1994, for example, a survey by the William M. Mercer Compensation Research Group reported that total annual compensation for chief executive officers rose by 11.4 percent, compared with merit raises for middle managers of 3.6 percent (Mercer, 1995).

A graphic example of rising inequality in compensation within companies comes from the Hay (1992) study described in an earlier chapter (see Figure 6.8). As the figure suggests, the group with the

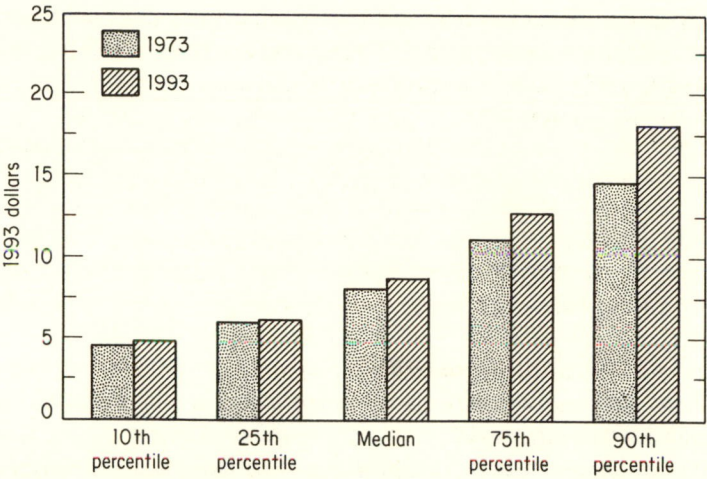

Figure 6.8. Real Hourly Wages for Women by Wage Percentile. *Source:* Economic Report of the President (1995).

largest increase in compensation was top executives, despite the fact that the increases in skills as measured by their job evaluation scores was nowhere near proportionate to their increase in compensation. Jobs in lower levels of management that did experience significant increases in requirements did not see significant increases in compensation.

Results like these suggest that in compensation as well as in job security, the important division inside companies is no longer between supervisors and front-line workers, who increasingly are treated in similar ways. Lower-level managers are squeezed on pay, by declining job security, and by reduced probabilities for promotion in flatter organizations. Now the important division is between top executives, who at least have the potential for enormous financial gains, and the rest of the organization.

Shift Toward Contingent Compensation

Another important change in the nature of pay has been the movement from straight-time compensation where pay is tied to the job, not to the individual, and varies little with the performance of the company, to a relationship that is contingent on organizational and individual performance. These developments have increased the variance and uncertainty of earnings not only across jobs *but for individuals* over time.

In a study of personnel practices in large companies during the late 1970s, Foulkes (1980) noted that pay rarely varied with individual performance even in companies with explicit merit pay programs. He found that these programs broke down for fear of the ramifications of generating inequality within work groups. By 1989, merit pay plans were making a comeback. The average merit pay increase, measured in percentage terms, that was associated with the highest level of performance reported in the Hay compensation database was 2.5 times higher than the increase associated with the lowest level of performance. By 1993, the difference between the highest and the lowest merit pay increases had risen to a factor of four.

Perhaps because they are more subject to market forces and to both firm and individual performance, the variance in individuals' earnings has risen markedly over the past decade. Gottchalk and Moffit (1994) report that the variance in individuals' earnings in the period 1980–1987 was 41 percent higher than it was in 1970–1978; the "transitory" variance in earnings, which measures individual earnings against the average earnings profile for others in the same age group, also rose by 52 percent. Shifts in employment to less stable industries or occupations does not explain the change in variance. The authors found an increase in transitory variance for individuals who stayed in the same jobs even after controlling for a wide range of other factors. Earnings inequality across workers with the same level of job experience (as measured by age of workers) also rose in every other industrialized country (except Japan) in the past decade (Organization for Economic Cooperation and Development, 1993a), suggesting once again that the forces pressing for more individualized compensation are widespread.

Other changes indicate that underlying pay structures may also be changing in ways that align pay more closely to productivity levels over an individual's lifetime, reducing the leveling effect that internal labor markets seemed to have on pay. A stylized fact of labor economics is that individual performance follows an inverted U-shaped relationship with job experience, rising initially and peaking toward the middle to later part of one's working life before declining as one approaches retirement. The pay practices of most internal labor markets typically smooth over these variations in performance so that pay does not decline when experience-related performance declines, and new entrants are paid much more than they are worth.

Recent evidence suggests that pay is shifting to conform more closely to performance. In the 1980s, workers with from one to five years of work experience saw their real wages decline by 7.7 percent, those near the peak of their experience-related productivity, with from sixteen to twenty years' experience, saw a slight gain, and those with more than thirty-five years of experience lost just under 3 percent of their real wages (Mishel and Bernstein, 1994).

As noted in chapter 1, efforts to align the interests of executives with those of stockholders contributed to sharp increases in the use of incentive pay for top executives. For employees at lower levels in the company, the use of incentive pay also increased, albeit for different reasons. Part of the explanation for the rise of incentive pay programs is the general interest in increasing motivation. These plans focus the attention of employees on particular issues, such as quality improvement, by tying pay to them. Figure 6.9 illustrates the range of special compensation programs and their growth over the last few years. A Towers Perrin (1995) survey found that 41 percent of companies offered variable or incentive pay to nonexecutive workers, a rise of 6 percent from 1994.

Contingent compensation programs are associated with the general restructuring trend in the following manner. First, they help motivate employees toward achieving the goals of restructuring; gain sharing and profit sharing, for example, give employees a direct financial stake in the outcome of restructuring efforts. Second, they help manage employees in downsized organizations with fewer layers of management and supervision. These financial incentives essentially operate as substitutes for direct supervision. They motivate employees toward specific goals that in the past might have been set for them and overseen by immediate supervisors.

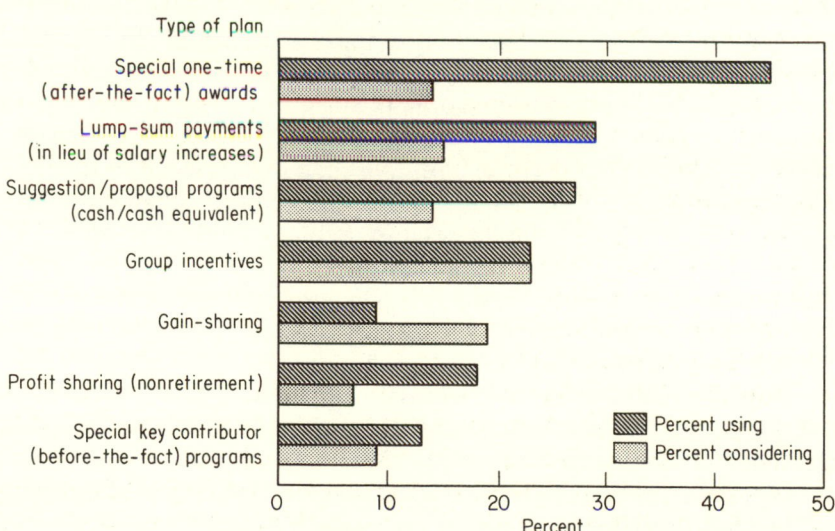

Figure 6.9. Use of Innovative Incentive Pay Systems, 1992. *Source:* 1992 Hay Compensation Conference Survey (Philadelphia: Hay Group, 1993).

Perhaps most important, incentive programs effectively shift much of the business risk of operations from the company to the employees. Increasing the percentage of total compensation that varies with performance essentially reduces the fixed costs of employment and operations. With lower fixed costs, the organization can be more flexible and can adapt more quickly to new opportunities.

Another aspect of changing compensation that illustrates the shifting of risk to employees concerns pensions. Defined-benefit plans, in which workers earn the right to predetermined benefit levels according to their years of service, accounted for 83 percent of all workers who had pensions in 1979. By 1988, that figure had fallen to 66 percent, a trend that experts expect to continue (Ippolito, 1995). The change was accounted for by growth in defined-contribution plans, in which employers make fixed contributions to a retirement fund for each employee and the benefits then vary. Most of the growth in these plans has been in 401(K) programs, which allow employees to contribute directly to their own retirement funds (Ippolito, 1995). (Employers often match part of their employees' contributions.)

While some part of the changing distribution of coverage is due to changes in the distribution of jobs across industries and employers, some other part of the change, perhaps half or more, is attributable to employers switching pension programs (Clark and McDermed, 1990). Unions appear to be an important source of resistance to the shift toward defined contribution plans.

Employers bear the risk of employee pensions in defined-benefit plans by guaranteeing a benefit stream for as long as each pensioner lives. Until the pension is vested, the employee has an incentive to stay with the employer (later, the incentives for the worker to quit increase as the employee can then take all of the pension benefits with him). Furthermore, these plans make employee turnover very costly to employers and create incentives to reduce it. If a worker quits or is laid off after her pension is vested, for example, the employer still bears the full pension liability for that worker but loses the benefit of her future performance out of which the costs of the pension would be earned.

With the shift to defined-contribution plans, the employer no longer bears the risk of guaranteeing a stream of benefits. That problem now falls to the employee. Because employer contributions and costs stop when an employee leaves, the fixed costs of employment drop dramatically with defined-contribution plans. There are no vesting requirements and, in turn, no incentives for the employee to stay. In 401(K) plans, risk is arguably pushed even further toward employees, who are allowed to share in the contributions and, in essence, control how large their retirement fund will be. Whether the shift toward defined-contribution and 401(K) plans was part of an effort to reduce fixed costs and move away from long-term employment relationships is a matter for speculation. But it clearly facilitated that move.

For employees, the move toward contingent pay and defined-contribution pensions is at best a mixed blessing. By expanding the variance in pay, contingent compensation plans offer greater earnings for high-performing employees in successful companies and lower incomes for those in the reverse circumstances. Linking performance and rewards more closely may seem to be fairer, although the fact that organizational performance (and the compensation associated with it) is not within an individual workers' control complicates that judgment. It also encourages mobility across companies. If pay varies with organizational performance, a worker doing the same job can get a big increase simply by moving to a company that looks as if it is going to perform well. Similarly, a worker can avoid a cut by bailing out of a company when its performance deteriorates.

The fact that risk and uncertainty in compensation have risen also complicates the lives of employees, especially when combined with the overall reduction in job security noted earlier. The ability to take on long-term obligations such as home ownership may become more difficult when income streams are less predictable. Capital markets may be able to find ways to address the variations in earnings (e.g., variable contributions on mortgages), but the uncertainty in income will inevitably find its way into the cost of borrowing. Overall consumer confidence may be reduced, with an adverse effect on consumption. How savings rates might be affected—whether a higher proportion of income in the form of bonuses will translate into more savings or whether greater uncertainty in earnings will lead to reduced planned savings—is an open question.

Hours of Work and Work Loads

Whether the work load that employees experience has changed is another part of the overall assessment of changes at work. The extent to which working hours have increased, by how much, and for whom are important questions that are hotly debated.

Recent research by Shor (1992) reports that working time has been rising significantly in recent decades and that the average employee now spends an additional 160 hours per year at work as compared to the equivalent worker in the 1960s. A Harris poll found that self-reported working hours rose from 40.6 per week in 1973 to 46.8 in 1987 (Harris, 1988); and a recent survey of business managers found that the average manager has a backlog of thirty-five hours' worth of work on his or her desk at any given time and now works ten hours per week longer than a comparable manager twenty years ago. The University of Maryland demographic study, "America's Use of Time," found that 35 percent of women and 23 percent of men reported that they were "constantly under pressure, trying to handle more than they can accomplish" (cited in Zemke, 1991). A Hay/Huggins survey (Hay Group, 1995) of company benefits reported a decline between 1989 and 1993 in holiday/vacation days provided, especially for workers with more than ten years of service; the proportion of companies offering twenty or more vacation days for these employees declined from 39 percent in 1989 to 10 percent in 1993.

Coleman and Pencavel (1993), on the other hand, examined census records, which appear more reliable than some of the other data we have reported, and found that the median number of hours worked remained virtually unchanged from 1940 to 1988; Robinson (1990) concluded that working hours have actually declined and that free time has risen (in part because of reduced housework) during the past twenty years. What can one make of these conflicting results?

As is often the case with labor market studies, much depends on how the sample is defined. Studies examining all workers, like that of Coleman and Pencavel (1993), reach different conclusions from those that concentrate on full-time workers, like that of Shor (1992). Overall, for example, the fact that workers are increasingly being pushed into involuntary part-time work has reduced the average and median hours worked for all employees even as those in full-time jobs are pushed toward longer and longer working hours.

Indeed, the main point in all of these studies is that the variance in hours worked has been rising. Robinson (1990) reported that the busiest segment of society in the 1980s reported a seven percentage point rise in working hours compared to the 1970s; Coleman and Pencavel (1993) concluded that working hours have risen for the most educated workers and have fallen for the least educated. Leete and Schor (1994) confirmed the general finding that the variance in hours has risen. They reported that hours have declined for those in the involuntary part-time workforce but have increased sharply for others, especially for women working full-time (by 20.4 percent).

The rise in inequality of working hours contributes to the growing inequality of total earnings noted earlier. And it is consistent with a vision of the workforce as increasingly divided between demanding but potentially enriching jobs held by educated workers—especially at the very top—and short-time, low-paid, low-skill, and often contingent work held by less-educated workers.

Those at the top of the working time distribution often find now that they have too little time for life outside work. A Roper poll (Deutschman, 1992) reported that for the first time since 1975, leisure was the most important aspect in the lives of respondents, no doubt because it was in such short supply. The conflict between work demands and family life is one of the key consequences of greater working time. In the Quality of Employment Survey (Galinsky et al., 1993), a national probability survey of individuals in full-time employment, 35 percent of those responding felt that they had to choose between paying attention to their personal lives and advancing in their jobs. Other studies found that stress was highest among two-career couples and in those aged 35 to 49 (Zemke, 1991). Yet it is not clear how much companies are doing to accommodate work and family tensions. The use of flex-time, for example, increased only slightly with 38 percent of employers offering it in 1990 and 41 percent in 1993 (Hay/Huggins, 1994).

Stress

Work loads, work and family conflicts, and the more general restructuring of employment discussed in earlier chapters all contribute to workplace stress. Research suggests that some stress is useful in helping individuals and organizations achieve important goals (Bardwick, 1991), and many individuals and organizations suffer from having too few consequences and pressures that contribute to success as well as to stress. But high levels of stress also contribute to a wide range of problems for individuals and for the organizations in which they work. The changes in organizations outlined in earlier chapters contribute to uncertainty and, in turn, to stress. At the individual level, the risk of job loss, declines in real income, increased hours, and the need to change how work is performed also increase stress.

The Quality of Employment Survey (Galinsky et al., 1993) noted that 43 percent of the employees surveyed reported that they had excessive amounts of work to do, and about the same proportion reported that they often felt "used up" at the end of the workday. A national survey conducted by the Northwestern National Life Insurance Company in 1991 found half of all workers worried about job security and feeling pressure to prove their value. More than one third of the women and 28 percent of men reported that they had thought about quitting their jobs because of stress. A comparison of this survey with the 1985 National Health Interview Survey, conducted by the National Center for Health Statistics, which asked similar questions, reveals that the number of workers reporting that they were highly or extremely stressed rose from 20 to 46 percent between 1985 and 1992; the number of stress-related illnesses reported by respondents rose from 13 to 25 percent. (Northwestern National Life Insurance Company, 1992).

The Health and Retirement Survey, a national probability sur-

Table 6.1.   Workplace Stress

Symptom	Percentage of American workers
Experience three or more stress-related conditions very or somewhat often	72%
Are required to work more than 40 hours per week very or somewhat often	53
Feel their job is very or extremely stressful	46
Feel more pressure to prove their value to their employer because of the recession	40
Thought seriously about quitting their job in 1990 because of workplace stress	34
Think they will burn out on the job in the next year or two	34
Say their job is the single greatest cause of stress in their lives	27

Source: Northwestern National Life Survey (1991).

vey conducted in 1993 by the Institute for Social Research at the University of Michigan, reported that 64 percent of those working said that their jobs involved stress (Gustman et al., 1995). In a Gallop survey of personnel executives, 72 percent reported that stress, anxiety, and depression were fairly or very pervasive among employees in their organizations (BNA 1989). Seventy-five percent of U.S. workers reported that their jobs were stressful, as opposed to 30 percent of workers in Sweden where perhaps the most aggressive steps have been taken to reduce stress.

The reports of stress appear to be related in part to the restructuring of organizations. The Northwestern National Life study found that reports of employee burnout were more than twice as high at companies where there had been reductions in force, compared to those that experienced no layoffs, and stress-related illnesses were 50 percent higher in such situations. Employees at companies where there had been major reorganizations had twice the rate of "burnout" and 50 percent more reported stress-related illnesses. A survey conducted by *Training* magazine (Zemke, 1991) found that the stress on middle managers peaked in 1987–1988—a period of accelerating corporate restructuring—and was between 50 and 100 percent higher at companies that had downsized or consolidated operations.

Stress, Illness, and Safety

Perhaps the most important manifestation of rising stress in the workplace is its effects on the health of employees. The government maintains good records on workplace accidents and illnesses, and the trend in accidents is clearly down. Accidental deaths at the workplace, for example, have fallen from 21 per 100,000 workers in 1912 to about 4 per 100,000 in the 1990s. Overall accidents have declined by as much as 20 percent since the 1970s. Car accidents still account for the biggest proportion of fatalities (35.5 percent), but overexertion is now the most important cause of injuries (31.3 percent). One in three injuries occur in manufacturing, and the shift away from manufacturing in the economy and toward safer, service industries has helped cut the accident rate (National Safety Council, 1991). (The injury and illness rate in U.S. manufacturing, however, is eleven times that of Japan. See Wokutch and McGlaughlin [1992].)

While occupational injuries have declined over time, illnesses associated with the workplace have virtually exploded, tripling in frequency since the 1980s (see Figure 6.10). A large part of this increase is associated with repeated trauma—repetitive motion syndrome and other afflictions that are classified as illnesses, not injuries. A study by the International Labour Organisation reported that stress-related worker compensation claims rose from 5 to 15 percent of all cases during the 1980s, and a study by Blue Cross-Blue Shield noted that five of six workers filing illness claims in the United States reported that stress is the major cause of their illness (ILO, 1993). Stress-related employee disabilities more than doubled during the 1980s and accounted for 13 percent of all cases by 1990 (Labs, 1992). While mental stress claims are only a small proportion of all worker compensation claims (1 percent), they increased five-fold from 1983 to 1988 (*Wall Street Journal*, 1988).

The rise of violence at work is a growing health hazard that may

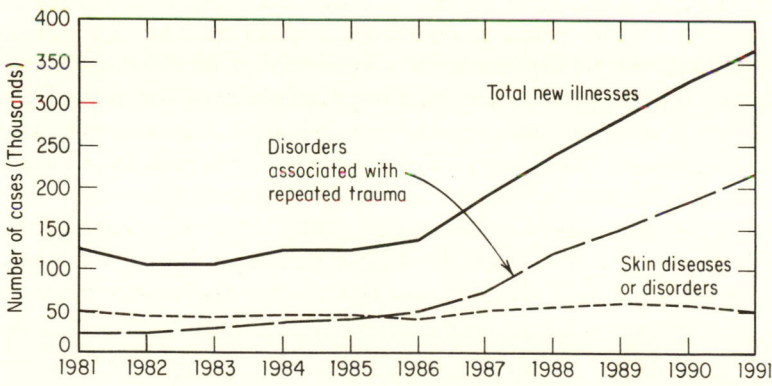

Figure 6.10. Number of New Occupational Illnesses, Private Industry, 1981–1991. *Source:* Bureau of Labor Statistics, *Occupational Injuries and Illnesses in the United States by Industry, 1991* (Washington, D.C., U.S. Department of Labor, Bureau of Labor Statistics, May 1993).

be related to some of the same factors that are contributing to increased stress. Another national survey by the Northwestern National Life Insurance Company (1991) found that one in four workers reported being physically harassed, threatened, or actually attacked at the workplace; one in six had been threatened with a deadly weapon. Workplace homicide is the fastest growing form of murder in the United States, having doubled in frequency since the 1970s. Just how much, if any, of this violence can be attributed to restructuring is open for debate. Forty-four percent of the attacks in the workplace are by customers, for example, which provides dramatic evidence about how problems from the outside society spill over into the workplace (Northwestern National Life Insurance Company, 1993). (Attacks by customers also helps explain why the industry in which employees are most at risk from violence is retail sales, because of employees' close contact with customers.)

The Northwestern survey provides some evidence, however, that violence by employees can be influenced by employment policies. That study found that violence was lower, for example, in companies in which the employer provided ways for workers to express discontent, such as grievance procedures.

Relations within the workplace and in particular the organization of work appear to be among the main causes—and cures—of excessive stress. Employee participation and control at the workplace seem particularly effective at reducing stress. Again, the Northwestern survey found that having supportive supervisors and some individual control over workplace issues were the main factors in reducing stress. Those reporting having little personal control over their work were twice as likely to experience stress-related "burnout" and more than twice as likely to have stress-related illnesses. These results suggest that the changes in work organization described in chapter 3 that push authority and autonomy down to individual employees may actually help reduce stress to the extent that they give employees greater control over their work. The fact these employees may have less control over other important matters such as job security works in the other direction.

The Northwestern survey also found that companies with supportive work and family policies had exactly half the rate of burnout and stress-related illnesses as companies with no such policies; roughly the same ratio operated for companies whose employee communication was rated effective compared to companies with no employee communication.

Morale and Attitudes Performance

Given many of the changes noted in this chapter—declining job security, declining real wages, increased work effort, hours, and stress—it would be surprising if employee morale had not declined in recent years. Some of the change in employee attitudes stems from factors that predate the current restructuring trend. The Yankelovich Partners organization, which has been tracking public opinion for decades, reports that the overly optimistic attitudes toward one's chances of economic success in the 1960s have given way in the 1990s to fear of losing affluence. The importance of the concept of "duty" in many aspects of life has declined, especially in the workplace, where the Protestant work ethic (the notion that working hard has intrinsic value) has given way to a view of work as a source of personal satisfaction. By the mid-1980s, 49 percent of respondents said that having a job they enjoyed was a measure of personal success, a factor that barely registered in surveys taken a decade earlier. Living up to one's potential has become a priority, and work is a means for doing that (Yankelovich, 1993).

S.R.A. Corporation has conducted employee attitude surveys every year since the 1950s, questioning approximately 500,000 U.S. workers across a range of industries and employers. The scores on the items, which included satisfaction measures with various aspects of employment and commitment to the organization, were remarkably stable until the early 1980s, when they began a sharp decline. By the mid-1980s, they were in a virtual free fall. The question "I believe that management is looking out for my interests" showed the sharpest drop, with only about half as many agreeing in the mid-1980s as in previous decades. Similar surveys conducted by the Mayflower Group, an informal collection of companies that compare employee attitude data, also reveal a decline in employee satisfaction during the 1980s. Employee surveys conducted by Hay Associates also show a sharp decline in employee attitudes in the 1980s, especially commitment to the employer.[5]

Employee surveys conducted by Roper Starch Worldwide found that the percentage of employees who were "extremely satisfied" with their work fields fell from 41 percent in 1976 to 27 percent in 1994. The percentage satisfied with their hours also fell, dropping from 46 to 30 percent over the same time period. In 1990, 38 percent of employees reported that the morale of their fellow employees was excellent; only four years later, that figure was down to 27 percent. The occupational group reporting the greatest sense of job security ("little danger of becoming unemployed") was professional/technical employees, perhaps reflecting the fact that their skills are readily transferable to other employers. The group with the greatest personal loyalty to the organization, in contrast, was executives, reflecting the considerable financial stake they typically have in their organizations.[6]

Middle managers appear to be the group that has experienced the sharpest drop in morale precisely because they appear to be the group whose psychological contract with the organization has been the most severely violated. As part of the management team, they expected job security, steady pay improvements, and promotion prospects in return for loyalty and adequate performance. And yet, as noted earlier, they have become more vulnerable to job loss than those in other occupational groups. It is therefore no surprise that the surveys that break out attitudes by occupational group find that managers have experienced the sharpest declines in morale, especially on measures of trust in the organization.

A survey of managers reported by *Training* magazine suggests that managers do not even pretend to believe in commitment to the organization. Only 2 percent reported that dedication to one's organization was the key to success (*Training*, 1992). Individual ambition, in contrast, was cited by 56 percent. A survey of 12,000 managers worldwide found a sharp decline in loyalty and commitment to the employer as compared to a similar survey done ten years earlier. Interestingly, the respondents were more satisfied with their work than with their employer (Kanter, 1991). Surveys at a regional operating company in the telephone system produced very similar results: satisfaction with work but dissatisfaction with job security and other terms and conditions of employment (Batt, forthcoming).

Perhaps the best news—possibly the only good news—about employee attitudes is the continuing interest in doing a good job at specific tasks. Fifty-two percent of those in the Quality of Employment Survey reported that they received personal satisfaction from doing a good job, and 99 percent said that they always tried to do their job well, "no matter what it takes." Fully 90 percent said that they were willing to work harder than they had been to help their company succeed (Galinsky et al., 1993). And, as noted in chapter 1, some of the changes associated with restructuring actually seem to improve workplace attitudes. A wide body of research (see Cotton, 1993) supports the idea that employee attitudes improve as a result of the changes in work organization described in chapter 3.

The Social Contract at Work

The decline in morale seems related not only to a general deterioration in some aspects of employment but also to a break in the implicit employment contract between employer and employee. Some think about this relationship as a contract that specifies the mutual obligations of the employer and the employee. These contracts are rarely explicit and sometimes not even acknowledged. They may be built up over time through a series of exchanges between employer and employee: Loyalty and retention by the employee are rewarded by stable employment and income. The norm of reciprocity runs deep in every society. Employees who have kept their side of the bargain with long service feel that the contract has been violated if the employer deviates from its obligations.[7] Describing the sharp decline in employee commitment observed over time in his polls, Daniel Yankelovich commented that "companies are unaware of the dreadful impact they are having. They don't realize they are violating an unwritten but important social contract they have with workers" (O'Reilly, 1994).

Management actions that literally break employment relations seem to have the most profound consequences on morale among employees who remain. In the 1994 American Management Association survey on downsizing, 86 percent of companies that had downsized reported that employee morale had declined. Those same companies reported that employee productivity had risen or held constant in 70 percent of downsized companies, while profits rose or held constant in 80 percent (American Management Association, 1994). A survey of employers that had restructured, conducted by the Wyatt Company, reported adverse effects on workloads, morale, and commitment but sharp increases in productivity, service levels, and workforce competence (Wyatt Company, 1993).

It would be reasonable to expect employees to want to break their side of the agreement as well. There is a well-documented body of research suggesting that employees act out this sense of inequity by reducing their efforts, being absent, or quitting altogether (e.g., Walster, et al., 1978), all of which have negative consequences for the organization.

Absenteeism, a manifestation of poor morale, rose slightly between 1992 and 1993 and then by 9 percent in 1994 to 2.6 percent of working days. The increase was greatest for larger companies (*Ideas and Trends*, 1994). But this appears to be about the only evidence of negative effects on performance that is traceable to poor morale. The extraordinary thing about the decline in morale, especially in restructured companies, is that it is apparently having so few negative effects on performance. Indeed, surveys of restructured companies, as noted earlier, seem to suggest the opposite.

The sharp declines in morale may come about in large measure because the employees cannot act out their frustration with the break in the psychological contract. If an organization were to act alone to downsize and restructure, breaking its psychological contract with employees, one might expect those employees to vote with their feet and go elsewhere. When all organizations appear to be downsizing at the same time, however, there is no place to go. The fact that one's organization is continuing to look for jobs and employees to cut makes it very risky to act out one's frustrations with any negative behavior. In short, employees are afraid of being tossed out into a job market that has few takers.

Middle managers are perhaps the group that has seen the biggest break in their psychological contact; yet, as we have noted, they are the occupational group in the Hay surveys with the greatest commitment to their employer as measured by intentions to remain. Their morale is low precisely because they feel that their contract was violated and yet they cannot leave. Companies generally do not hire middle managers from the outside labor market. They promote them from within. A similar problem now afflicts law firms. Senior lawyers who can take clients with them can find jobs, as can young associates at the beginning of their careers, whose lack of specialized skills makes them transferable and relatively cheap to hire. Lawyers in between, those with six or more years of experience, have a much more difficult time finding jobs now that law firms are scaling back (Stevens, 1994).

So the survivors of restructuring often see their morale decline because of broken psychological contracts. They sometimes suffer guilt as well when colleagues and friends are forced out of jobs. Furthermore, the people doing the restructuring—specifically, those doing the downsizing—often suffer enormously from making layoff decisions. Executives and top managers who make the decisions in principle to restructure draw comfort and financial rewards from improvements in financial performance associated with those cuts; the managers down the line who make the face-to-face layoff decisions appear to suffer much more, not only because they know the people who will be departing but because they have a smaller stake in the financial benefits deriving from such changes (see Smith, 1994, for examples).

Another factor depressing employee morale is the move toward contingent arrangements in jobs and pay. One of the best-known results in behavioral research is that individuals do not like to risk losses and will pay a considerable price to avoid that risk. (Khanaman and Tversky, 1979). Employment arrangements that shift more of the risk of job loss and income variation onto employees seem to make employees worse off. In addition to the fact that the old contracts appear to have been broken, mainly by layoffs, then, the new arrangements being offered seem to be worse for employees. Robinson et al. (1994) found that, other things equal, the longer one is on the job, the more one comes to expect of one's boss and the less one expects of oneself. Here, long-service employees are finding that, while their expectations are rising, what they are being offered is declining.

Management does not seem especially worried about the decline in worker attitudes. Employee morale ranks eighth out of a possible nine management priorities for the next five years in a Conference Board survey of executives (Conference Board, 1992).

Human resource executives admit in private that concerns about declining morale have little effect on top-management decision making. Indeed, some suggest that if employee attitudes have not suffered, there is a sense at the top of organizations that painful restructuring has not gone far enough.[8]

The sharp division between the experience of executives and that of other employees on these restructuring issues is illustrated in the results of another survey conducted by Kepner-Tregoe (1995). In this survey, 70 percent of executives reported that restructuring efforts met their expectations, while only 40 percent of workers so reported; similar figures for downsizing were 73 and 45 percent, respectively. Executives estimated that morale was worse for 27 percent of their workers as the result of restructuring initiatives, while 51 percent of workers reported that morale was down. Executives reported that the most troubling issue for the future was "people issues" such as employee commitment (50 percent), but fewer than 4 percent reported that responding to these issues was among their goals for the next year.

Rewriting the Psychological Contract

Many companies are attempting to rewrite the social contract at work explicitly in ways that reduce the employer's obligations. At the Intel Corporation, a vice president described the new arrangement as follows: "You own your own employability. You are responsible" (*Fortune* 1994a). J. P. Morgan produced a pamphlet titled, "Guiding Principles of the Relationship between Morgan and You" that identifies the new agreement. For employees, perhaps the most important change is they are now expected to "take the initiative in your own professional development."

Efforts to change the contract are also under way for top executives although, as with pay, the arrangements for top management are substantially different from those for other employees. Executives are facing an increase in explicit employment contracts that spell out in legal terms the obligations of the employer to the employee. A 1989 Hay/Huggins survey found 29 percent of companies providing these contracts for executives and 27 percent offering executive severance pay; by 1993, those figures had risen to 36 and 39 percent, respectively. Employees in lower-level positions are almost never offered employment contracts; in fact, an important factor in the declining use of employee handbooks that identify company procedures with respect to employment is that the courts have interpreted those handbooks as establishing contractual rights for employees.

The element of trust is crucial in all social or psychological contracts. Because exchanges between parties take place at different times, the last party to make an exchange has an incentive to cheat—to get the exchange from the first party and then not give his or her share. The first party needs to trust that the second party will not cheat in order to make the deal go ahead. Consider, for example, an implicit contract in which the employer has offered career development and stable earning and employment in return for the employee's commitment and loyalty in the future. The employer trusted that the commitment would come, just as the employees who provided that level of commitment trusted that stable employment opportunities would continue. Once these contracts are broken and trust is shattered, the contracts may be redrafted. But the element of trust is unlikely to be part of the new arrangements. Contracts without trust between the parties have to either be legal documents that can be enforced by the courts—what one sees for executives—or so short-run and transactional that trust is less necessary to make them go.

These examples of the new "employability" notion of a psychological contract at work illustrate clearly the transactional approach that reduces the role of trust. A main feature of the employability argument is that it reduces employees' expectations about employers' responsibility to them and suggests that employees take responsibility for their own futures. (Interestingly, these statements rarely suggest that the employee's responsibility to the employer has also diminished.) What this means in practice might include increased negotiations between employer and employee inside companies whenever a project changes, negotiations over issues such as the nature of the tasks to be performed, training opportunities, and measures of and rewards for performance.

The more important issue concerning the new employability contract is how employers will ever get long-term commitments from employees and, in turn, how they will justify investments in such employees. Presumably, asking employees to focus on their own employability will focus their attention more on opportunities elsewhere. When opportunities develop outside the company, what is to stop them from moving, taking with them any employer investments in them in the process? As we noted in the discussion on morale, the relative shortage of alternatives in the labor market, especially for traditional management jobs, means that employers have not had to worry that much yet about employees breaking their commitments. But a tighter labor market may find employers suddenly furious about the lack of employee commitment. To paraphrase Keynes, however, many of us will be dead before the oversupply in the labor market abates. And in the meantime, employees will continue to absorb most of the costs of the restructured employment relationship.

Attitudes in the Future

What about the next generation of workers? Those in the generation behind the "baby boom," sometimes referred to as "Generation X," are currently in their teens and twenties and have never experienced the old social contract at work. They come into the workforce with different expectations, and there is some evidence already that their attitudes and behavior may be quite different.

Douglas Coupland, author of the book *Generation X*, used the term "McJobs" to describe the kind of career-free work that faces this age cohort. American youth have faced these kind of entry-level jobs for decades, but eventually—after about six or eight years in the labor force—they moved into jobs with some future. Whether that will happen for the next generation and, if so, for how many workers and how long will it take are the important questions. It is certainly the case that the younger workers are not doing as well financially as previous generations. In 1970, only about 15 percent of twenty-one-year-olds were living with their parents. By 1990, that figure had risen to 21 percent, largely because declining real wages, especially for noncollege graduates, and rising housing costs have made it difficult to set up households (Goldschneider and Goldschneider, 1993).

Some argue that this generation has adapted to the fact that the jobs they initially see do not seem to offer chances for career development and advancement. Because these jobs all look the same to them, moving between them becomes much easier. Reports from employers suggest that these workers have adapted extremely well to the lack of employer commitment, especially to new hires, by becoming exceptionally nomadic in their own employment decisions. They are much more transactional at the workplace, judging a job by what it offers right now, not possibly in the future, and are extraordinarily willing to hop from job to job if a new position offers some advantage (Filipczak, 1994).

There is some evidence that people have adjusted their expectations to a tougher workplace reality. A Harris poll in 1992 (Vanos, 1992) found that 29 percent of respondents thought that their children's generation would have a worse life than their own, up from 18 percent in 1989. A recent Roper poll reports that leisure is the most important outcome for this younger generation, the first time in fifteen years that leisure came out at the top. The emphasis on leisure may represent a response to diminishing workplace oppor-

tunities. Perhaps because their expectations have already been lowered, young adults are reasonably optimistic about their future
prospects (Deutschman, 1992).

Summary

While there are some bright spots associated with restructuring for
employees, mainly the potential of more autonomy and interesting
work, most of the outcomes noted in this chapter appear quite negative. Some, like declining real wages, can be linked only in a minor
way to the restructuring decisions of companies. Others, like stress
and declining morale, are much more closely tied to those decisions.
Current trends suggest that employees are increasingly confronted
with greater risk, often longer hours, increased work loads, and
stress and are offered less by employers in return. The biggest short-
term challenge associated with these developments that is facing
employers is how to manage workforces that lack commitment. The
long-term challenge is how to manage the significant reversals that
are likely to occur in the workforce if something like a labor shortage appears.

For employees and for society, the problems appear both more
immediate and more dramatic. Employees seem to have borne a
very large share of the costs of restructuring companies, and they
are suffering for it. For society as a whole, the adjustments associated with changes (e.g., increased worker mobility) are difficult to
foresee clearly, although they may well be widespread. Perhaps the
main issue for society raised by these findings is the consequences
of increased inequality of income and opportunity in employment,
consequences that will clearly spill over from the workplace into all
aspects of life.

Notes

1. Controlling for age and education, the relationship between tenure
on the job and displacement did not change over the period, however (Farber, 1993).

2. See Brown and Light (1992) for a discussion of the problems with
using the CPS data and questions asking for length of employment.

3. Young workers on average have far higher turnover rates than other
workers, and new entrants by definition have zero job tenure. The end of the
baby boom and the arrival of the smallest youth cohort since World War II
suggests a sharp shift in the distribution of the labor force away from
young, new entrant workers with high turnover rates and low tenure, which
should have *increased* average tenure, other things equal, in the most recent
periods.

4. As Farber (1995) notes, if one looks at changes in tenure for the

whole population (a calculation that incorporates business cycle variations) and not just for those currently employed, the declines in tenure across all of these categories are considerably more dramatic.

5. These results, from proprietary surveys, were made available by the organizations to the author.

6. See Chilton and Weidenbaum (1994) for these results, as well as for an excellent survey of many of the issues raised throughout this volume.

7. For a discussion of these implied contracts in the workplace, see Rousseau (1989).

8. We are indebted to Robert McKersie for this observation.

7

Conclusions

The changes in employee relations described throughout this volume were caused in large measure by pressures on employers to restructure themselves, pressures that are massive and appear unlikely to go away. Comparisons with the private sector are pushing restructuring into new areas, such as government and the nonprofit sector, where competitive pressures are clearly different. It is doubtful that any sector of the economy will escape unchanged.

A thumbnail sketch of the changes described in the earlier chapters of this book includes sharp moves toward downsizing and growth of a contingent workforce; redesign of tasks and work systems that both make greater demands on employees and allow them opportunities for more meaningful work; and training arrangements that distribute opportunities for learning skills in an unbalanced manner, contributing to unequal outcomes in the labor market. The sharp decline in labor market opportunities for men in recent years, especially for those with little education, is perhaps the most important political development of our era. It lies behind not only the broad-based attacks on redistributive programs such as affirmative action but more general trends, such as efforts to reduce tax burdens and the programs they fund.

From the evidence accumulated so far, it appears that there have been important changes in the nature of the employment relationship. The nature of the pressures for change described in chapter 1 are crucial to understanding the long-term implications of these changes in employment. Specifically, will the restructuring of organizations and employment be a one-shot adjustment in which employers all scale back to some new norm of operating efficiency? Under this scenario, at least some core of the workforce will have employment relationships that look at least something like the traditional model. Or will it be a more continuous process in which companies keep restructuring in response to changes in markets and in competitors' strategies? In this case, it is much less likely that the relationship between employers and employees will settle down and resemble the traditional arrangements described in chapter 1.

When we talk about typical practices or trends, it is important to acknowledge the wide variance in employment relationships across the economy. The traditional model was applicable probably only to employees in larger organizations, and the changes in that model therefore also apply mainly to larger operations. We might expect even large employers to vary in the extent to which they follow the trends noted earlier depending on the nature of the pressures they face to restructure. And it is not at all clear what the "best" strategy for restructuring is, even from the perspective of improving organizational performance. As noted earlier, some businesses succeed with deep cuts in jobs while others succeed without them.

Not all of the types of changes described in this volume have the same long-term impact. Downsizings of the magnitude seen over the past decade cannot continue forever, or the organizations doing them will eventually disappear altogether. But other changes seem more permanent. It seems clear, for example, that employers will continue to change the mix of skills that they need. Indeed, the rate at which those skills change will probably increase. Furthermore, changes in organizational structures and in the way work is organized seem to have long-term implications for issues such as promotion prospects and employee development. The fact that similar restructuring efforts are now beginning in Europe, and that pressures for change are mounting even in Japan, suggests that the forces driving them are indeed powerful and widespread.

But there is something of a pattern among most restructuring efforts that is perhaps best described as a contrast to the previous employment relationship. The new model makes individual employment relationships more sensitive to market forces. Pressures from the product market are brought inside the company to employees by making compensation and job security contingent on organizational performance. Pressures from the labor market manifest themselves through more hiring from outside, career development increasingly across (rather than within) organizations, and greater use of contingent and contract labor. These changes push more of the risk of doing business onto employees at the same time that changes in work organization are demanding substantially more from them.

The new employment arrangements have important implications for workers, employers, and the economy as a whole. The question raised earlier—whether these new arrangements will continue to expand or be replaced by some alternative arrangement, possibly even a return to more traditional employee relationships—may depend in large measure on the internal contradictions raised by these new employment arrangements.

Implications of the New System

Meeting Higher Skill Demands

Many of the challenges associated with new employment relationships begin with the work systems described in chapter 3 that push authority down in the organization and demand more from employees. The rise of teamwork and related changes in work organization create reasonably idiosyncratic skills that may not translate well to other settings. Getting a group of people to cooperate and function as a team is not easy. It requires learning about each other, establishing trust, and developing good methods of communication. Practices such as job rotation, an important component of these new work systems, also make unique demands by requiring workers to learn how to perform many of the different tasks in their area. If a worker moves out of a team, this investment in learning about the team and its tasks does not translate elsewhere and is lost. When a replacement worker is brought into a team work system, that new worker must make a big investment in learning these specific skills before he or she can begin to contribute. And until the individual worker can contribute, the entire team—indeed, the entire system —suffers.

These arguments seem to suggest that in order to make the new work arrangements pay off, employment has to be reasonably stable. The investment in learning required to make employees competent in new work systems is costly for employers, who recoup that investment only when the systems settle down and start performing well. If employees are continually moving in and out of these systems, the cost of the investments in learning goes through the roof and cannot be recouped. Having a constant stream of new workers coming in, being trained, and then leaving means that the investment in learning is simply wasted. Furthermore, the work systems in which these employees sit while they are learning are constantly disrupted and never perform well. Downsizings and other restructurings that move employees around inside organizations also disrupt these work systems and seem incompatible with them.

It would seem that some kind of employment stability and perhaps even explicit job security would be a necessary condition for these new work systems to succeed. But the trends described in chapters 2 and 5 suggest otherwise, that in fact employee attachment and commitment to individual employers is weakening. So the trend toward new work systems and the trend toward reduced employee attachment seem to be creating a contradiction.

Keeping current employees in their jobs is not something that is entirely within the control of an individual employer. As employees gain more experience and skills, it is natural to expect them to want to move on to new, more challenging jobs. And as organizations trim down, broaden jobs, and flatten hierarchies, the opportunity for workers to move up and yet stay in the same company may diminish. Chapter 5 noted that about two thirds of all employee turnover is voluntary quits, and most workers quit to pursue opportunities elsewhere. An employer with an explicit job security program reduces only a part of its turnover—dismissals other than for cause. If other employers increase their hiring from the outside labor market or if employees get used to exploring opportunities elsewhere and see career opportunities as extending more across than within employers, then quit rates will rise. To reduce quit rates when job shopping has increased, an individual employer has to make its jobs more desirable than those elsewhere.

Osterman (1995) suggested that compensation structures can be used to bind trained employees to employers. He found that the presence of internal labor market structures to foster job security is not related to the extent of company-provided skills training but that those establishments that provide more training are also more likely to pay above-market "efficiency wages" that tend to reduce turnover. Paying above-average wages or otherwise being a better than average employer is obviously not a strategy that all employers can use simultaneously, however.

Declining attachment to individual employers raises more general issues for the development of company-specific skills. If employees come to see their experience with an employer as temporary at best, and if employers meet skill needs by hiring from the outside—in effect "poaching" skilled workers from other employers—then the incentive for companies to provide training evaporates. Employers earn an economic return on investments in training over time through the improvement in performance made possible by training. The incentive to train erodes as attachment to employers declines because of the difficulty in earning a return on that investment.

The problem, therefore, is how to create skills that are largely specific to an individual employer, skills that cannot be purchased in the outside market, when the employer's ability to recoup an investment in those skills may well have eroded because of declining employee-employer attachment. One alternative is that employers may have to adjust production processes and work systems to make them more generic, relying less on skills that are specific to the company and more on general skills available in the labor market. The move away from proprietary information and computer systems to more generic ones is one example. Moving even further by pushing functions to the outside market is another alternative. Outsourcing functions or working with vendors to develop proprietary systems that the vendors might then support is yet another example. These are obviously only partial solutions that are not applicable for those tasks that are truly part of an organization's core competencies.

Employee Development

As organizations flatten their hierarchies, opportunities for training and development within the same organization will likely diminish. The breakdown of narrow job ladders and the incorporation of the simplest tasks into existing jobs raises questions as to how unskilled workers in particular can enter and work their way up an organization. One tremendous advantage of scientific management-based work systems is that they created simple entry-level positions where unskilled workers could make a contribution while learning something about work. The notion of broadly skilled, cross-functional teams basically eliminates lower-skilled, entry-level positions and makes it difficult to see how new workers could develop those skills. On the management side, movement across employers to secure promotion and advancement may be more common as a result.

The declining attachment to employers but increasing attachment to occupations noted in chapter 5 complicates the problem. An investment in occupation-specific skills pays off even more for an individual now because that worker will have more time over which to recoup the costs of learning those skills. Such investments are less attractive to individual employers, however, because employees are less likely to spend enough time with them to allow the employers to recoup their investment. One might therefore expect employees to demand more training but employers to offer less of it. And employees have an even stronger interest in learning skills, especially skills that are portable across employers, when they will have to find new jobs and career prospects on the outside market. (Unions have pushed for skills retraining programs in downsizing companies in large part because of this concern among their members.) Jobs that can provide skills and the credentials to certify them will be in demand, and employees will increasingly compete to secure them.

Other things being equal, employers that can offer skills training and credentials for employee development should therefore be able to hire better employees for less. The problem is how to pay for that training. Employee development implies skills that can be used in other jobs, skills that can walk out the door and be used elsewhere. The typical way of providing such skills is to make the employees pay for them while they are working by paying them wages that are substantially below the value of the work they are producing. Examples at the high end of the employment spectrum are reasonably common—doctors who take low-paid residencies in order to earn a further credential, lawyers who take low-wage clerkships or government jobs in order to get exposure to case work, college students who take summer research jobs to help get references for graduate school. The military has long been seen as an avenue where one can trade lower wages for training and experience that will pay off later in the labor market.

But these situations are unique in that the credentials secured are well known and valuable. Employees understand that there is a big return from completing their training and have incentives to finish it. Most employers cannot expect such supportive circumstances, and the general trend toward reduced attachment noted earlier pulls in the other direction, making employee training and development more difficult. Again, more traditional forms of work organization associated with scientific management not only allowed unskilled employees to learn a little bit while doing unskilled jobs where they were making a contribution but created jobs that were reasonably insensitive to turnover. Because no specific skills were required for these jobs, it did not matter much if a worker/trainee quit. The new work systems, in contrast, not only make it more difficult for unskilled, untrained workers to contribute but are also quite vulnerable to turnover. As we have noted, the company- and job-specific skills required in these jobs are lost if an employee walks out the door.

The problem of how to pay for training and skills is compounded by public policy. The Fair Labor Standards Act prohibits employees from explicitly sharing the costs of training; an employer must pay workers for time spent in training that the employer requires and cannot require them to contribute to the costs of training.[1] Similarly, the tax treatment of training and education for individuals is such that investments to improve performance in one's current job are not deductible.

Many employers essentially get around these problems by re-quiring that applicants receive (and pay for) specific training pro-grams at community colleges or similar vendors before they are hired. Indeed, the increased interest in postsecondary education in general may well reflect the growing incentives for employees to receive such training and the growing disincentives for employers to provide it. As Bishop (1994) concluded, education can be a substi-tute for training for specific jobs. Preliminary results from the Na-tional Employer Survey (National Center on the Educational Qual-ity of the Workforce, 1995) suggest a similar trade-off for employers; those who provide less training are significantly more likely to work with local schools to develop better educated graduates that they could hire.

Partly because of the difficulty in securing skill development in many organizations, temporary help agencies have taken over some of the tasks of helping entry-level workers secure training and work their way into permanent jobs. A 1994 survey conducted by the National Association of Temporary Staffing Services (National As-sociation of Temporary Staffing Services, 1994) reported that about 30 percent of temporary workers received twenty or more hours of formal training from their agencies. Seventy-six percent reported that seeing temporary help as "a way to get a full-time job" was an important factor in their decision to become a temp, and 38 percent of those who were still in temporary jobs had been offered full-time jobs at the organizations to which they were assigned.

The changes in both work organization and tenure patterns sug-gest, first, that it will be increasingly difficult for employees to work their way up a skills hierarchy through on-the-job training and, second, that employers will have less incentive to pay for training, especially formal training where the employee is not contributing. The increased use of training provided by vendors may in part be a response to the first problem. Small employers in particular, who lack the scale to make training programs efficient or where skills are likely to change over time, may rely on vendors to provide the skills training that their employees cannot get on the job. But the problem of how to pay for that training remains.

Some efforts are under way to construct new arrangements for developing skills. Employer-generated skill standards, for example, that are in effect credentials for skills that should facilitate work-based training are being drafted by some industry associations. But the current surplus of skilled workers resulting from downsizing may at least delay the development of a market for training, and there may be certain work processes or technologies for which training cannot be efficiently provided by vendors or schools.

We might expect to see employers pursue very different strategies in the area of developing skills, depending on their circumstances and on the nature of their work. Some employers will continue to invest in company-specific skills and training when they can be reasonably certain that their employees will not leave. Unionized operations where superior employment practices and seniority-based provisions bind organized workers to the business are the most prominent examples. Other employers will become net exporters of skill, relying on the productive work of trainees who then move on to other organizations for their competitive edge. Still other employers may do no training at all and rely on poaching workers from other employers to get the skills they need.

Managing with a New Psychological Contract

Employee commitment is currently an important factor in the effective operation of most organizations. Under more traditional arrangements, especially with "good" employers, employee commitment developed as part of a set of mutual obligations that included long-term employment security and career development offered by the employer. As job security and other perceived employer obligations dissolved, so did employee commitment. How organizations will function in the absence of employee commitment, where workers have a more individualistic orientation, is an open question.

The apparent paradox of declining employee commitment and work-related attitudes without a concommitant decline in employee performance was explained earlier by the "reserve army of the unemployed"; the threat of layoff, the comparison with the jobless, and the fact that most alternative employers were undergoing the same restructuring helped keep employees from quitting and performance up. Operating with sharply lower employee commitment raises a series of long-run challenges, however, even given these countervailing pressures from the market. The challenge of managing with lower commitment is exacerbated by other internal contradictions within the new employment systems. The changes in work organization noted earlier have led most employers to cut back sharply on supervision and the monitoring of employees that can provide a substitute for commitment. At the same time, they are also introducing new work systems that empower employees, give them autonomy in decision making, and make far greater demands on their commitment. The opportunities for and the costs of shirking responsibilities or of simply not making extra efforts are enormous under these new arrangements.

The peer pressures generated by teams are in part a substitute for commitment to the organization. Even if workers have no commitment to the employer, they may still put in the extra effort to

avoid letting their work team down, especially if the team is autonomous and accountable in ways that make the missing effort more
obvious. For example, the decision in many organizations to get rid
of relief workers means that whenever a team member is absent
from a work group, the other members of the team must "cover" for
the absentee, an unpleasant situation that puts peer pressure on
individual workers to show up.

A second way that organizations are attempting to cope with
reduced employee commitment is by creating short-term contracts
with employees that link performance to the organization's goals.
Compensation packages that are heavily leveraged on individual or
team performance, described in chapter 5, are the most obvious of
these. In addition to raising the proportion of pay that is contingent,
another part of the effort toward a more explicit performance contract is to rearrange jobs to make individual and team performance
more observable. Perhaps the most obvious of such efforts are in the
management ranks, where work may be organized around reasonably autonomous "projects"—the design of a marketing campaign
or the production of a brochure on procedures—that employees can
include as part of their portfolio to be shown to potential employers.

More explicitly contractual employment relationships inevitably mean that conflicts will increasingly be resolved outside the
organization in the courts through civil law suits. The courts have
already held that personnel practices in employee handbooks can be
enforced as legal contracts, and the trend at the state level to reduce
the "at will" employment doctrine has expanded the range of issues
over which employees can sue. Bringing the courts further into
employment relationships may well enhance justice in the workplace, but all parties seem to recognize that litigation is an expensive, time-consuming, and typically unsatisfying way to address
workplace problems.

Finally, there are always some self-equilibrating aspects to systems issues, and this may be so for the issue of declining employee
morale. Expectations will eventually adjust to lower levels of job
security and employer commitments, if only because new workers,
whose expectations are different, will replace the old ones. As Robinson, Kraatz, and Rousseau (1994) noted, workers with less tenure
expect less of management and think they owe more to the organization than do more senior workers, so perhaps the reduction in
tenure inside organizations will produce some average improvement in worker commitment.

But there are still situations where the lack of commitment is
likely to be a big problem, where the long-term interests of the
organization cannot be easily reconciled with the self-interest of
uncommitted employees. Consider, for example, a common situa-

tion in which employees are asked to contribute ideas to improve organizational productivity. Unless output is growing, productivity improvements mean that the organization will need fewer employees to do the same amount of work. In the absence of job security, it is difficult to imagine that employees will volunteer suggestions for productivity improvements that would put their own jobs at risk.

One of the most important developments associated with the restructuring of employment is that the new contract between employer and employee has been written very differently for executives than for other employees. In the past, the important division in the workplace was between supervisory employees and their supervisees. Employment legislation followed this division and reflected the common understanding that the employer was offering better protections to supervisory employees than to other workers.

That is no longer the case. Lower-level and middle managers have been hit about as hard by restructuring as the workers that they supervise, and by some measures even harder. In unionized settings, it has been very common for employees covered by collective bargaining agreements to have better protections against the costs of restructuring than management. Indeed, in some organized companies like NYNEX, there have been modest efforts to provide greater protection for blue-collar workers and to internalize their employment relationships along the lines of the traditional model for managers. Overall, then, the distinctions in the treatment between supervisors and their supervisees have largely eroded, and there has been something of a convergence in the structure of blue- and white-collar labor markets.

The contract with top executives has also been rewritten, but in a very different way. While the changes associated with lower-level management have been dominated by the use of sticks, the new contracts for executives are distinguished by the use of carrots. Executives face enormous pressures from investors for increased performance. Formal employment contracts, which are highly unusual for other employees, are becoming almost the rule for top executives. They provide financial protections against the risks of job loss and related risks that have been associated with restructuring efforts and specify in legal terms what is expected of the executives and of the employer.

The most important changes for executives have been efforts to secure their commitment to the goals of investors by giving them extraordinary financial stakes in the success of the organization. Base compensation has risen disproportionately for executives, as noted in chapter 5, but the contingent rewards associated with stock performance represent the most important efforts to build executive commitment. While contingent compensation has also increased for other employees, it is on an entirely different level than that for executives. And in a big year, a CEO's contingent compensation can be sufficient to set up the future generations of his or her family for life.

These new compensation arrangements do seem to be successful in ensuring the commitment of executives to the goals of shareholders. The downside is that they have created a new and important division within organizations. While there still may be tensions between front-line workers and supervisors, the real division now is between executives and everyone else. Employees clearly understand that their company's leadership is playing a very different game than they are, one with very different rules. It is difficult for the leadership to persuade employees that "we are all in this together" and to motivate them to get behind the executive's goals for the company when employees understand how different the stakes for meeting those goals are for them and for the brass.

Employee Outcomes

The last but arguably the most important issue concerning these new arrangements is how employees—and ultimately society—will adapt to them. U.S. employees are taking naturally to work systems that give them greater autonomy and authority, but other aspects of the new employment system represent more difficult adjustments. The first of these are arrangements that make both employment security and pay more contingent not only on individual performance but also on the performance of the organization as a whole. These arrangements essentially shift much of the risk of doing business onto employees and may create substantial hardship when that performance is poor. And the risks associated with business are increasingly being pushed onto employees with no apparent compensating advantages. Once in jobs, employees have much greater responsibility for managing their own careers—securing skills and training, identifying opportunities for advancement, often outside the company, and dealing with job insecurity—than they have been accustomed to.

How employees will adjust to this greater uncertainty is an important issue for society. Major investments such as home ownership or college educations for the middle and working classes have typically been funded by borrowing and paid back in small increments from a steady stream of earnings. These investments have become central to the way that middle-class society operates. Whether they will still be possible or what will have to change in order for them to continue if jobs and income become more variable is a question with some potentially profound implications.

Another issue is the greater difficulty and complexity associated with managing one's career in a world where internal systems of development have declined. Employees need to negotiate for skills and then to identify and pursue opportunities across organizations. These new tasks require new skills and abilities and better information about the world of work. We might expect to see, for example, increased demand for education about career management in schools as workers struggle to find their own paths through the workplace.

A third and more general issue is the inequality of opportunity and outcomes potentially associated with these new developments. Employees with good skills, superior information about opportunities, and an overall high level of marketability may find that their job prospects are enhanced under the new market-oriented system; those who lack skills and information and are less marketable are already finding their prospects deteriorating. The rising inequality in compensation within organizations has already contributed to the growth in economic inequality in society as a whole. The changes we have noted may further accelerate this trend, given that the growth in earnings inequality is already associated with education and skill differences.

Another aspect of the ongoing change is the increasing difficulty of the transition from school to work as employers become less inclined to make investments in new entrants. The shift in employment away from unskilled, entry-level jobs in high paying industries like manufacturing is perhaps the most important part of that development, discussed in chapter 6. But even college graduates are facing similar problems now that many of the less demanding supervisory jobs that served as entry-level management positions have been cut.

Employers that restructure successfully maintain jobs and contribute to improved economic performance. The question at hand concerns who bears the cost in the mean time. Perhaps an important question for society as a whole concerns the distributive aspects of these developments. Wages have fallen, especially for jobs that had been protected by internal labor markets; risk in job security and compensation have increased for employees; long-term unemployment and involuntary part-time work have increased. Yet organizational performance appears to have gained. Bargaining power seems to have shifted to employers in most (but not all) jobs at present because of the large supply of skill on the outside market, made possible in part by widespread organizational downsizing that has both increased the supply of skilled and available workers while reducing the demand for them.

A tightening of the labor market may well lead to a very different situation in which employee turnover escalates rapidly and wages follow as employers scramble to retain key skills. One might expect employers to demand action about skill shortages when the labor market tightens. The behavioral consequences of poor morale (e.g., high turnover and absenteeism, sabotage) will also escalate when a more buoyant labor market makes workers less concerned about losing their current jobs.

In short, if internal labor markets buffered employment from changes in the outside labor market, then the move to more market-mediated employment relationships may well be associated with increased volatility in workplace issues. Issues like wages, turnover, and morale may be much more sensitive to market circumstances, which vary job by job and region by region and with the business cycle. Especially in large, diverse organizations, managing this variability will represent an enormous challenge.

These developments also raise some interesting issues for unions. Industrial unionism has been built around reasonably stable employment patterns and an identification with particular employers. The tenets of traditional collective bargaining have been based on adapting the features of internal labor markets to accommodate employee interests. Arguments to reform current labor relations through enterprise-based union models also rely on traditional and possibly even stronger ties to an employer (Kochan and Osterman, 1994). A decrease in attachment to a single employer may reduce employees' interest in unions as a means of addressing workplace problems rather than simply moving on to a job elsewhere.

On the other hand, U.S. unions also have a long history of craft-based union organization in occupations where the attachment to individual employers is weak at best. Craft-style unions have not flourished in recent years, however, and whether they could be adapted to other kinds of jobs that are traditionally found inside organizations is an open question.

It is also an open question whether the evolving arrangements will produce a stronger or a weaker economic system. There may well be gains in terms of better matches between employees and jobs resulting from increased worker mobility (assuming that the mobility is voluntary). On the other hand, it is also possible, as noted earlier, that the incentives to employers for providing training may be reduced relative to the growing demand for skills. A scaling back of employer investments in worker training and skills may lead to levels of skill that are not optimal for the economy as a whole. The employment system could adjust to reductions in training relative to demand—by substituting additional education for training or redesigning work, for example—but such adjustments may be far from optimal from the perspective of economic performance. Imperfect capital markets and other institutional impediments may make it difficult for individual employees to invest in their own skills and manage their own careers effectively.

Options for the Parties

Do the implications of the changes in the employment relationship that we have outlined shed any light on how far these changes will go? Are the drawbacks and internal contradictions enough to restrain the trend toward these new arrangements? Part of the answer turns on the fact that the changes themselves are driven mainly by the actions of employers while many of the costs are borne by employees and society as a whole. In the absence of a labor shortage, it seems likely that the present trend in restructuring will continue.

Situations in which decisions that make perfect sense for the individual actors have negative spillover effects for those not making the decisions are a classic problem in political economy. Whether U.S. society has both the will and the ability to provide such restraints in this context is another matter.

The traditional means for restraining the potentially adverse actions of employers have involved legal regulations to prevent undesirable actions. But legal regulations on employers are not currently a popular approach for addressing social problems, in part because of the distortions associated with such regulations in the past. As illustrated in chapter 1, efforts by employers to get around previous legislative restraints helped create aspects of these new employment relationships. And in Europe, legislative prohibitions on developments such as an increase in part-time work and in downsizing seem only to have slowed—not stopped—restructuring efforts.

To what extent can we rely on the parties themselves, particularly employers, to take actions that at least ameliorate the more unpleasant aspects of restructuring? Simply resisting the pressures to restructure is probably not a reasonable option for employers, particularly for publicly held companies. For companies, the pressures to restructure are at least in part beyond their control. Once the investment community was persuaded that cutting jobs improved performance, for example, it created a new pressure to cut, independent of the preferences of individual employers; once employees are persuaded that the best career path is to change companies, employee attachment erodes, independent of any change in employer policies.

Employers do have some discretion as to how they respond to these pressures. Chapter 1 suggests that characteristics such as the values of the leaders do shape the paths taken to restructuring, and some employers have chosen strategies that are less disruptive of the lives of employees and their communities.

One of the problems for employers who choose approaches that protect employees is the perception that such choices represent a costly trade-off, that the more radical restructurings are better for organizational performance, and that efforts to protect employees simply hurt the bottom line. This perception is especially common in the investment community, and it puts business executives in the difficult position of having a particularly nasty conflict of duties: the fiduciary responsibility to maximize shareholder value versus the moral responsibility of minimizing the damage inflicted on employees. Perhaps the most unfortunate aspect of this conflict is that it is most troublesome for those leaders who feel the greatest responsibility toward their employees.

The perceived conflict between employee interests and organizational performance has also been the greatest problem for trade unions in their efforts to protect their members from the costs of restructuring. By representing the interests of employees and forcing companies to address them, labor unions have been the most important source of protection for workers in organizations that are undergoing changes of the kind described throughout this volume. The nature of that protection has been to impose contractual obligations that make it costly for companies to restructure along traditional lines—outright job guarantees, compensation for laid-off employees, or retraining for workers whose jobs are eliminated, for example. These contractual obligations reinforce the notion that protecting employees is costly, and it means that trade unions have to pay a price, often a large price, to secure that protection. Sometimes the price is strikes and other industrial action; in other cases, it is giving up other benefits, such as wage increases, to secure protections against restructuring costs.

The great irony here is that there is no real evidence that protecting employees when restructuring has to cost the employer in terms of performance. While companies rush to restructure in ways that appease the investment community, analysts and experts in that investment community in fact have no systematic information about what works or does not work in terms of performance. An obvious recommendation is to disseminate better what we do know about the consequences of restructuring and to focus research attention specifically on the consequences of employee protections. We need to know, for example, whether it really costs a company in the long run to retrain its workers as opposed to laying them off and hiring new ones.

At the moment, then, unions that press employers to protect

worker interests and executives who see extending those protections as part of their obligations both pay a price for doing so. If we believe that the current restructuring is a one-time event, then perhaps we can expect, and should encourage, the parties to pay that price and protect their employees. If we believe that the pressures to restructure will be ongoing, it is more difficult to expect the parties on their own to keep paying that price again and again.

One conceptual alternative is to organize companies in ways that make it possible to restructure in the future with less cost to employees. The best known of these alternatives is the "core-periphery" model, in which job security is explicitly redistributed away from permanent employees toward more casual workers. Central to this model is the assertion that employment will have to flex in the future and that the way to accommodate that reality is to create a "peripheral" workforce of employees that can be adjusted to meet changes in demand conditions. This can be done by having employees who can be easily replaced (based on their abundance in the labor pool), using part-time and contingent workers, and having subcontracting arrangements. Hewlett Packard, where outsourcing is manipulated to maintain stable employment and product market strategies are chosen to reduce employment swings (e.g., avoiding contract work), has long been seen as a successful application of this approach.

There is little evidence that the core-periphery model is widespread in the United States. Abraham's (1990) survey, for example, asked employers about their reasons for using temporary help, outsourcing, and subcontracting. "Providing a buffer for regular staff against downturns in demand" was one of the least frequently cited choices. Of the nine options, only the inability to recruit regular employees was cited less often as a reason (respondents were free to cite more than one choice).

One problem with the core-periphery models is that in practice they do not in fact increase job security within the organization. They simply redistribute it from one group of employees to another, much as the system of seniority-based layoffs distributes the risk of job loss toward junior and away from senior workers. Introducing temporary or contingent employees requires a decision to replace permanent workers with more casual ones, an effort that seems counter to the theme of protecting the permanent employee workforce. The remaining core employees would have been buffered under the old arrangements as well, given that only some of the permanent employees (the ones replaced by the temporaries) would have been at risk. The main advantage to employees under the new system is that they have a better idea up front about the likelihood of job loss based on where their jobs are. Other aspects of the changing employment relationship (i.e., more contingent compensation, reduced promotion and development prospects) are unchanged.

From the perspective of an employer in the nonunion sector, it is hard to see that a core-periphery model offers any advantages over what they could do without it. Assuming that the employer can identify which workers it believes are crucial to retain and which are not, it can simply use selective dismissals and layoffs when necessary and protect the crucial employees. Targeting individual workers is arguably better from this perspective than trying to identify a priori which *jobs* should be included in a "core" group. In short, it is difficult to see models like the core-periphery as representing the solution to the costs associated with restructuring.

Public Policy

It seems that employers and trade unions, given the current environment, can at best be expected only to soften some of the employee and community costs associated with restructuring. And it is highly unlikely that public policy will be brought to bear in ways that significantly restrain employer restructuring options. Rather than attempting to block restructuring, the other option for policy is to help individuals and society deal with the costs.

Some of the more obvious policy initiatives would be aimed at reducing the costs associated with increased employee mobility. A high level of information is needed to allow employees to move efficiently across employers. Employers need to be able to judge the skills of an applicant, just as the applicants need to understand clearly the requirements of jobs. Systems of employment within an organization offered this kind of information. They will be difficult to duplicate in the outside labor market. One consequence, then, is that there may be more "slippage" with these new arrangements—employees with the necessary abilities and talent who are passed over because they lack the necessary credentials or jobs for which qualified workers do not apply because they do not know about them.

Efforts to identify job requirements for jobs across the economy and to establish employee credentials for knowing the skills required in those jobs are an important aspect of reducing the information problems that hinder the movement of employees across jobs. The National Skills Standards Board is currently embarked on such an effort. Whether a system can be created that will convey the appropriate information without creating burdensome bureaucracies and restrictive rules (e.g., different industry boards should not generate wildly different standards for comparable jobs like secretaries) is a formidable burden.

Making pensions and health care more portable and less tied to individual employers is another obvious recommendation that would reduce the problems associated with employee mobility. It is important to note, however, that initiatives that reduce the costs and burdens of mobility are also likely to increase further the movement of workers across employers.

Efforts to improve the school-to-work transition are primarily designed to address long-standing problems facing youth when they enter the labor market. But they have additional relevance now, given that the problem of finding entry-level jobs that offer training and a career path may be worsening. In particular, school-to-work programs may increasingly be called on to provide some of the work-based learning that trainees in the past received in entry-level employment.

The great political advantage of using school-to-work interventions as a means of addressing the problems associated with a changing employment relationship is that schooling is already accepted as an established point of intervention. Public schools and state higher education are already instruments of public policy. We may therefore expect to see education initiatives in a variety of areas as a means of addressing changes in employment relationships. In many states, for example, community colleges are being used as instruments for economic development, training workers for targeted employers in advance of their employment. Initiatives like these essentially encourage hiring by providing employment subsidies for companies through the use of state funds for employee training.

Public policy initiatives designed to ameliorate some of the adverse employee experiences associated with restructuring are more controversial. Income subsidies for workers who experience job losses, for example, exist under a range of programs. The most important of these, such as unemployment insurance, are designed to address temporary and short-term job loss. If the nature of unemployment has changed in ways that make it a long-term problem for more workers, then perhaps the nature of the policies must also change. But long-term income subsidies on their own may create disincentives for participants to find new jobs, which is one reason that many analysts have advocated retraining as the main policy instrument for addressing the problems of workers who have lost their jobs through restructuring. And many of the arguments presented in this volume suggest that skill mismatches and incentives to reduce employer-provided training relative to demand are among the central causes of restructuring related difficulties for employees.

The relatively poor results associated with the more important retraining programs currently in operation, however, have called into question the efficacy of training as a solution to the employee-related problems of restructuring. Government-sponsored training to help workers secure new jobs has suffered from a range of drawbacks (e.g., training for jobs that no longer exist) and has not been very successful. Initiatives in California and, more recently, in New Jersey, in contrast, have attempted to *prevent* restructuring-related job loss by retraining workers before they are laid off. These programs use unemployment insurance funds to assist employers in retraining their current workforces when restructuring has occurred.

The relationship between employees and employers stands, at present, on something like a brink. Clearly there have been important changes in the expectation of job security, work organization, and career development, especially for large employers. Compelling arguments suggest that pressures on employers to restructure may continue the changes in employment, perhaps even accelerate them. On the other hand, the costs and potential drawbacks associated with these new arrangements seem substantial enough at least to slow, or possibly even halt, these trends. It seems difficult to imagine how large, complex organizations in particular can function without the traditional employment relationships that long supported them. Again, employers pursuing these new arrangements confront two daunting problems: how to manage without significant employee commitment and how to provide training and skills to meet the growing demands of jobs.

As authors, we are frankly divided as to how far these developments will go, with the division turning on the relative weight given to the pressures to restructure and the drawbacks of the new arrangements. There is agreement that we have already experienced significant changes. As market circumstances and business strategies change, we should expect individual employers to adjust their employment strategies, some moving back toward the traditional model after a period of restructuring, others moving further out the continuum toward market-based relationships, in an effort to find the path that suits them best. The change at work will continue, as will the search for the best way to accommodate its implications.

Notes

1. Employees may well contribute in the sense that wages can be lower for jobs that offer training, but employers cannot lower wages during periods when training is being provided. They may create a formal structure, however, where wages are lower initially during periods when training is offered.

References

Chapter 1

Abegglen, J. C., and G. Stalk Jr. 1985. *Kaisha: The Japanese Corporation.* New York: Basic Books.

American Management Association. 1993. "1993 AMA Survey on Downsizing." New York: American Management Association.

Applebaum, Eileen, and Rose Batt. 1994. *Transforming Work Systems in the United States.* Ithaca, N.Y.: ILR Press.

Auerbach, James A., and Jerome T. Barrett, eds. 1993. *The Future of Labor-Management Innovation in the United States.* Washington, D.C.: National Planning Association.

Barnevik, Percy. 1991. "The Logic of Global Business." *Harvard Business Review* (March).

Baron, James N., Frank R. Dobbins, and P. D. Jennings. 1986. "War and Peace: The Evolution of Modern Personnel Administration in U.S. Industry." *American Journal of Sociology* 92: 350–383.

Batt, Rosemary. 1996. "From Bureaucracy to Enterprise? The Changing Jobs and Careers of Managers in Telecommunications Services." In *Broken Ladders: Managerial Careers in the New Economy,* ed. Paul Osterman. New York: Oxford University Press.

Becker, Gary S. 1964. "Investments in Human Capital: A Theoretical Analysis." *Journal of Political Economy* 70: 9–49.

Beckman, Sara L. 1996. "The Evolution of a Networked Organization: An Insider's View of the Hewlett-Packard Company." In *Broken Ladders: Managerial Careers in the New Economy,* ed. Paul Osterman. New York: Oxford University Press.

Berger, Joseph. 1993. "The Pain of Layoffs for Ex-Senior I.B.M. Workers." *New York Times*, December 22, B1, B5.

Berger, Lance A., and Martin J. Sikora, ed. 1994. *The Change Management Handbook*. New York: Irwin Professional Publishing.

Bethel, Jennifer E., and Julia Liebeskind. 1993. "The Effects of Ownership Structure on Corporate Restructuring." *Strategic Management Journal* 14: 15–31.

"Beware the IPO Market." 1994. *Business Week*, April. 84–90.

Bhagat, S., A. Shleifer, and R. Vishny. 1990. "Hostile Takeovers in the 1980s: The Return to Corporate Specialization." *Brookings Papers on Economic Activity*. Washington, D.C.: Brookings Institution.

Blair, Margaret M., and Martha A. Schary. 1993. "Industry-Level Pressures to Restructure." In *The Deal Decade*, ed. Margaret M. Blair. Washington, D.C.: Brookings Institution.

Bounds, Wendy. 1993. "Kodak Gives Fisher Options to Purchase 750,000 of Its Shares." *New York Times*, December 20, B2.

Bowman, Edward H., and Harbir Singh. 1990. "Overview of Corporate Restructuring: Trends and Consequences." In *Corporate Restructuring*, ed. Milton L. Rock and Robert H. Rock. New York: McGraw-Hill.

Bowman, Edward H., and Habir Singh. 1993. "Corporate Restructuring: Reconfiguring the Firm." *Strategic Management Journal* 14: 5–14.

Brockner, Joel, Steven Grover, Michael N. O'Malley, Thomas F. Reed, and Mary Ann Glynn. 1993. "Threat of Future Layoffs: Self-Esteem, and Survivors' Reactions: Evidence from the Laboratory and the Field." *Strategic Management Journal* 14: 153–166.

Brockner, Joel, Steven Grover, Thomas F. Reed, and Rocki Lee DeWitt. 1992. "Layoffs, Job Insecurity, and Survivors' Work Effort: Evidence of an Inverted-U Relationship." *Academy of Management Journal* 35: 413–425.

Byrne, John A. 1993. "The Horizontal Corporation." *Business Week*, December 20, 76–81.

Business Failure Record. 1992. New York: Dunn & Bradstreet.

Cameron, Kim S., Sarah J. Freeman, and Aneil K. Mishra. 1993. "Downsizing and Redesigning Organizations." In *Organizational Change and Redesign*, ed. George P. Huber and William H. Glich. New York: Oxford University Press.

Cappelli, Peter, and K. C. O'Shaughnessey. 1995. "Changes in Skill and Wage Structures in Corporate Headquarters, 1986–1992." Philadelphia: National Center on the Educational Quality of the Workforce (EQW).

Coase, Ronald H. 1953. "The Nature of the Firm." *Economica*. 4.

Cole, Robert E., Paul Bacdayan, and B. Joseph White. 1993. "Quality, Participation, and Competitiveness." *California Management Review* (Spring) 35: 68–81.

Conference Board. 1993. "Does Quality Work? A Review of Relevant Studies." New York: Conference Board Report # 1034.

Conte, Michael A., and Jan Svejnar. 1990. "The Performance Effects of Employee Ownership Plans." In *Paying for Productivity: A Look at the Evidence*, ed. Alan S. Blinder. Washington, D.C.: Brookings Institution.

Davis, Gerald F., Kristina A. Diekman, and Catherine H. Tinsley. 1994. "The Decline and Fall of the Conglomeration Firm in the 1980s: Deinstitutionalization of an Organizational Form." Evanston, Ill.: Kellogg Graduate School of Management, Northwestern University.

Davis, Gerald F., and Suzanne K. Stout. 1992. "Organization Theory and the Market for Corporate Control: A Dynamic Analysis of the Characteristics of Large Takeover Targets, 1980–90." *Administrative Science Quarterly* 37 (1992): 605–633.

Dennard, H. Lane Jr., and Herbert R. Northrup. 1994. "Leased Employment: Character, Numbers, and Labor Law Problems." *Georgia Law Review* 23: 683–728.

Doeringer, Peter B., Kathleen Christensen, Patricia M. Flynn, Douglas T. Hall, Harry C. Katz, Jeffrey H. Keefe, Christopher J. Ruhm, Andrew M. Sum, and Michael Useem. 1991. *Turbulence in the American Workplace.* New York: Oxford University Press.

Donaldson, Gordon. 1994. *Corporate Restructuring: Managing the Change Process from Within.* Boston: Harvard Business School Press.

Dyer, Lee, Felician Foltman, and George Milkovich. 1985. "Contemporary Employment Stabilization Practices." In *Human Resource Management and Industrial Relations: Text, Readings, and Cases,* ed. Thomas A. Kochan and Thomas A. Barocci. Boston: Little, Brown.

Economic Report of the President. 1995. Washington, D.C.: GPO. Tables B-22 and B-23.

Edwards, Richard, Michael Reich, and David Gordon. 1979. *Labor Market Segmentation.* New York: Basic Books.

Ehrlichman, John. 1993. "Who Will Hire Me Now?" *Parade,* August 29, 4–6.

Foulkes, Fred. 1980. *Personnel Practices of Large, Non-Union Companies.* Englewood Cliffs, N.J.: Prentice-Hall.

Galinsky, Ellen, James T. Bond, and Dana E. Friedman. 1993. *The Changing Workforce.* New York: Families and Work Institute.

Garone, Stephen J. 1993. *Building a High-Performance Organization.* New York: Conference Board.

Ghemawat, Pahkaj. 1986. "Sustainable Advantage." *Harvard Business Review* (May-June): 69–74.

Griffin, Abbie. 1993. "Metrics for Measuring Product Development Cycle Time." *Journal of Production Innovation Management* 10: 112–125.

Hall, Gene, Jim Rosenthal, and Judy Wade. 1993. "How to Make Reengineering *Really* Work." *Harvard Business Review* (November-December): 191–131.

Hammer, Michael, and James Champy. 1993. *Reengineering the Corporation: A Manifesto for Business Revolution.* New York: Harper Business.

Hay Group. 1993. *1993 Hay Executive Compensation Report—Industrial.* Philadelphia: Hay Group.

Hays, Laurie. 1994. "IBM's Finance Chief, Ax in Hand, Scours Empire for Costs to Cut." *Wall Street Journal,* January 26, A1, A6.

Hays, Laurie, and Gautam Naik. 1993. "Xerox to Cut 10,000 Jobs, Shut Facilities." *Wall Street Journal,* December 9, A2, A4.

Hewitt Associates. 1994. Personal communication.

Hiam, Alexander. 1993. *Does Quality Work? A Review of Relevant Studies.* New York: Conference Board.

Holusha, John. 1993. "A Profitable Xerox Plans to Cut Staff by 10,000." *New York Times,* December 9, D1, D5.

Horwitz, Tony. 1993. "Jobless Male Managers Proliferate in Suburbs, Causing Subtle Malaise." *Wall Street Journal,* September 20, A1, A6.

Hoskisson, Robert E., Richard A. Johnson, and Douglas D. Moesel. 1993. "Corporate Restructuring Intensity: Effects of Governance, Strategy and Performance." College Station, Texas: College of Business Administration, Texas A&M University.

Howard, Robert. 1992. "The CEO as Organizational Architect." *Harvard Business Review* (September-October): 107–119.

Jacoby, Sanford M. 1985. *Employing Bureaucracy: Managers, Unions, and the Transformation of Work in American Industry, 1900–1945.* New York: Columbia University Press.

Janger, Allen. 1989. *Measuring Managerial Layers and Spans.* New York: Conference Board.

Jensen, M. C. 1989. "Eclipse of the Public Corporation." *Harvard Business Review* (September-October): 61–74.

Jensen, Michael C., and Kevin J. Murphy. 1990. "CEO Incentives—It's Not How Much You Pay, but How." *Harvard Business Review* (May-June): 138–153.

Johnson, Arlene S., and Fabian Linden. 1992. *Availability of a Quality Workforce.* New York: Conference Board.

Kaplan, Steven. 1989. "The Effects of Management Buyouts on Operating Performance and Value." *Journal of Financial Economics* 11: 5–50.

Kaplan, Steven N., and Jeremy C. Stein. 1992. "The Evolution of Buyout Pricing and Financial Structure." Paper presented at a conference on "Efficiency and Ownership: The Future of the Corporation," sponsored by University of California, Davis, May, 1992.

Katz, Harry C., and Jeffrey H. Keefe. 1993. "Final Report on a Survey of Training and the Restructuring of Work in Large Unionized Firms." Ithaca, N.Y.: New York State School of Industrial and Labor Relations, Cornell University (mimeographed).

Kekre, Sunder, and Kannan Srinivasan. 1990. "Broader Product Line: A Necessity to Achieve Success?" *Management Science* 30: 12–16.

Kilborn, Peter T. 1993. "The Workplace, After the Deluge." *New York Times,* September 5, Business section, 3–4.

Kochan, Thomas A., and Peter Cappelli. 1984. "The Transformation of the Industrial Relations and Human Resources Functions." In *Internal Labor Markets,* ed. Paul Osterman. New York: Oxford University Press.

Lambert, Richard A., David F. Larcker, and Robert E. Verrecchia. 1991. "Portfolio Considerations in Valuing Executive Compensation." *Journal of Accounting Research* 29: 129–149.

Lawler, Edward E. III, Susan Mohrman, and Gerald Ledford. 1992. *Employee Involvement and Total Quality Management: Practices and Results in Fortune 500 Companies.* San Francisco: Jossey-Bass.

Lichtenberg, Frank R., and Donald Siegel. 1987. "Productivity and Changes of Ownership of Manufacturing Plants." *Brookings Papers on Economic Activity.* Washington, D.C.: Brookings Institution.

Lohr, Steve. 1994. "I.B.M. May Quit Hilltop Headquarters." *New York Times,* January 13, A1, D3.

Lubin, Joann. 1993. "Survivors of Layoffs Battle Angst, Anger, Hurting Productivity." *Wall Street Journal,* December 6, A1, A16.

MacDuffie, John Paul, and John Krafcik. 1992. "Integrating Technology and Human Resources for High Performance Manufacturing: Evidence from the International Auto Industry." In *Transforming Organizations,* ed. Thomas Kochan and Michael Useem. New York: Oxford University Press.

MacDuffie, John Paul, Kannan Sethuraman, and Marshall L. Fisher. 1996. "Product Variety and Manufacturing Performance: Evidence from the International Automotive Assembly Plant Study." *Management Science,* 42, 3: 350–369.

Macy, Barry A., and Hiroaki Izumi. 1993. "Organizational Change, Design, and Work Innovation: A Meta-Analysis of 131 North American Field Studies—1961–1991." In *Research in Organizational Change and Development,* ed. Richard W. Woodman and William A. Pasmore. Greenwich, Ct: JAI Press.

Marglin, Stephen A. 1974. "What Do Bosses Do? The Origins of Hierarchy in Capitalist Production." *Review of Radical Political Economics.* 4: 60–112.

Markides, Constantine C. 1993. "Diversification, Restructuring, and Economic Performance." London Business School working paper.

McKinsey & Company. 1993. *Manufacturing Productivity.* Washington, D.C.: McKinsey Global Institute.

Medoff, James E., and Katharine G. Abraham. 1980. "Experience, Performance, and Earnings." *Quarterly Journal of Economics* 90: 703–736.

Mercer, David. 1987. *IBM: How the World's Most Successful Corporation Is Managed.* London: K. Page.

Mills, D. Quinn. 1985. "Seniority Versus Ability in Promotion Decisions." *Industrial and Labor Relations Review* 38: 421–427.

Mirvis, Philip H., ed. 1993. *Building a Competitive Workforce: Investing in Human Capital for Corporate Success.* New York: John Wiley.

"More than a Dying Fad?" 1993. *Fortune,* October 18, 66.

Morris, Charles E. 1993. "Why New Products?" *Chilton's Food Engineering* 6: 130.

Nadler, David A., Marc S. Gerstein, Robert B. Shaw, and Associates. 1992. *Organizational Architecture: Designs for Changing Organizations.* San Francisco: Jossey-Bass.

Nadler, David A., and Michael Tushman. 1988. *Strategic Organization Design.* Glenview, Ill.: Scott, Foresman.

Newman, Katherine S. 1989. *Falling from Grace: The Experience of Downward Mobility in the American Middle Class.* New York: Random House.

Osterman, Paul. 1986. "The Impact of Computers on the Employment of Clerks and Managers." *Industrial and Labor Relations Review* 39: 175–186.

Osterman, Paul. 1994. "How Common Is Workplace Transformation and How Can We Explain Who Adopts It?" *Industrial and Labor Relations Review* 47: 173–188.

Osterman, Paul, ed. 1996. *Broken Ladders: Managerial Careers in the New Economy.* New York: Oxford University Press.

Ouchi, William G. 1981. Theory Z: How American Business Can Meet the Japanese Challenge. Reading, MA: Addison-Wesley.

Pfeffer, Jeffrey, and James N. Baron. 1988. "Taking the Workers Back Out: Recent Trends in the Structuring of Employment." *Research in Organizational Behavior* 10: 251–303.

Piore, Michael J., and Charles F. Sabel. 1984. *The Second Industrial Divide.* New York: Basic Books.

Prahaled, C. K. and G. Hamel. 1990. "The Core Competence of the Corporation." *Harvard Business Review,* May–June, 79–91.

Reich, Robert B. 1993. "Companies are Cutting Their Hearts Out." *New York Times Magazine,* December 19, 54–55.

Reilly, Anne H., Jeane M. Brett, and Linda K. Stroh. 1993. "The Impact of Corporate Turbulence on Managers' Attitudes." *Strategic Management Journal* 14: 167–179.

Richman, Louis S. 1993. "How Jobs Die—And Are Born." *Fortune* 128: 26.

Riverside Economic Research. 1994. *Brancato Report: Equity Turnover & Investment Strategies.* Fairfax, Va.: Victoria Group.

Rogers, Rolf E. 1993. "Managing for Quality: Current Differences Between Japanese and American Approaches." *National Productivity Review* 12, no. 4: 503.

Rosenau, Milton D. Jr. 1988. "From Experience: Faster New Product Development. *Journal of Production Innovation and Management* 5: 150–153.

Scott, Elizabeth D., K. C. O'Shaughnessey, and Peter Cappelli. 1996. "The Changing Structure of Management Jobs in the Insurance Industry." In *Broken Ladders: Managerial Careers in the New Economy,* ed. Paul Osterman. New York: Oxford University Press.

Scott Morton, Michael S., ed. 1991. *The Corporation of the 1990s: Information Technology and Organizational Transformation.* New York: Oxford University Press.

Slater, Stanley F. 1993. "Competing in High Velocity Markets." *Industrial Marketing Management* 22: 255–263.

Stalk, George Jr. 1988. "Time—The Next Source of Competitive Advantage." *Harvard Business Review* (July-August): 41–51.

Slichter, Sumner H., James J. Healy, and E. Robert Livernash. 1960. *The Impact of Collective Bargaining on Management.* Washington, D.C.: The Brookings Institution.

Tully, Shawn. 1993. "The Real Key to Creating Wealth." *Fortune,* Sept. 20, 1993, 38–50.

Uchitelle, Louis. 1993a. "Strong Companies Are Joining Trend to Eliminate Jobs." *New York Times,* July 26, A1, D3.

Uchitelle, Louis. 1993b. "More Are Forced into Ranks of Self-Employed at Low Pay." *New York Times,* November 15, A1, B8.

United Nations. 1995. *World Investment Report: Transnational Corporations and Integrated International Production.* New York: United Nations.

United Shareholders Association. 1993. *Executive Compensation 1,000.* Washington, D.C.: United Shareholders Association.

U.S. Department of Labor. 1993. "High Performance Work Practices and Firm Performance." Washington, D.C.: U.S. Department of Labor.

Useem, Michael. 1993. "Management Commitment and Company Policies on Education and Training." *Human Resource Management* 32: 411–434.

Useem, Michael. 1996. *Investor Capitalism: How Money Managers Are Changing the Face of Corporate America.* New York: Basic Books (Harper Collins).

Williamson, Oliver E. 1975. *Markets and Hierarchies.* New York: Free Press.

Williamson, Oliver E. 1980. "The Organization of Work: A Comparative Institutional Assessment." *Journal of Economic Behavior and Organization* 1: 5–38.

Womack, James, Daniel Jones, and Daniel Roos. 1990. *The Machine that Changed the World.* New York: Rawson-MacMillan.

Worrell, Dan L., Wallace N. Davidson III, and Varinder M. Sharma. 1991. "Layoff Announcements and Stockholder Wealth." *Academy of Management Journal* 34: 662–678.

Wyatt Company. 1993. "Wyatt's 1993 Survey of Corporate Restructuring— Best Practices in Corporate Restructuring." New York: Wyatt Company.

Yago, Glenn. 1991. *Junk Bonds: How High Yield Securities Restructured Corporate America.* New York: Oxford University Press.

Chapter 2

Abraham, Katharine G. 1990. "Restructuring the Employment Relationship: The Growth of Market-Mediated Work Arrangements." In *New Developments in the Labor Market,* ed. Katharine Abraham and Robert McKersie. Cambridge, Mass.: MIT Press.

American Management Association. 1990. *Annual Survey on Downsizing and Worker Assistance.* New York: American Management Association.

American Management Association. 1994. "1994 AMA Survey on Downsizing: Summary of Key Findings." New York: American Management Association.

Baily, Martin Neal, Eric J. Bartelsman, and John Haltiwanger. 1994. "Downsizing and Productivity Growth: Myth or Reality." National Bureau of Economic Research, Working Paper No. 4741.

Bassi, Laurie J. 1993. "Reorganization of Work and Workplace Education: Scope and Impact." Washington, D.C.: Southport Institute for Policy Analysis.

Belous, Richard S. 1989. *The Contingent Economy.* Washington, D.C.: National Planning Association.

Brockner, Joel. 1988. "The Effects of Work Layoffs on Survivors: Research, Theory, and Practice." In *Research in Organizational Behavior,* ed. M. Staw and L. L. Cummings. Greenwich, CT.: JAI Press.

Bureau of National Affairs. 1994. "New BLS Data Shows Displaced Workers

Generally Not Helped By Advance Notice." *Daily Labor Report* (September 15): B-4–B-12.

Callaghan, Polly, and Heidi Hartmann. 1991. *Contingent Work.* Washington, D.C.: Economic Policy Institute.

Cameron, Kim S., Sarah J. Freeman, and Aniel K. Mishra. 1993. "Downsizing and Redesigning Organizations." In *Organizational Change and Redesign,* ed. G. P. Huber and W. H. Glick. New York: Oxford University Press.

Cappelli, Peter. 1992. "Examining Managerial Displacement." *Academy of Management Journal* 35, no. 1: 203–217.

Cascio, Wayne F. 1993. "Downsizing: What Do We Know? What Have We Learned?" *Academy of Management Executive* 7, no. 1: 95–104.

Farber, Henry S. 1993. "The Incidence and Costs of Job Loss: 1982–91." *Brookings Papers on Economic Activity: Microeconomics.* Washington, D.C.: The Brookings Institution.

Fisher, Anne B. 1991. "Morale Crisis." *Fortune,* November 18, 70–80.

Greenberg, Eric Rolfe. 1991. "Downsizing: AMA Survey Results." *Compensation and Benefits Review* 23, no. 4: 33–38.

Harris, Louis, and Associates. 1991. *Laborforce 2000 Survey.* New York: Harris Associates.

Herz, Diane E. 1991. "Worker Displacement Still Common in the Late 1980s." *Monthly Labor Review* (May): 3–9.

Katz, Harry C., and Jeffrey H. Keefe. 1993. "Final Report on a Survey of Training and the Restructuring of Work in Large Unionized Settings." Philadelphia: National Center on the Educational Quality of the Workforce.

Katz, Harry C., and Charles F. Sabel. 1985. "Industrial Relations and Industrial Adjustment in the Car Industry." *Industrial Relations* 24 (Fall): 295–315.

Keefe, Jeffrey, and Karen Boroff. 1995. "Telecommunications Labor-Management Relations After Divestiture." In *Contemporary Collective Bargaining in the Private Sector,* ed. Paula Voos. Madison, Wis.: IRRA.

Kletzer, Lori G. 1991. "Job Displacement, 1976–86: How Blacks Fared Relative to Whites." *Monthly Labor Review* (July): 17–25.

Osterman, Paul. 1988. *Employment Futures: Reorganization, Dislocation, and Public Policy.* New York: Oxford University Press.

Osterman, Paul, and Rosemary Batt. 1992. *Public Policy and Workplace Centered Training.* Washington, D.C.: Economic Policy Institute.

Podgursky, Michael. 1992. "The Industrial Structure of Job Displacement, 1979–89." *Monthly Labor Review* (September): 17–25.

Rose, Stephen. 1995. "Declining Job Security and the Professionalization of Opportunity," Research Report No. 95-04, National Commission for Employment Policy, Washington, D.C. (May).

Sharpe, Rochelle. 1993. "In Latest Recession Only Blacks Suffered Net Employment Loss." *Wall Street Journal,* September 14, A-1, A-12, A-13.

Swinnerton, Kenneth A., and Howard Wial. 1995. "Is Job Stability Declining in the U.S. Economy?", *Industrial and Labor Relations Review* 48, no. 2 (January): 293–304.

Tilly, Chris. 1991. "Reasons for the Continuing Growth in Part-Time Employment." *Monthly Labor Review* (March): 10–18.

Useem, Michael. 1993. "Management Commitment and Company Policies on Education and Training." *Human Resource Management* 32, no. 4 (Winter): 411–434.

Wyatt Company. 1993. "Wyatt's 1993 Survey of Corporate Restructuring—Best Practices in Corporate Restructuring." New York: Wyatt Company.

Chapter 3

Adler, Paul. 1991. "The New 'Learning Bureaucracy': New United Motor Manufacturing, Inc." Mimeo, University of Southern California.

AFL-CIO. 1994. "The New American Workplace: A Labor Perspective." Report by the AFL-CIO Committee on the Evolution of Work. Washington, D.C.: AFL-CIO.

Applebaum, Eileen, and Rose Batt. 1994. *The New American Workplace: Transforming Work Systems In The United States.* Ithaca, N.Y.: Cornell University Press.

Bailey, Thomas. 1994. " 'High Performance' Work Organization and the Apparel Industry: The Extent and Determinants of Reform." New York: Columbia University Institute on Education and the Economy.

Bassi, Lauri. 1993. "Reorganization of Work and Workplace Education: Scope and Impact." Washington, D.C.: Southport Institute for Policy Analysis.

Berg, Peter, Eileen Appelbaum, Thomas Bailey, and Arne Kalleberg. 1994. "The Performance Effects of Modular Production in the Apparel Industry." Washington, D.C.: Economic Policy Institute.

Cappelli, Peter, and Nikolai Rogovsky. 1993. "Work Systems and Individual Performance." Mimeo. Philadelphia: National Center on the Educational Quality of the Workforce.

Commission on the Skills of the American Workforce. 1990. *America's Choice: High Skills or Low Wages.* Washington, D.C.: National Center on Education and the Economy.

Cotton, J. L. 1993. *Employee Involvement: Methods for Improving Performance and Work Attitudes.* Newbury Park, Calif.: Sage.

Cutcher-Gershenfeld, Joel. 1991. "The Impact on Economic Performance of a Transformation in Workplace Relations." *Industrial and Labor Relations Review* 44 (January): 241–260.

Dore, Ronald. 1973. *British Factory, Japanese Factory.* Berkeley: University of California Press.

Ehrenberg, Ronald, and George Milkovich. 1987. "Compensation and Firm Performance." In *Human Resources and the Performance of the Firm,* ed. Morris Kleiner. Madison, WI: Industrial Relations Research Association.

Goodman, Paul S. 1980. "Quality of Work Life Projects in the 1980s." Industrial Relations Research Association Proceedings of the 1980 Spring Meeting. Philadelphia: IRRA.

Harris, Louis and Associates. 1991. *Laborforce 2000 Survey.* New York: Louis Harris.

Huselid, Mark. 1995. "The Impact of Human Resource Management Practices Upon Turnover, Productivity, and Corporate Financial Performance." *Academy of Management Journal* 38 (June): 635–672.

Ichniowski, Casey. 1986. "The Effect of Grievance Activity on Productivity." *Industrial Labor and Relations Review* 40: 75–89.

Ichniowski, Casey, Katherine Shaw, and Giovanna Prennushi. 1994. "The Effects of Human Resource Management Practices Upon Productivity." Graduate School of Business, Columbia University, mimeograph.

Katz, Harry. 1985. *Shifting Gears: Changing Labor Relations in the U.S. Auto Industry.* Cambridge, Mass.: MIT Press.

Katz, Harry, Thomas Kochan, and Mark Weber. 1985. "Assessing the Effects of Industrial Relations Systems and Efforts to Improve the Quality of Work Life on Organizational Performance." *Academy of Management Journal* 28: 509–526.

Katz, Harry, Thomas Kochan, and Kenneth Gobeille. 1983. "Industrial Relations Performance, Economic Performance, and QWL Programs: An Interplant Analysis." *Industrial and Labor Relations Review.* 37: 1, 3–17.

Kaufman, Roger. 1992. "The Effects of Improshare on Productivity." *Industrial and Labor Relations Review* 45 (January): 311–322.

Kochan, Thomas, and Paul Osterman. 1994. *The Mutual Gains Enterprise.* Cambridge, Mass.: Harvard Business School Press.

Kruse, Douglas. 1988. "Essays on Profit Sharing and Unemployment." Ph.D. dissertation, Harvard University Department of Economics.

Lawler, Edward, Susan Mohrman, and Gerald Ledford. 1992. *Employee Involvement and Total Quality Management: Practices and Results in Fortune 1000 Companies.* San Francisco: Jossey-Bass.

Levine, David, and Laura D'Andrea Tyson. 1990. "Participation, Productivity, and the Firm's Environment." In *Paying for Productivity*, ed. Alan Blinder. Washington, D.C.: Brookings Institution.

Lincoln, James, and Arne Kalleberg. 1990. *Culture, Control, and Commitment: A Study of Work Organization and Work Artifacts in the United States and Japan.* Cambridge: Cambridge University Press.

MacDuffie, John Paul. 1995. "Human Resource Bundles and Manufacturing Performance: Flexible Production Systems in the World Auto Industry." *Industrial and Labor Relations Review* 48 (January): 197–221.

MacDuffie, John Paul, and Thomas Kochan. 1995. "Do U.S. Firms Invest Less in Human Resources Training in the World Auto Industry." *Industrial Relations*, 34: 2, 147–168.

Mark, Carolyn. 1993. "High Performance Production in Small Firms." Master's Thesis, Department of Urban Studies and Planning, Massachusetts Institute of Technology.

Milkman, Ruth. 1991. "California's Japanese Factories; Labor Relations and Economic Globalization." Los Angeles: UCLA Institute of Industrial Relations.

Miller, Katherine, and Peter Monge. 1986. "Participation, Satisfaction, and Productivity: A Meta-Analytic Review," *Academy of Management Journal* 29 (December): 727–753.

Mitchell, Daniel J. B., David Lewin, and Edward Lawler. 1990. "Alternative Pay Systems, Firm Performance, and Productivity." In *Paying for*

Productivity, ed. Alan Blinder. Washington, D.C.: Brookings Institution.

National Center on the Educational Quality of the Workforce. 1995. "The EQW National Employer Survey: First Findings." Philadelphia: National Center on the Educational Quality of the Workforce.

New York Stock Exchange. 1982. *People and Productivity: A Challenge to Corporate America*. New York: New York Stock Exchange.

Osterman, Paul. 1987. "Choice Among Alternative Internal Labor Market Systems." *Industrial Relations* 26 (February): 46–67.

Osterman, Paul. 1988. *Employment Futures: Reorganization, Dislocation, and Public Policy*. New York: Oxford University Press.

Osterman, Paul. 1994. "How Common Is Workplace Transformation and How Can We Explain Who Does It?" *Industrial and Labor Relations Review* (January): 173–188.

Piore, Michael, and Charles Sabel. 1984. *The Second Industrial Divide*. New York: Basic Books.

Russell, Raymond. 1988. "Forms and Extent of Employee Participation in the Contemporary United States." *Work and Occupations* 15: 374–395.

Schuster, Michael. 1984. "The Scalon Plan: A Longitudinal Analysis. *Journal of Applied Behavioral Science* 20 (February): 23–38.

Streeck, Wolfgang. 1988. "Successful Adjustment to Turbulent Markets: The Automobile Industry," Berlin, Wissenschaftszentrum Berlin Fur Sozialforschung, FSI88-1, June.

Walton, Richard. 1985. "From Control to Commitment in the Workplace." *Harvard Business Review*, March/April, pp. 77–84.

Wall, Toby, Nigel Kemp, Paul Jackson, and Chris Clegg. 1986. "Outcomes of Autonomous Work Groups: A Long Term Field Experiment." *Academy of Management Journal* 29 (June): 280–304.

Weitzman, Martin, and Douglas Kruse. 1990. "Profit Sharing and Productivity." In *Paying for Productivity*, ed. Alan Blinder. Washington, D.C.: Brookings Institution.

Chapter 4

American Society for Training and Development. 1994. *U.S. Business Views on Workforce Training*. Washington, D.C.: Price Waterhouse (mimeographed).

Baker, Richard. 1991. "Joint State-Level Responses to Worker Dislocation." In *Joint Training Programs: A Union-Management Approach to Preparing Workers for the Future*, ed. Louis A. Ferman, Michele Hoyman, Joel Crutcher-Gershenfeld, and Ernst J. Savoie. Ithaca, N.Y.: ILR Press.

Barley, Stephen R. 1992. "The New Crafts: The Rise of the Technical Labor Force and Its Implication for the Organization of Work." Philadelphia: National Center on the Educational Quality of the Workforce.

Baron, James N., and William T. Bielby. 1984. "The Organization of Work in a Segmented Economy." *American Sociological Review* 49:454–473.

Baron, James N., Frank R. Dobbin, and P. Devereux Jennings. 1986. "War and Peace: The Evolution of Modern Personnel Administration in U.S. Industry." *American Journal of Sociology* 92: 350–383.

Barron, John M., Dan A. Black, and Mark A. Lowenstein. 1989. "Job Matching and On-the-Job Training." *Journal of Labor Economics* 7: 1–19.

Bassi, Laurie J. 1993. "Reorganization of Work and Workplace Education: Scope and Impact." Washington, D.C.: Southport Institute for Policy Analysis.

Becker, Gary S. 1964. *Human Capital: A Theoretical and Empirical Analysis with Special Reference to Education.* New York: National Bureau of Economic Research.

Berg, Ivar. 1970. *Education and Jobs: The Great Training Robbery.* New York: Praeger.

Bishop, John. 1991. "On-the-Job Training of New Hires." In *Market Failure in Training*, ed. David Stern and Josef Ritzen. New York: Springer-Verlag.

Bishop, John H. 1994a. "The Incidence and Payoff to Employer Training: A Review of the Literature." Philadelphia: Center on the Educational Quality of the Workforce.

Bishop, John H. 1994b. "The Impact of Previous Training in Schools and on Jobs on Productivity, Required OJT, and Turnover of New Hires." In *Private Sector and Skill Formation: International Comparisons*, ed. Lisa Lynch. Chicago: University of Chicago Press.

Black, Dan, Mark Berger, and John Barron. 1993. *Job Training Approaches and Costs in Small and Large Firms.* Lexington: University of Kentucky, Department of Economics (mimeographed).

Boston, Thomas D. 1990. "Segmented Labor Markets: New Evidence from a Study of Four Race-Gender Groups." *Industrial and Labor Relations Review* 44: 99–115.

Bowers, Norman, and Paul Swaim. 1992. "Probing (Some of) the Issues of Employment-Related Training: Evidence from the CPS." Washington, D.C.: U.S. Department of Agriculture, Economic Research Service.

Brown, Charles. 1990. "Empirical Evidence on Private Training." *Research in Labor Economics* 11: 97–113.

Cappelli, Peter, and K. C. O'Shaugnessey. 1993. "What's Behind the Skills Gap?" *IRRA 45th Annual Proceedings*, 296–303.

Carnevale, Anthony P., and Leila J. Gainer. 1989. *The Learning Enterprise.* Washington, D.C.: U.S. Government Printing Office.

Carnevale, Anthony P., Leila J. Gainer, and Janice Villet. 1990. *Training in America: The Organization and Strategic Role of Training.* San Francisco: Jossey-Bass.

Congressional Quarterly. 1994. "Worker Retraining." *CO Researcher* 4: 49–72.

Constantine, Jill M., and David Neumark. 1994. "Training and the Growth of Wage Inequality." Philadelphia: National Center on the Educational Quality of the Workforce.

Ferman, Louis A., Michele Hoyman, and Joel Crutcher-Gershenfeld. 1990. "Joint Union-Management Training Programs: A Synthesis in the

Evolution of Jointism and Training." In *New Developments in Worker Training: A Legacy for the 1990s*, ed. Louis A. Ferman, Michael Hoyman, Joel Crutcher-Gershenfeld, and Ernst J. Savoie. Madison, Wis.: Industrial Labor Relations Research Association.

Ferman, Louis A., Michele Hoyman, Joel Crutcher-Gershenfeld, and Ernst J. Savoie, eds. 1991. *Joint Training Programs: A Union-Management Approach to Preparing Workers for the Future*. Ithaca, N.Y.: ILR Press.

Frazis, Harley J., Diane E. Herz, and Michael W. Horrigan. 1995. "Employer-Provided Training: Results from a New Survey." *Monthly Labor Review* 188: 3–18.

Goldstein, A. P. 1981. *Psychological Skill Training: The Structured Learning Technique*. New York: Pergamon.

Goldstein, Mark L. 1980. "Training in Work Organizations." *Annual Review of Psychology* 31: 229–272.

Granovetter, Mark. 1985. "Economic Action and Social Structure: The Problem of Embeddedness." *American Journal of Sociology* 91; 481–510.

Hoyman, Michele, and Louis A. Ferman. 1991. "Scope and Extent of Joint Training Programs." In *Joint Training Programs: A Union-Management Approach to Preparing Workers for the Future*, ed. Louis A. Ferman, Michele Hoyman, Joel Crutcher-Gershenfeld, and Ernst J. Savoie. Ithaca, N.Y.: ILR Press.

Kalleberg, Arne L., David Knoke, Peter V. Marsden, and Joe L. Spaeth. 1996. *Organizations in America: Analyzing Their Structures and Human Resource Practices*. Thousand Oaks, Calif.: Sage.

Katz, Harry C., and Jeffrey H. Keefe. 1993. "Final Report on a Survey of Training and the Restructuring of Work in Large Unionized Firms." Ithaca, N.Y.: New York State School of Industrial and Labor Relations, Cornell University (mimeograph).

Knoke, David. 1994. "Cui Bono? Employee Benefits Packages." *American Behavioral Scientist* 37: 963–978.

Knoke, David, and Yoshito Ishio. 1994. "Occupational Training in Organizations: Job Ladders and Unions." *American Behavioral Scientist* 37: 992–1016.

Knoke, David, and Arne Kalleberg. 1994. "Job Training in U.S. Organizations." *American Sociological Review* 59: 537–546.

Loveman, Gary W., Michael J. Piore, and Werner Sengenberger. 1990. "The Evolving Role of Small Business and Some Implications for Employment and Training Policy." In *New Developments in the Labor Market: Toward a New Institutional Paradigm*, ed. Katherine G. Abraham and Robert B. McKersie. Cambridge, Mass.: MIT Press.

Lynch, Lisa M. 1991. "The Private Sector and Skill Formation in the United States." *Advances in the Study of Entrepreneurship, Innovation, and Economic Growth* 5: 115–144.

MacDuffie, John Paul, and Thomas A. Kochan. 1995. "Do U.S. Firms Invest Less in Human Resources? Training in the World Auto Industry." *Industrial Relations* 34: 147–168.

Monahan, Sue, John W. Meyer, and W. Richard Scott. 1994. "Employee Training: The Expansion of Organizational Citizenship." In *Institutional Environments and Organizations: Structural Complexity and*

Individualism, ed. W. Richard Scott and John W. Meyer. Newbury Park, Calif.: Sage.

National Center on the Educational Quality of the Workforce. 1995. "The EQW National Employer Survey: First Findings." Philadelphia: National Center on the Educational Quality of the Workforce.

Osterman, Paul, ed. 1984. *Internal Labor Markets*. Cambridge, Mass.: MIT Press.

Osterman, Paul. 1995. "Skill, Training, and Work Organization in American Establishments." *Industrial Relations* 34: 125–146.

Patrick, J. 1992. *Training: Research and Practice*. London: Academic Press.

Phillips, J. J. 1990. *Handbook of Training Evaluation and Measurement Measures*. London: Kogan Page.

Pines, Marion, and Anthony Carnevale. 1991. "Employment and Training." In *Human Capital and America's Future*, ed. David W. Hornbeck and Lester M. Salamon. Baltimore: Johns Hopkins University Press.

Roberts, Markley, and Robert Wozniak. 1994. "Labor's Key Role in Workplace Training." Washington, D.C.: AFL-CIO Economic Research Department.

Rumberger, Russell W. 1984. "The Incidence and Wage Effects of Occupational Training Among Young Men." *Social Science Quarterly* 65: 775–788.

Schurman, Susan J., Margrit K. Hugentobler, and Hal Stack. 1991. "Lessons from the UAW-GM Paid Education Leave Program." In *Joint Training Programs: A Union-Management Approach to Preparing Workers for the Future*, ed. Louis A. Ferman, Michele Hoyman, Joel Crutcher-Gershenfeld, and Ernst J. Savoie. Ithaca, N.Y.: ILR Press.

Scott, W. Richard. 1992. "Institutions and Organizations: Attempting a Theoretical Synthesis." Stanford, Calif.: Stanford University (mimeograph).

Scott, W. Richard, and John W. Meyer. 1991. "The Rise of Training Programs in Firms and Agencies: An Institutional Perspective." *Research in Organizational Behavior* 13: 297–326.

Spence, Michael. 1974. *Market Signalling: Information Transfer in Hiring and Related Processes*. Cambridge, Mass.: Harvard University Press.

Thurow, Lester C. 1975. *Generating Inequality: Mechanisms of Distribution in the U.S. Economy*. New York: Basic Books.

Tomasko, Elizabeth S., and Kenneth K. Dickinson. 1991. "The UAW-Ford Education, Development and Training Program." In *Joint Training Programs: A Union-Management Approach to Preparing Workers for the Future*, ed. Louis A. Ferman, Michele Hoyman, Joel Crutcher-Gershenfeld, and Ernst J. Savoie. Ithaca, N.Y.: ILR Press.

U.S. Bureau of Labor Statistics. 1985. *How Workers Get Their Training*. Washington, D.C.: U.S. Government Printing Office.

U.S. Bureau of Labor Statistics. 1992. *How Workers Get Their Training: A 1991 Update*. Washington, D.C.: U.S. Government Printing Office.

U.S. Bureau of Labor Statistics. 1994. "BLS Reports on Employer-Provided Training." Washington, D.C.: U.S. Department of Labor (press release 94–432).

U.S. Commission on Excellence in Education. 1983. *A Nation at Risk: The*

Imperative for Educational Reform. Washington, D.C.: The Commission.

Useem, Michael. 1993. "Company Policies on Education and Training." In *Building a Competitive Workforce: Investing in Human Capital for Corporate Success,* ed. Philip Mirvis. New York: Wiley.

Veum, Jonathan R. 1993. "Training Among Young Adults: Who, What Kind, and for How Long?" *Monthly Labor Review* 116: 27–32.

Wartzman, Rick. 1995. "A Clinton Potion to Restore Middle Class's Love, Brewed by Labor Secretary, Stresses Job Training." *Wall Street Journal,* February 11, A16.

Wexley, Kenneth N. 1984. "Personnel Training." *Annual Review of Psychology* 35: 519–551.

Chapter 5

Barley, Stephen R. 1992. "The New Crafts: The Rise of the Technical Labor Force and Its Implications for the Organization of Work." Philadelphia: National Center on the Educational Quality of the Workforce.

Bartel, Ann P., and Nachum Sicherman. 1993. "Technological Change and the on-the-job Training of Young Workers." New York: Columbia University Press.

Berliner, David C. 1993. "Mythology and the American System of Education." Phi Delta Kappan 74: 632.

Berman, Eli, John Bound, and Zvi Griliches. 1993. "Changes in the Demand for Skilled Labor Within U.S. Manufacturing Industries: Evidence from the Annual Survey of Manufacturing." Cambridge, Mass.: N.B.E.R. working paper no. 4255.

Bishop, John B. 1992. "High School Performance and Employee Recruitment." *Journal of Labor Research.* 13.1: 41–44.

Bishop, John B. 1990. "Incentives for Learning: Why American High School Students Compare So Poorly to Their Counterparts Overseas." *Research in Labor Economics.*

Bracey, Gerald W. 1992. "How Bad Are Our Schools?" *Principal* 71 (March): 14–18.

Burtless, Martin N. 1993. *Growth with Equity: Economic Policymaking for the Next Century.* Washington, D.C.: The Brookings Institution.

Cappelli, Peter, and K. C. O'Shaughnessey. 1995. "Skill and Wage Changes in Corporate Headquarters, 1986–1992." Philadelphia: National Center on the Educational Quality of the Workforce.

Cappelli, Peter, and Nikolai Rogovsky. 1994. "New Work Systems and Skill Requirements." *International Labour Review* 133: 205–220.

Cappelli, Peter, and K. C. O'Shaughnessey. 1993. "Are Skill Requirements Rising? Evidence from Production and Clerical Jobs." *Industrial Labor Relations Review* 46: 515–530.

The Condition of Education. 1994. Washington, D.C.: National Center for Educational Statistics.

General Accounting Office. 1990. *Training Strategies: Preparing Noncollege Youth for Employment in the U.S. and Foreign Countries.* Washington, D.C.: GAO, HRD-90-88. May.

Howell, D. R., and E. N. Wolff. 1991. "Trends in the Growth and Distribution of Skills in the U.S. Workplace, 1960–1985." *Industrial and Labor Relations Review* 44: 486–502.

Hudson Institute. 1986. *Workforce 2000.* Washington, D.C.: Hudson Institute.

Kelley, Maryellen. 1989. "Unionization and Job Design Under Programmable Automation." *Industrial Relations* 28 (Spring): 174–187.

Komiyo, Fumito. 1991. "Law of Dismissal and Employment Practices in Japan." *Industrial Relations Journal* 22: 59–66.

Levy, Frank, and Richard Murmane. 1992. "Earnings Levels and Earnings Inequality: A Review of Recent Trends and Proposed Explanations." *Journal of Economic Literature* 303: 1333–1381.

Long, David A., Charles Maller, and Craig V.D. Thornton. 1981. "Evaluating the Benefits and Costs of the Job Corps." *Journal of Policy Analysis and Management* 1: 1.

Mavrinac, Sarah C., Neil R. Jones, and Marshall W. Meyer. 1994. "The Financial and Non-Financial Returns to Innovative Workplace Practices: A Critical Review." Washington, D.C.: U.S. Department of Labor.

Mishel, Lawrence, and Ruy A. Texeira. 1991. "The Myth of the Coming Labor Shortage: Jobs, Skills, and Incomes of America's Workforce 2000." Washington, D.C.: Economic Policy Institute.

Monthly Labor Review. 1986. "Unemployment Rate by Sex and Age, Seasonally Adjusted Annual Averages." 109: 12, 62.

Monthly Labor Review. 1994. "Unemployment Rate by Sex and Age, Seasonally Adjusted Annual Averages." 117: 12, 81.

Murnane, Richard J., John B. Willet, and Frank Levy. 1995. "The Growing Importance of Cognitive Skills in Wage Determination." *Review of Economics and Statistics* 77: 251–266.

Nation at Risk, A. 1984. Cambridge, Mass.: USA Research.

National Center for Education Statistics. 1993. *Digest of Education Statistics.* Washington, D.C.: U.S. Department of Education.

National Center for Education Statistics. 1995. *Digest of Education Statistics.* Washington, D.C.: U.S. Department of Education.

National Center on the Educational Quality of the Workforce. 1995. "The EQW National Employer Survey: First Findings." Philadelphia: National Center on the Educational Quality of the Workforce.

Osterman, Paul. 1993. *Economic Futures.* New York: Oxford University Press.

Organisation for Economic Co-operation and Development. 1988. *Living Conditions in OECD Countries 1986.* Paris. OECD.

Shelley, Kristina J. 1992. "The Future of Jobs for College Graduates." *Monthly Labor Review* 115 (July): 13–20.

Sherer, Peter D. 1992. "Beyond the Standard Employment Relationship: The Character and Determinants of Risk-Involved Teams, Altered-Time Arrangements, and the Contracting-In of Retirees." Philadelphia: National Center on the Educational Quality of the Workforce.

Chapter 6

Abraham, Katharine G. 1990. "Restructuring the Employment Relationship: The Growth of Market-Mediated Work Arrangements." In *New*

Developments in the Labor Market, ed. Katharine Abraham and Robert McKersie. Cambridge, Mass.: MIT Press.

Advisory Council on Unemployment Compensation. 1994. *Findings and Recommendations.* Washington, D.C., Advisory Council on Unemployment Compensation.

American Management Association. 1990. *Annual Survey on Downsizing and Worker Assistance.* New York: American Management Association.

American Management Association. 1994. "1994 AMA Survey on Downsizing: Summary of Key Findings." New York: American Management Association.

Baily, Martin Neal, Eric J. Bartelsman, and John Haltiwanger. 1994. "Downsizing and Productivity Growth: Myth or Reality." National Bureau of Economic Research Working Paper No. 4741.

Bardwick, Judith. 1991. *Danger in the Comfort Zone: From Boardroom to Mailroom—How to Break the Entitlement Habit That's Killing American Business.* New York: AMACOM.

Batt, Rosemary. "Management Labor Markets in Telecommunications." In *White Collar Internal Labor Markets,* ed. Paul Osterman. New York: Oxford University Press (forthcoming).

Belous, Richard S. 1989. *The Contingent Economy.* Washington, D.C.: National Planning Association.

Bishop, John. 1991. "On-the-job Training of New Hires." In *Market Failure in Training,* ed. David Stern and Josef Ritzen. New York: Springer-Verlag.

Bishop, John. 1994. "The Incidence of and Payoff to Employer Training: A Review of the Literature with Recommendations for Policy." Philadelphia: National Center on the Educational Quality of the Workforce.

Blackburn, McKinley L., David E. Bloom, and Richard B. Freeman. 1990. "The Declining Economic Position of Less-Skilled American Men." In *A Future of Lousy Jobs? The Changing Structure of U.S. Wages,* ed. Gary Burtless. Washington, D.C.: Brookings Institution.

Bluestone, Barry, and Bennett Harrison. 1982. *The De-Industrialization of America: Plant Closings, Community Abandonment, and the Dismantling of Basic Industry.* New York: Basic Books.

BNA's Employee Relations Weekly. 1989. "Workforce Stress, Depression Common, Personnel Executives Report in Survey." October 23.

Boisjoly, Johanne, Greg J. Duncan, and Timothy Smeeding. 1994. "Have Highly-Skilled Workers Fallen from Grace? The Shifting Burdens of Involuntary Job Losses from 1968 to 1992." University of Quebec (Rimouski) (unpublished Manuscript).

Bok, Derek. 1993. *The Cost of Talent.* New York: Free Press.

Bowers, Norman, and Paul Swaim. 1992. "Probing (some of) the Issues of Employment Related Training: Evidence from the CPS." Washington, D.C.: U.S. Department of Agriculture, Economic Research Service.

Bridges, William. 1994. "The End of the Job." *Fortune,* September 19, 62–74.

Brown, James, and Richard Light. 1992. "Interpreting Panel Data on Job Tenure." *Journal of Labor Economics* July 10: 219–257.

Bureau of National Affairs. 1994. "New BLS Data Shows Displaced Workers Generally Not Helped by Advance Notice." *Daily Labor Report*, September 15: B-4–B-12.

Burtless, Gary. "Meeting the Skill Demands of the New Economy." Washington, D.C.: Brookings Institution (mimeographed).

Callaghan, Polly, and Heidi Hartmann. 1991. *Contingent Work*. Washington, D.C.: Economic Policy Institute.

Cappelli, Peter. 1992. "Examining Managerial Displacement." *Academy of Management Journal* 35: 203–217.

Cappelli, Peter. 1993. "Are Skill Requirements Rising? Evidence for Production and Clerical Workers." *Industrial and Labor Relations Review* 46: 515–530.

Cappelli, Peter, and K. C. O'Shaughnessey. 1995. "Skill and Wage Changes in Corporate Headquarters, 1986–1992." Philadelphia: National Center on the Educational Quality of the Workforce.

Cascio, Wayne F. 1993. "Downsizing: What Do We Know? What Have We Learned?" *Academy of Management Executive* 7: 95–104.

Cascio, Wayne F. 1995. *A Guide to Sensible Restructuring*. Washington, D.C.: U.S. Department of Labor, Office of the American Workplace.

Chauvin, Keith W. 1994. "Firm-Specific Wage Growth and Changes in the Labor Market for Managers." *Managerial and Decision Economics*, 15: 21–37.

Chilton, Kenneth, and Murray Weidenbaum. 1994. "A New Social Contract for the American Workplace: From Paternalism to Partnering." St. Louis, MO: Washington University, Center for the Study of American Business.

Clark, Robert, and Ann McDermed. 1990. *The Choice of Pension Plans in a Changing Economy*. Washington, D.C.: American Enterprise Institute.

Coleman, Mary T., and John Pencavel. 1993. "Changes in Work Hours of Male Employees, 1940–1988." *Industrial and Labor Relations Review* 46, no. 2 (January): 262–283.

Commerce Clearing House. 1994. "Mean Absenteeism Rate up by Nine Percent to 2.68 Percent," *Ideas and Trends*, no. 326 (April 27).

Commission on the Skills of the American Workforce. 1989. *America's Choice: High Skills or Low Wages!* Rochester: National Center on Education and the Economy.

Conference Board. 1992. "Availability of a Quality Workforce." Report no. 1010. New York: Conference Board.

Constantine, Jill M., and David Neumark. 1994. "Training and the Growth of Wage Inequality." Philadelphia: National Center on the Educational Quality of the Workforce.

Cotton, J. L. 1993. *Employee Involvement: Methods for Improving Performance and Work Attitudes*. Newbury Park, Calif.: Sage Publications.

Council of Economic Advisors. 1994. *Economic Report of the President*. Washington, D.C.: U.S. Government Printing Office.

Council of Economic Advisors. 1995. *Economic Report of the President*. Washington, D.C.: U.S. Government Printing Office.

Daily Labor Report. 1993. "Use of Contingent Workers Rising." Report no. 150 A-16. August 6.

Davis, Steven J., and John Haltiwanger. 1991. "Wage Dispersion Between and Within U.S. Manufacturing Plants, 1963–1986." Chicago: University of Chicago Graduate School of Business.

Deutschman, Alan. 1992. "The Upbeat Generation." *Fortune*, July 13, 42–54.

Diebold, Francis X., David Neumark, and Daniel Polsky. 1995. "Changes in Job Stability in the United States." Philadelphia: National Center on the Educational Quality of the Workforce.

Doeringer, Peter B., and Michael J. Piore. 1971. *Internal Labor Markets and Manpower Analysis.* Lexington, Mass.: D.C. Heath.

Easterlin, Richard A. 1980. *Birth and Fortune: The Impact of Numbers on Personal Welfare.* New York: Basic Books.

Farber, Henry S. 1993. "The Incidence and Costs of Job Loss: 1982–91." *Brookings Papers on Economic Activity: Microeconomics.*

Farber, Henry S. 1995. "Are Lifetime Jobs Disappearing? Job Duration in the United States: 1973–1993." Princeton, N.J.: Industrial Relations Section Princeton University Working Paper #341.

Filipczak, Bob. 1994. "It's Just a Job: Generation X at Work." *Training* 31 (April): 21–27.

Foulkes, Fred. 1980. *Personnel Practices of Large, Non-Union Companies.* Englewood Cliffs, N.J.: Prentice-Hall.

Freeman, Richard B. 1976. *The Over-Educated American.* New York: Basic Books.

Freeman, Richard B., and Lawrence Katz. 1995. *Differences and Changes in Wage Structures.* Chicago: University of Chicago Press.

Galinsky, Ellen, James T. Bond, and Dana E. Friedman. 1993. "The Changing Workforce." New York: Families and Work Institute.

Gardner, Jennifer M. 1993. "Recession Swells Count of Displaced Workers." *Monthly Labor Review* (June): 14–23.

Gardner, Jennifer M., and Diane E. Herz. 1992. "Working and Poor in 1990." *Monthly Labor Review* (December): 20–28.

Gittleman, Maury B., and David R. Howell. 1995. "Changes in the Structure and Quality of Jobs in the United States: Effects by Race and Gender." *Industrial and Labor Relations Review* 48: 420–440.

Golden, L., and E. Applebaum. 1992. "What Was Driving the 1982–1988 Boom in Temporary Employment? Preferences of Workers or Decisions and Power of Employers." *Journal of Economy and Society* 51: 473–493.

Goldin, Claudia, and Robert A. Margo. 1992. "The Great Compression: Wage Structure in the United States at Mid-Century." *Quarterly Journal of Economics* 107: 1–34.

Goldschneider, Francis, and Calvin Goldschneider. 1993. *Leaving and Returning Home in 20th Century America.* Providence: Brown University Press.

Gottschalk, Peter, and Robert Moffit. 1994. "The Growth of Earnings Instability in the U.S. Labor Market." *Brookings Papers on Economic Activity.*

Greenberg, Eric Rolfe. 1991. "Downsizing: AMA Survey Results." *Compensation and Benefits Review* 23, no. 4: 33–38.

Groshen, Erica. 1993. "HRM Policy and Increasing Inequity in a Salary

Survey." *Industrial Relations Research Association 44th Annual Proceedings.* Madison, Wisc.: Industrial Relations Research Association, pp. 216–224.

Grubb, W. Norton, and Robert H. Wilson. 1992. "Trends in Wage and Salary Inequality, 1967–1988." *Monthly Labor Review* 115: 23–39.

Gustman, Alan, Olivia Mitchell, and Thomas Steinmeier. 1995. "Retirement Measures in the Health and Retirement Survey," *Journal of Human Resources,* 30: 557–583.

Harris, Louis, and Associates. 1991. *Laborforce 2000 Survey.* New York: Louis Harris and Associates.

Harris, Louis, and Associates. 1988. "America and the Arts V." New York: Harris Associates.

Hay Group. 1993. *1993 Hay Executive Compensation Report.* Philadelphia: Hay Group.

ILO. 1993. "Stress at Work." In *World Labor Report.* Geneva: International Labor Organization.

Ippolito, Richard A. 1995. "Toward Explaining the Growth of Defined Contribution Plans." *Industrial Relations* 34: 1–20.

Ideas and Trends. 1994. "Mean Absenteeism Rate up by Nine Percent to 2.68 Percent." Commerce Clearing House, no. 326 (April 27).

Jacoby, Sanford M. 1985. *Employing Bureaucracy: Managers, Unions, and the Transformation of Work in American Industry, 1900–1945.* New York: Columbia University Press.

Kahneman, D., and A. Tversky. 1979. "Prospect Theory: An Analysis of Decision Under Risk." *Econometrica* 47: 263–291.

Kanter, Rosabeth Moss. 1991. "Transcending Business Boundaries: 12,000 World Managers View Change." *Harvard Business Review* (May–June): 151–163.

Katz, Lawrence F., and Alan B. Krueger. 1991. "Changes in the Structure of Wages in the Public and Private Sectors." In *Research in Labor Economics,* ed. Ronald G. Ehrenberg, vol. 12. Greenwich, Conn.: JAI Press.

Kepner-Tregoe, Inc. 1995. "House Divided: Views on Change from Top Management—and their Employees." Princeton, N.J.: Kepner Tregoe, Inc.

Kletzer, Lori G. 1991. "Job Displacement, 1976–86: How Blacks Fared Relative to Whites." *Monthly Labor Review* (July): 17–25.

Krueger, Alan. 1993. "How Computers Have Changed the Wage Structure: Evidence from Microdata, 1984–1989." *Quarterly Journal of Economics* 108: 33–60.

Labs, Jennifer J. 1992. "Perspectives: Job Stress." *Personnel Journal* (April): 43.

Leete, Laura, and Juliet B. Schor. 1994. "Assessing the Time-Squeeze Hypothesis: Hours Worked in the United States, 1969–1989." *Industrial Relations* 33, no. 1 (January): 25–43.

Levy, Frank, and Richard J. Murnane. 1992. "U.S. Earnings Levels and Earnings Inequality: A Review of Recent Trends and Proposed Explanation." *Journal of Economic Literature* 30, no. 3.

Marcotte, Dave. 1994. "Evidence of a Fall in the Wage Premium for Job

Security." Bloomington, Ill.: Northern Illinois University, Center for Governmental Studies.

Marnum, G., D. Mayhall, and K. Nelson. 1985. "The Temporary Help Industry: A Response to the Dual Internal Labor Market." *Industrial and Labor Relations Review* 38: 599–611.

Medoff, James. 1993. "Middle-Aged and Out of Work: Growing Unemployment Due to Job Loss Among Middle-Aged Americans." Washington, D.C.: National Study Center.

Medoff, James E., and Katharine G. Abraham. 1980. "Experience, Performance, and Earnings." *Quarterly Journal of Economics* 95: 703–736.

Mercer, William M., Inc. 1995. "Wall Street Journal/William M. Mercer CEO Compensation Study." New York: William M. Mercer, Inc. Compensation Research Group.

Mills, D. Quinn. 1985. "Seniority Versus Ability in Promotion Decisions." *Industrial and Labor Relations Review* 38: 421–427.

Mishel, Lawrence, and Jared Bernstein. 1992. "Job Destruction: Worse than We Thought." *Challenge* (September-October): 4–8.

Mishel, Lawrence, and Jared Bernstein. 1994. *The State of Working America, 1994–1995.* Washington, D.C.: Economic Policy Institute.

Mowday, R. T., L. W. Porter, and R. M. Steers. 1982. *Employee-Organization Linkages.* New York: Academic Press.

Murnane, Richard J., John B. Willett, and Frank Levy. 1995. "The Growing Importance of Cognitive Skills in Wage Determination." *Review of Economics and Statistics* 77: 251–266.

Nardone, Thomas, Diane Herz, Earl Mellor, and Steven Hipple. 1993. "1992: Job Market in the Doldrums." *Monthly Labor Review* (February): 3–14.

National Safety Council. 1991. *Accident Facts.* Washington, D.C.: National Safety Council.

National Association of Temporary and Staffing Services. 1994a. "Profile of the Temporary Workforce." Alexandria, Va.: National Association of Temporary and Staffing Services.

National Association of Temporary and Staffing Services. 1994b. "Temporary Help/Staffing Services Industry Continues to Create Employment Opportunities." Alexandria, Va.: National Association of Temporary and Staffing Services.

National Center on the Educational Quality of the Workforce. 1995a. "The EQW National Employer Survey: First Findings." Philadelphia: National Center on the Educational Quality of the Workforce.

National Center on the Educational Quality of the Workforce. 1995b. "Employers who Work with Schools." Philadelphia: National Center on the Educational Quality of the Workforce.

Northwestern National Life Insurance Company. 1992. "Employee Burnout: Causes and Cures." St. Paul, Minn.: Northwestern National Life Insurance Company.

Northwestern National Life Insurance Company. 1993. "Fear and Violence in the Workplace." St. Paul, Minn.: Northwestern National Life Insurance Company.

Oi, Walter Y. 1983. "The Fixed Employment Costs of Specialized Labor." In

The Measurement of Labor Cost, ed. Jack Triplett. Chicago: University of Chicago Press.

Organization for Economic Cooperation and Development. 1993a. *1993 Issues: The OECD Response.* Paris: Organization for Economic Cooperation and Development.

Organization for Economic Cooperation and Development. 1993b. *Employment Outlook.* Paris: Organization for Economic Cooperation and Development.

O'Reilly, Brian. 1994. "The New Deal: What Companies and Employees Owe One Another." *Fortune,* June 13: 44–52.

Osterman, Paul. 1994. "How Common Is Workplace Transformation and How Can We Explain Who Does It?" *Industrial and Labor Relations Review* (January): 173–188.

Osterman, Paul. 1995. "Skills, Training, and Work Organization in American Establishments." *Industrial Relations* (April): 125–146.

Osterman, Paul. Forthcoming. "Work Organization." In *Change at Work,* ed. Peter Cappelli. New York: Oxford University Press.

Piore, Michael J., and Charles F. Sabel. 1984. *The Second Industrial Divide.* New York: Basic Books.

Podgursky, Michael. 1992. "The Industrial Structure of Job Displacement, 1979–89." *Monthly Labor Review* (September): 17–25.

Robinson, John. 1990. "The Time Squeeze." *American Demographics* 12: 30–33.

Robinson, Sandra L., Matthew S. Kraatz, and Denise M. Rousseau. 1994. "Changing Obligations and the Psychological Contract." *Academy of Management Journal* 37: 137–152.

Rose, Stephen. 1995. "The Decline of Employment Stability in the 1980s." Washington, D.C.: National Commission on Employment Policy.

Rousseau, Denise. 1989. "Psychological and Implied Contracts in Organizations." *Employee Responsibilities and Rights Journal* 2, no. 2: 121–139.

Ryscavage, Paul, and Peter Henle. 1990. "Earnings Inequality Accelerates in the 1980s." *Monthly Labor Review* 113: 3–16.

Shor, Juliet B. 1992. *The Overworked American.* New York: Basic Books.

Smith, Lee. 1994. "Burned-Out Bosses: The Other Victims of Restructuring." *Fortune,* July 25, 44–55.

Smith, Robert S. 1988. "Comparable Worth: Limited Coverage and the Exacerbation of Inequality." *Industrial and Labor Relations Review* 41: 227–239.

Stevens, Amy. 1994. "Lawyer with Six Years of Experience, Top Credentials, Seeks Job, Any Job at All." *Wall Street Journal,* July 22, B1.

Swinnerton, Kenneth A., and Howard Wial. 1995. "Is Job Stability Declining in the U.S. Economy?" *Industrial and Labor Relations Review* 48, no. 2 (January): 293–304.

Thompson, J. D. 1977. *Organizations in Action.* New York: McGraw-Hill.

Time. 1993. "What Ever Happened to the Great American Job?" November 11, 22.

Towers Perrin. 1995. "Salary Management Planning Survey Results." Valhalla, N.Y.: Towers Perrin.

Vanos, Mark N. 1992. "Time for Uncle Sam to Pitch In?" *Business Week,* April 6, p. 76.

Wall Street Journal. 1988. "Mental Stress Exacts a Rising Toll in the Workplace." December 12, p. 1.

Walster, Elaine, G. William Walster, Ellen Berscheid, et al. 1978. *Equity: Theory and Research.* Boston: Allyn and Bacon.

Wellington, Alison J. 1993. "Changes in the Male/Female Wage Gap." *Journal of Human Resources* 28, no. 2: 383–411.

Wokutch, Richard E., and Josetta S. McGlaughlin. 1992. "The U.S. and Japanese Work Injury and Illness Experience." *Monthly Labor Review* (April): 2–37.

Wyatt Company. 1993. "Wyatt's 1993 Survey of Corporate Restructuring—Best Practices in Corporate Restructuring." New York: Wyatt Company.

Wyatt Company. 1995. "Measuring Change in the Attitudes of the American Workforce." New York: Wyatt WorkUSA, Wyatt Company.

Yankelovich, Daniel. 1993. "How Changes in the Economy Are Reshaping American Values." In *Values and Public Policy,* ed. Henry J. Aaron, Thomas E. Mann, and Timothy Taylor. Washington, D.C.: Brookings Institution.

Zemke, Ron. 1991. "Workplace Stress Revisited." *Training* (November): 28: 35.

Chapter 7

Abraham, Katharine G. 1990. "Restructuring the Employment Relationship: The Growth of Market-Mediated Work Arrangements." In *New Developments in the Labor Market,* ed. Katharine Abraham and Robert McKersie. Cambridge, Mass.: MIT Press.

Bishop, John. 1994. "The Incidence and Payoff to Training: A Review of the Literature and Recommendations for Public Policy." Philadelphia: National Center on the Educational Quality of the Workforce.

EQW (National Center on the Educational Quality of the Workforce). 1995. "Employers Who Do: Working With Schools." Philadelphia: National Center on the Educational Quality of the Workforce.

Kochan, Thomas A., and Paul Osterman. 1994. "Mutual Gains Bargaining." Boston: Harvard Business School Press.

National Association of Temporary Staffing Services (NATSS). 1994. "Profile of the Temporary Workforce." Alexandria, Va.: NATSS.

Osterman, Paul. 1995. "Skill, Training, and Work Organization in American Establishments." *Industrial Relations* 34: 125–146.

Robinson, Sandra L., Matthew S. Kraatz, and Denise M. Rousseau. 1994. "Changing Obligations and the Psychological Contract." *Academy of Management Journal* 37: 137–152.

Index

subsidies, 225; job mobility and, 225; job training, 151–153, 213–214, 225–226; pensions, portability, 13, 225; restructuring and, 13–14, 224–226; school-to-work transition and, 165–166, 225; schools and, 225; skills gap and, 154–155, 169–172; unemployment, 225; work skills and, 154, 169–172, 224

quality: benchmarking, 94; downsizing and, 71, 83, 139; employee empowerment and, 92; high-performance work systems and, 108, 112; job training and, 123, 139–140, 143, 145; standards, 94; work organization and, 105–106
quality circles, 94; competitive strategies and, 105–106; core employees, 94–95, 97, 100–101; defined, 120; diffusion, 90–91, 97; employee involvement, 92; influence of, 41–42; internal labor market, job training and, 123; Japanese transplants, 98–99; leadership and, 55; penetration rate, 94–96; performance and, 109–110; surveys, 98–99
quality control: employee empowerment and, 92; in Japan, 41–42; statistical process control, 41–42
Quality of Employment Survey: employee attitudes, 200; hours of work, 195; stress, 195
quitting (employment): employer costs, pension plans and, 192; restructuring and, 201; stress and, 195; voluntary, 211

railroad industry: competition and, 27; law and legislation, 16
recession: cyclical, layoffs and, 67
reengineering, 45; contingent workforce and, 51; defined, 48;

Ford Motor Company, 49; insurance industry, 48–49; internal labor market and, 51; job security and, 51; leadership, importance of, 55–56, 64; management information systems and, 48–49; market relationships and, 50–51; performance, requirements for sustaining, 54–55; profitability and, 6; virtual organization, 51; work skills and management, demand, 156; work systems, change in, 49
Reich, Robert, 152
restructuring, 3; absenteeism and, 201; apprenticeships and, 124; Bell operating companies, 58–59; benefits of, for employers, 57–59; blue-collar workers, 60, 62, 217; business risks, transfer to employees, 10, 15, 192, 202–206, 209–210, 220–221; California, 226; career development and, 209, 226; collective bargaining and, 217; company size and, 53; competition and, 5–6, 27–29, 38, 53, 63, 158; conditions of work and, 89, 92; consumer demand and, 5, 29–32; contingent compensation and, 26, 191–193, 224; continuing education and, 11; contradictions in, 210, 221; core competencies and, 6, 33, 43–44; core-periphery model, response to, 223–224; cost cutting, 33–34, 36, 38; costs, 58, 173, 218–221; debt financing and, 32–33; decision making and, 8, 45–47, 54; definitions, 44; dismissal and, 224; distribution of, 53; drawbacks of, 226; duration, 6–7, 209, 221, 223, 226; early-out offers, 79, 176–177; Eastman Kodak, 44; economic